# Pro SharePoint 2010 Development for Office 365

**Bart McDonough**

**Dave Milner**

**Paul Stork**

Apress®

## Pro SharePoint 2010 Development for Office 365

ISBN-13 (pbk): 978-1-4302-4182-9

ISBN-13 (electronic): 978-1-4302-4183-6

President and Publisher: Paul Manning
Lead Editor: Jonathan Hassell
Developmental Editor: Kate Blackham
Technical Reviewer: Jim Duncan
Editorial Board: Ste ve An glin, Ewan Buckin gham, Gary Corn ell, Louise Corrigan , Morgan Erte l, Jon athan Gennick, Jon athan Hassell, Robert Hutchin son, Michelle Lowman, James Markh am, Matthew M oodie, Jeff Olson, J effrey P epper, D ouglas Pundick, Ben R enow-Clarke, D ominic Sha keshaft, G wenan Sp earing, M att Wade, Tom Welsh
Coordinating Editor: Jill Balzano
Copy Editor: Nancy Sixsmith, ConText Editorial Services
Compositor: Bytheway Publishing Services
Indexer: SPi Global
Artist: SPi Global
Cover Designer: Anna Ishchenko

Distributed to the book trade worldwide by Springer Scie nce+Business Media New York, 233 Spring Street, 6th Floor, New Y ork, NY 10013. Phone 1-80 0-SPRINGER, f ax (2 01) 348 -4505, e-mail orders-ny@springer-sbm.com, or visit www.springeronline.com.

For information on translations, please e-mail rights@apress.com, or visit www.apress.com.

Apress and friends of ED book s may be purchased in bulk f or academic, corporate, or promo tional use. eBoo k versions and licenses are also available for most ti tles. For more information, reference our Special Bulk Sales–eBook Licensing web page at www.apress.com/bulk-sales.

Any source code or other supplementary materials referenced by the author i n this te xt is av ailable to re aders at www.apress.com. For detailed information about how to locate your book's source code, go to www.apress.com/source-code.

*To my wonderful wife, Cathy, and our children Caitlin, John, and Kevin, for your patience, love, and support while I wrote this book. I love you all!*

*–Bart McDonough*

# Contents at a Glance

# Contents

# Foreword

Now is an exciting time to be a developer for the Microsoft platform. Cloud-based technologies such as Office 365 offer businesses a way to contain their IT costs and focus on what they do best. That means there will be more opportunities to develop targeted solutions for those businesses that help them to be more effective and more competitive. And with the rapid adoption of mobile devices and an invitation to a broader developer base by emphasizing client-side technologies such as HTML and jQuery, it's now easier than ever to develop solutions at a relatively low cost that can be marketed to a broader range of customers than in the past. That's exciting!

With that said, an important aspect of developing for the cloud is gaining a firm understanding of this new environment. The cloud represents a new environment with new boundaries that many developers of traditional on-premise applications are just beginning to grasp. The primary goal of this book is to get readers up to speed as quickly as possible on what the boundaries are in SharePoint Online and what's possible in the realm of customization and development. We also tried to cover best practices and potential pitfalls as much as possible. After all, that's one of the biggest reasons for buying a book like this, in our opinion.

We wish you the best in your endeavors with SharePoint Online and hope you'll find this book to be a valuable resource on your journey!

Bart McDonough

# About the Authors

**Bart McDonough** is a Principal Consultant at Neudesic as well as the owner of Incline Technical Group. Neudesic is a Microsoft National Systems Integrator and Gold-Certified partner specializing in providing reliable and effective solutions on Microsoft's technology platform. Incline Technical Group is a Microsoft partner specializing in providing high-quality training around modern Microsoft technologies. Bart has been working with Microsoft technologies for more than 12 years and has been working with SharePoint since 2007. In recent years, he has chosen to focus heavily on Office 365 and SharePoint Online as well as client-side development for SharePoint. He is also a Microsoft-Certified Technology Specialist (MCTS) in SharePoint 2010 application development.

An avid hiker and skier, Bart moved with his wife from northwest Florida to Colorado Springs, Colorado, in 2005 and has never looked back. The Colorado Front Range has a vibrant technology community and an innovative, business-friendly atmosphere that offers a lot of opportunities. Bart has always been a fan of sharing ideas and knowledge, which he has been able to do as an active member of the Colorado SharePoint User Group (COSPUG) that meets in both Colorado Springs and Denver. He has also presented at conferences such as SharePoint Saturday and SharePoint Fest.

When Bart isn't working with clients, producing training materials, or presenting at a user group or conference, he's probably hiking one of Colorado's "14-ers" (mountains that peak at 14,000+ feet above sea level) or cruising down the ski slopes along the Continental Divide.

**Dave Milner** is a Senior SharePoint Architect and the Products Lead at ShareSquared where he builds SharePoint products and helps companies implement their SharePoint solutions. Dave is a technology professional with deep understanding of Microsoft technologies, including 19 years of IT experience and experience with Microsoft technologies spanning over a decade.

Dave has an MBA with a technology management focus, and is a Microsoft Certified Trainer as well as having obtained other advanced Microsoft certifications in the .NET and SharePoint areas. He also is a Certified Scrum Master, having successfully implementing Scrum methodologies with several application development and solution teams. In the technology community, Dave is a frequent speaker and trainer at local and national SharePoint and .NET related events. He serves on the leadership team of COSPUG (the Colorado SharePoint User Groups) and helps run the local branch in Colorado Springs; he's also involved in other local technology groups. When he's not working on technology, Dave enjoys the outdoors of Colorado Springs where he lives with his wife and two children.

 **Paul Stork** is a Senior Solution Architect, serving as chief technical architect within the Portals and Collaboration team at Blue Chip. He has an MBA from the Weatherhead School of Management and has been active in the IT industry for over twenty-five years. His primary focus for the last eight years has been Microsoft SharePoint products and technologies. Paul's is a "Jack of all Trades" who has developed expertise as a network administrator, architect, developer, and DBA. He has worked with SharePoint in many roles including chief architect, solution developer, and trainer. His broad and deep experience is frequently requested by customers who are designing and implementing applications based on Microsoft SharePoint. Paul has been a contributor or co-author on several books about SharePoint. He has been recognized by Microsoft with a SharePoint Server MVP award for the last five years in recognition of his contributions to the SharePoint community

# About the Technical Reviewer

 Based in California, **Jim Duncan** is a former Microsoft SharePoint MVP and Senior SharePoint Architect at ShareSquared. Jim has been working with the SharePoint product since its initial release in 2001. He is a SharePoint Certified Technology Specialist (MCTS) and has recently attended the Microsoft Certified Master training course.

Jim has served as a Senior Architect and Project Lead on numerous SharePoint implementations, ranging from large-scale enterprise portals to line of business systems built on the SharePoint platform. He is a pioneer in extending SharePoint beyond portal software by leveraging the SharePoint framework to construct mission-critical web-based business applications.

# Introduction

Welcome to the world of customization and development for SharePoint Online in Office 365. Although Office 365 offers lots of opportunities for businesses and developers, it also represents a different development and deployment paradigm from what most SharePoint developers are accustomed to in a traditional on-premise environment. Our purpose in writing this book is to help bridge the gap between on-premise and cloud-based SharePoint development and get developers up to speed as quickly as possible on what can be done and how to do it.

## Who This Book Is For

This book is intended for .NET/ASP.NET developers who have never developed for SharePoint Online before. Notice that we said .NET developers, not SharePoint developers. Although being a SharePoint developer will certainly be helpful, it's not a requirement for getting through this book. The idea is that anyone with existing Microsoft development skills can apply those skills to developing for SharePoint Online. Part of the reason we targeted this audience is that Office 365 tends to attract a lot of small and mid-size businesses that might already have .NET development expertise in-house, but are often lacking SharePoint developers. SharePoint developers, however, will still find this book useful because it covers some key differences in developing for the cloud rather than an on-premise environment.

## Conventions

Throughout this book, we use the terms *online* and *cloud-based* interchangeably to refer to SharePoint Online and the Office 365 environment. We use the term *on-premise* to refer to traditional SharePoint 2010 environments that are hosted internally by a business or organization.

As we discuss in Chapter 1, we also sometimes use plan names and plan categories interchangeably while discussing available features in Office 365. For example, the terms *E plans*, *enterprise-level plans*, and *Office 365 for enterprises* all mean the same thing and refer to the same set of available features.

While we included some reference material in this book, the book is not intended to be a reference manual for Office 365 or SharePoint Online. Microsoft has its own set of help/reference documentation, and we provide links to it when appropriate. Our focus here is more on the tools and techniques involved in SharePoint development as well as sharing some real-world tips and best practices with our readings that we've learned through years of experience.

## Downloading the Code

The code for the examples shown in this book is available on the Apress website: http://www.apress.com. A link can be found on the book's information page under the Source Code/Downloads tab. This tab is located underneath the Related Titles section of the page.

## Contacting the Author

We love to hear from our readers and welcome your feedback about the book. Bart can be contacted by visiting his blog at http://www.SharePointTapRoom.com or by e-mailing him at bart@inclinetechnical.com.

# CHAPTER 1

# Introduction to Office 365 and SharePoint Online

If you're reading this book, you've probably heard phrases such as *cloud computing* and *moving to the cloud* being tossed around over the last few years. These terms have often been associated with the strategic planning efforts of medium-to-large IT organizations. However, that's beginning to change. As cloud computing evolves, it's becoming more and more accessible to smaller and midsize companies as well as individuals (for example, independent consultants). In fact, one of the major benefits behind cloud computing is that it can help smaller businesses grow larger by giving them access to the same IT resources "the big guys" use, but at a much smaller cost. Now that's leverage!

Because more and more businesses are moving to the cloud, the way we develop software will continue to evolve as well. In cloud-based environments multiple companies share the same infrastructure; there are considerations and restrictions that don't apply when developing traditional desktop and web applications. Microsoft refers to this type of infrastructure sharing as *multitenancy*, and you can think of it as being similar to many tenants renting apartments in a single apartment building. Each apartment has its own kitchen and bathroom, but resources such as elevators and swimming pools are shared. Office 365 is a multitenancy environment, so that topic will play heavily into our customization and development discussions throughout the rest of this book.

---

## WHAT IS THE CLOUD?

The *cloud* refers to IT services and infrastructure (software, computers, storage devices, and so on) that's hosted outside of your organization and made available to you over the web. As opposed to the traditional *on-premise* model of hosting software and services in-house, the cloud-based model offloads the burden of maintaining those resources to someone else. In the case of Office 365, that "someone else" is Microsoft.

---

This chapter introduces you to Office 365 and SharePoint Online by covering the following topics:

- What Are Office 365 and SharePoint Online?

- What's Included in Office 365?

- Plan Types in Office 365

- Plan Comparison

- Signing Up for a Trial

- Converting Your Trial to a Paid Subscription

- Purchasing a Paid Subscription

- How to Manage Your Account

- Accessing SharePoint Online

- Managing SharePoint Online

If you're already familiar with signing up for a plan and managing an account in Office 365, you may want to skip ahead to Chapter 2 and start looking at what's possible in the realm of customization and development for SharePoint Online. Chapter 3 will then walk you through setting up a development environment so you have a place to develop and test your customizations.

## What Are Office 365 and SharePoint Online?

Office 365 is a subscription-based offering from Microsoft that includes cloud-based software for managing and running a business. One of the software products offered is SharePoint Online, which is the focus of this book. SharePoint Online is very similar to SharePoint 2010, but has some key differences due to the multitenant nature of the Office 365 environment.

## What's Included in Office 365?

Depending on which plan you purchase, your Office 365 environment will include one or more of the following products:

- SharePoint Online (for collaboration and websites)

- Exchange Online (for e-mail and calendaring)

- Lync Online (for web conferencing and messaging)

- Microsoft Office desktop software (for desktop productivity)

- Office Web Apps (for online productivity)

At the time of this writing, these products are all based on the Microsoft Office 2010 product suite (though Office 365 Preview was just released as well, which correlates to the Office 2013 product suite). One important thing to remember with Office 365 is that the online version of each of these products is *not* exactly like its on-premise counterpart. SharePoint Online looks and functions a lot like SharePoint 2010, but they are *not* the same product. There are some differences in features and functionality, and they're technically considered to be two different products. The same is true for Exchange Online and Lync Online.

As an example, consider the simple public website you can create in SharePoint Online. SharePoint 2010 has no equivalent, nor does it contain the special Page Designer ribbon that's included for editing this type of site in SharePoint Online.

# Plan Types in Office 365

Customers subscribe to plans in Office 365, and each plan is a little different in terms of the software and features it offers. At a high level, the plans offered can be broken down into three categories:

- Office 365 for professionals and small business (P plans)

- Office 365 for enterprises (E plans)

- Individual product plans

Plans in the first category are often called *P plans* because the plan names begin with the letter *P*. Plans in the second category are often called *E plans* because the plan names begin with the letter *E*. The last category of plans typically uses names containing the product name and a plan number (e.g., SharePoint Online Plan 1). There are also educational plans, government plans, and kiosk plans (which are mostly specialized versions of the plans we already mentioned).

The edition of SharePoint Online in the P plans is very much like SharePoint Foundation 2010. The E plans, however, use an edition that's very much like SharePoint Server 2010 (it has publishing, user profiles, and so on). We chose to focus primarily on the E plans in this book because we want to discuss the broadest possible range of customization options for SharePoint Online. We've done our best to note throughout the book where significant differences exist between plan types. However, some differences aren't explicitly called out if they're well-known. For example, we don't mention that SharePoint publishing features are not available in the P plans because SharePoint Foundation does not have that capability.

---

■ **Note** Sometimes we use the terms *P plans* and *Office 365 for professionals and small business* interchangeably. We do the same for *E plans* and *Office 365 for enterprises*. We also occasionally use specific plan names such as *P1* or *E3* when relevant.

---

# Plan Comparison

Table 1-1 summarizes the differences in features across some common Office 365 plans.

*Table 1-1. Office 365 Plan Comparisons*

| Plan Name | Features |
| --- | --- |
| P1 | • E-mail<br>• Shared calendars<br>• Instant messaging, PC-to-PC calling, and video conferencing<br>• Web-based viewing of Excel, Word, PowerPoint, and OneNote files<br>• A team site for sharing files<br>• A simple public website<br>• Antivirus and anti-spam filtering<br>• Microsoft community support |
| E1 | *Everything in P1 plus:*<br>• Active Directory synchronization<br>• Configurable antispam filtering<br>• SharePoint intranet (supporting up to 300 websites)<br>• Live 24/7 phone support |
| E3 | *Everything in E1 plus:*<br>• Office Professional Plus 2010 desktop software subscription (for up to five devices per user)<br>• Unlimited e-mail storage and archiving<br>• Hosted voicemail support<br>• Web-based *editing* (not just viewing) of Word, Excel, PowerPoint, and OneNote files |

■ **Note** Microsoft also offers *dedicated* plans that provide customers with their own dedicated servers, but those plans are not covered in this book.

## Service Descriptions

Looking for in-depth descriptions of what's supported by each type of plan in Office 365? At the time of this writing, the best descriptions available are provided by Microsoft in their Office 365 *Service Description* documents. Here are the links to the Service Descriptions:

- Service description for *Office 365 for professionals and small businesses*: http://bit.ly/Li6sbk

- Service description for *Office 365 for enterprises*: http://bit.ly/JvWrFD

The Service Descriptions cover many of the most frequently asked questions about the plans, including these:

- Overview of services and features in the plan

- System requirements

- Security

- Office web apps

- Administration

- Help and support

- Licensing

- Buying your subscription (or upgrading from a different one)

- Data center information

- Service level agreements (SLAs)

## Signing Up for a Trial

If you're brand new to Office 365 and have never tried it before, a good first step is to sign up for a trial account and find out which features and software you really need. To sign up for a free trial, you can visit http://www.office365.com and click the Free Trial link. You'll see a page similar to the one shown in Figure 1-1.

*Figure 1-1. Office 365 trial sign-up page*

As you saw in Figure 1-1, there are two trial plans available: P1 and E3. If you're interested in a different enterprise-level plan such as E1, you'll still have to sign up for the E3 plan during the trial period. You can convert to a paid subscription when the trial period ends, but be aware that you may lose some features if you convert to a paid plan with fewer features than your trial plan has.

Also, be aware that trial plans limit the number of licenses that are available to you. You are given 25 user licenses with the E3 trial and 10 user licenses with the P1 trial. If you need more licenses during your trial period, one approach you can try is calling Office 365 support and asking for more. If you can present a valid reason and are legitimately interested in converting to a paid subscription later, Microsoft will often grant you more licenses during your trial period.

■ **Note** Curious about the differences in SharePoint Online between the E1 and E3 plans? SharePoint Online in E1 is essentially equivalent to SharePoint Server 2010 *Standard*. SharePoint Online in E3 is essentially equivalent to SharePoint Server 2010 *Enterprise*.

## Converting Your Trial to a Paid Subscription

If you decide to purchase an Office 365 plan subscription when your trial period (normally 30 days) expires, the process is pretty straightforward. Basically all that's involved is purchasing the appropriate types and number of licenses you need and then assigning those licenses to your users. The administration portal used to manage your account will show you a link at the top that lets you purchase paid licenses and begin the conversion process (see Figure 1-2).

*Figure 1-2. Link to convert trial to paid subscription*

For example, let's suppose you're interested in purchasing the E1 plan. E1 isn't available as a trial, so you sign up for E3 during the trial period so you can test out Office 365 with some of your users. Your trial period has now ended, and you decide to go ahead and purchase the E1 plan. If you have 50 users and you want them all to remain active after the switch, you simply need to buy 50 E1 plan licenses and assign them to your existing users. If you do that, your data will be retained and the transition will be seamless. The only difference would be a loss of features that were available in the E3 plan but are not included in the E1 plan.

But wait! What about converting your trial to one of the individual product plans such as the SharePoint Online Plan 1 subscription? That's possible, too. You would just need to buy one or more SharePoint Online Plan 1 licenses and assign them before your trial expires. As long as you do that, the conversion should be pretty seamless. You would simply lose the other software and features that were present in the E3 plan but aren't included in the SharePoint Online Plan 1 subscription. Along those same lines, a conversion usually results in an eventual loss of data for any users who are *not* assigned licenses from a paid subscription once the trial period ends. If you have a user mailbox in Exchange Online, for example, and no paid license is assigned to that user for Exchange Online after the conversion, the user's mailbox will eventually be deleted.

If you have questions about a specific trial-to-paid conversion scenario, we suggest visiting http://www.office365.com and contacting Microsoft directly. Its sales and support staff will be able to tell you whether a given scenario is supported and what the process is for doing the conversion.

■ **Note** Office 365 only supports migrations *within* plan types. That means, for example, that you can switch from one E plan to another (e.g., E3 to E1), but *not* from an E plan to a P plan. Please consider this when signing up for a trial subscription!

## Purchasing a Paid Subscription

There are two ways to purchase a paid subscription to Office 365:

- Buy a plan subscription from the main Office 365 website
- Buy a plan subscription through the administration portal

A *paid subscription* simply consists of one or more licenses purchased for a given plan over a specified period of time. The options are spelled out for you when you purchase the subscription.

### Purchasing Multiple Subscriptions

You can have multiple Office 365 subscriptions in your account simultaneously. For example, you can purchase 50 licenses for a SharePoint Online Plan 2 subscription and an additional 25 licenses for a Lync Online Plan 2 subscription if only 25 users in your organization need to use Lync.

The good news is you have some flexibility in terms of what you purchase and how you assign features and functionality to your user base. The potential downside is you need to do some due diligence in managing the subscriptions to make sure you have the right licenses assigned to the right users. Otherwise a user may lose data or functionality you expect him or her to have. (For example, if a user has an Exchange Online license and then that license is removed, the mailbox will eventually be deleted.)

## How to Manage Your Account

Your Office 365 account is managed through the Microsoft Online Customer Portal, or MOCP. You may also hear it referred to as the *administration portal* (a term we use in this book because it's more intuitive than *MOCP*).

Once you've sign up for a subscription (whether paid or a trial), you'll receive a confirmation e-mail like the one shown in Figure 1-3.

*Figure 1-3. Subscription confirmation e-mail*

As seen in the figure, the e-mail includes a sign-in link and the User ID of the user account you will use to sign in. The sign-in link takes you to the administration portal (see Figure 1-4).

The user ID was created based on information you entered when signing up for your subscription. During the sign-up process, you're asked to provide a domain name and user ID. Microsoft takes those values and constructs an initial administrator account user ID of the form *[UserID]@[Domain]*.onmicrosoft.com, so we recommend choosing a short user ID for your initial account (e.g., Admin). Otherwise, you'll find yourself typing a very long name to sign in to the portal.

# Admin Overview Page

When you sign in to the administration portal, you'll initially be presented with the Admin Overview page, as shown in Figure 1-4.

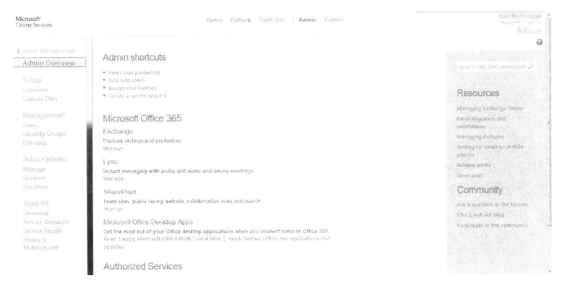

*Figure 1-4. Admin Overview page in the administration portal*

The Admin Shortcuts section at the top of the page contains links for common tasks such as adding users or creating a service request (a *service request* is a support ticket to get help from Microsoft).

The Microsoft Office 365 section in the middle of the page contains links to manage the various pieces of software associated with your account. Use these links to navigate to the administration pages for Exchange Online, Lync Online, and SharePoint Online. If your subscription includes Microsoft Office desktop software, there will be links related to it in this section as well.

---

■ **Note** The main content area of this page looks a little different if you have a P plan subscription. For example, Exchange is titled Outlook, and SharePoint is titled Team sites and documents. There is also a direct link to edit the simple public website that's automatically created for you.

---

The links on the left side of the page are divided into four sections: Setup, Management, Subscriptions, and Support. (The Setup section is omitted from this page if you have a P plan subscription.) We'll take a moment now to cover what you can do using the links in each one of these sections.

## Setup

The Setup section is designed to help you in setting up and managing Office 365. The Overview page contains information and links about the following topics:

- Using the Microsoft Online Services Module for Windows PowerShell to accomplish many administrative tasks using PowerShell

- Configuring single sign-on so your Active Directory users can sign into Office 365 using their existing on-premise credentials

- Synchronizing Active Directory so that users, contacts, and groups from your on-premise Active Directory installation can be automatically imported into Office 365

- Adding a registered domain name (a vanity domain) to your account

- Updating users' desktops so they can sign in to Office 365 and use cloud-based software seamlessly

- Migration of existing e-mail accounts to Exchange Online

- Using SharePoint Online

- Using Lync Online

The Custom Plan link takes you to a page that lets you build a deployment checklist for rolling out Office 365 to your organization. You can choose which steps you need to complete and then mark them as finished when you complete them.

## Management

The Management section lets you manage your users, security groups (unless you have a P plan subscription), and domains.

Clicking the Users link takes you a page in which you can create users, edit users, reset passwords, and perform other tasks related to user accounts. If you have an enterprise-level plan subscription (e.g., an E3 plan), you'll also see links here about setting up single sign-on and Active Directory synchronization (because both those tasks relate to users). As shown in Figure 1-5, you can use the View drop-down to apply different filters to the list of users. (For example, you can choose to display only unlicensed users to quickly see which ones need licenses assigned.)

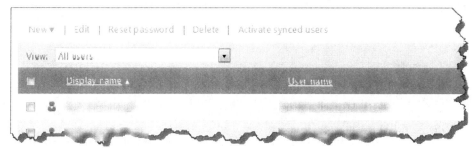

*Figure 1-5. The View drop-down for the user list*

You can edit a user by clicking the person's name or by checking the box on the same row and then clicking the Edit link in the toolbar. Editing users allows you to make changes such as these:

- Modify users' personal details (first and last name, user name, job title, and so on)

- Assign administrative roles to users if you want them to manage all or a portion of your Office 365 account

- Assign licenses to users

- Change service-specific settings for users

---

**Note** If your plan is configured for single sign-on with directory synchronization, personal details of synchronized users must be edited in your on-premise Active Directory environment.

---

The Security Groups link in the Management section allows you to create security groups and add users to those groups. Some groups (such as AdminAgents) are system groups created automatically by Office 365 and cannot be edited. Likewise, any groups that are imported from Active Directory (assuming that you have directory synchronization configured) will be displayed but cannot be edited here.

Finally, the Domains link in the Management section allows you to associate registered domains with your account. Doing so will allow you to use custom domains for e-mail, your public-facing SharePoint site, and your user ID suffixes (e.g., *admin@mycompany.com* rather than *admin@mydomain.onmicrosoft.com*). Note that adding a domain here requires that it be *verified*. The verification process will involve adding some specific DNS records that Microsoft will check, so make sure that you can edit DNS records for any domain you add here.

## Subscriptions

The links in this section allow you to manage your existing plan subscriptions and licenses. The Manage link lets you add licenses to a subscription and edit some of the billing settings. The Licenses link lets you view the number of valid, expired, and assigned licenses for each subscription. The Purchase link lets you purchase new subscriptions.

## Support

The links in this section are for helping you with support and maintenance for your Office 365 subscriptions. The Overview page provides quick links for solutions to common issues, a summary of service requests Microsoft has worked on for you, and information about how to contact Microsoft support. It also provides a link for getting help from the Microsoft Online Community (forums).

The Service Health and Planned Maintenance links give you information about the current status of Office 365 services and what maintenance events are coming up.

If you have an enterprise-level plan subscription, you'll also see a Service Requests link that lets you submit service requests directly to Microsoft support online.

# Accessing SharePoint Online

Regardless of whether you signed up for a small business-level or enterprise-level subscription, the administration portal for your account will have a Team Site link at the top (see Figure 1-6) if your subscription includes SharePoint Online. Clicking this link will take you to your team site.

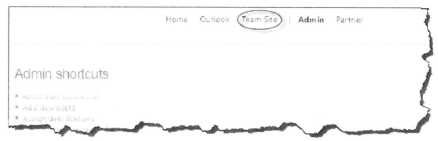

*Figure 1-6. Team Site link on an administration portal*

Exactly where this link takes you within SharePoint, however, *does* depend on what type of subscription you have, as described in Table 1-2.

*Table 1-2. Team Site Link Behavior by Plan Type*

| Plan Type | Team Site Link Behavior |
| --- | --- |
| Office 365 for professionals and small business (P plans) | Navigates to http://*yourdomain*.sharepoint.com/teamsite. |
| | Notice that the team site is a *subsite* of the main site collection, which is your public-facing website if you have a small business plan. |
| Office 365 for enterprises (E plans) | Navigates to http://*yourdomain*.sharepoint.com. |
| | In this case, you're taken to your main team site. We say *main* because it's possible to create additional team sites with an enterprise-level plan. Additional team sites will include */sites/* in the URL; for example, http://*yourdomain*.sharepoint.com/sites/teamsite2. |
| | The public-facing site (if created) for enterprise-level plans is given a URL of http://*yourdomain-web*.sharepoint.com. |

# Managing SharePoint Online

If you have a small business plan, the Admin Overview page in your administration portal will show the SharePoint Online management links pictured in Figure 1-7.

*Figure 1-7. SharePoint Online management links for P plans*

The Manage team sites link will take you to the Site Settings page of your team site, in which you can manage all the settings for your site. The Change permissions link will take you to the Site Permissions page of your team site, in which you can control who has access to your site. The Add sites and templates link will take you to a page in which you can add new structural elements to your site (lists, libraries, subsites, and so on).

If you have an enterprise-level plan, you'll see the SharePoint Online management link pictured in Figure 1-8.

*Figure 1-8. SharePoint Online management link for E plans*

Clicking the Manage link shown in Figure 1-8 will take you to the SharePoint Online administration center shown in Figure 1-9. Think of this page as a replacement for Central Administration in an on-premise SharePoint 2010 environment.

administration center

Manage site collections

A SharePoint site collection is a group of related Web sites organized into a hierarchy. A site collection often shares common features, such as
can be managed together.

Configure InfoPath Forms Services

InfoPath Forms Services enables users to open and fill out InfoPath forms in a browser without requiring Microsoft InfoPath installed on their c

Manage User Profiles

The User Profile service provides a central location where administrators can configure user information, including user profiles, organization

Manage Business Data Connectivity

Business Connectivity Services bridges the gap between SharePoint sites and other web services, databases, and external business application
to external data in lists, and to display external information in Web Parts.

Manage Term Store

A Term Store contains a set of related keywords (called managed terms) organized into a hierarchy of information, such as a well-defined pro
control the entry of list values. A Term Store helps improve the consistency, reliability, and discoverability of information within a site collectior

Manage Secure Store Service

The Secure Store contains credentials such as account names and passwords, which are required to connect to external business applications.
credentials, and associating them to an identity or group of identities.

*Figure 1-9. SharePoint Online administration center*

The administration center is designed to let you access a subset of what you'd normally be able to
access and manage through Central Administration. From here, you create and manage site collections,
configure InfoPath Forms Services, manage user profiles (but not the User Profile Service Application or
the User Profile Synchronization Service), manage Business Connectivity Services (BCS), manage the
term store (managed metadata), and manage the Secure Store Service (SSS). Subsequent chapters will
delve into more detail about several of these areas.

For more information about the SharePoint Online administration center, you can also click the
help icon (not pictured in Figure 1-9) in the upper-right corner of the page.

# Summary

This chapter introduced you to Office 365 and SharePoint Online. We talked about how to sign up for an
Office 365 subscription plan (paid or trial) and how to manage your account with the Microsoft Online
Customer Portal (MOCP). We also covered the core set of plans offered for Office 365 and discussed
some key differences in the management of your account and SharePoint Online depending what plan
you have. The rest of this book, beginning with Chapter 2, will focus on customizing and developing
solutions for SharePoint Online.

# CHAPTER 2

# SharePoint Online Development Overview

There are many who mistakenly believe that Office 365 heralds the end of custom development because of its limitations. Nothing could be farther from the truth. In this chapter, we will take a look at how the rules of development have changed with the advent of Office 365. Although you will need to learn new ways to do things, customizing and extending SharePoint through development will still be an integral part of what companies want to do with SharePoint Online.

Okay, let's get started. In this chapter we will cover the following topics:

- The different approaches and tools available

- Limitations that apply to development and customization

- Customizations available in the browser

- Using SharePoint Designer 2010 (SPD)

- Creating custom code with Visual Studio 2010

## Three Customization Approaches

There are three basic toolsets available when customizing SharePoint Online. First, you can use the web browser to change configuration and customize elements in SharePoint. After you've reached the limit of what is available in the browser you can apply additional customizations to individual sites using SharePoint Designer 2010. If you want to make changes that affect the entire site collection, you will inevitably turn to writing custom code using Visual Studio 2010.

## Customization Through the Browser

Customizing SharePoint Online using only the browser is the easiest and most convenient way to modify how SharePoint Online looks and operates. You can make significant changes in both the look and feel of a site and the functionality available using only a web browser. Possible customizations include, but are not limited to, the following:

- Changing the site title, description, or icon

- Modifying top-level or quick-launch navigation

- Applying themes to change the look and feel

- Creating site columns and content types for storing different kinds of content

- Adding functionality by activating existing site collection or site-level features

- Configuring shared services applications provided in SharePoint Online

- Adding a Content Editor Web Part to embed client-side code (JavaScript/jQuery) on a page

The focus for making most of these changes will be the links found on the Site Settings page shown in Figure 2-1. Site collection administrators and site owners can reach this screen through the Site Actions menu.

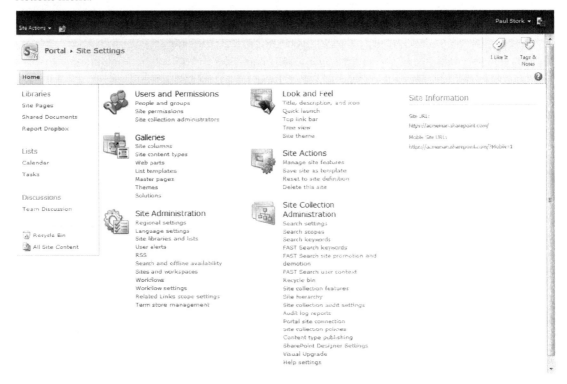

*Figure 2-1. The Site Settings page in a SharePoint Online site*

SharePoint Online also includes a subset of the shared service applications available in an on-premise installation. These services include the following:

- InfoPath forms service

- User profile service

- Managed metadata service

Global administrators can configure these services from links on the SharePoint Online administration center page, shown in Figure 2-2.

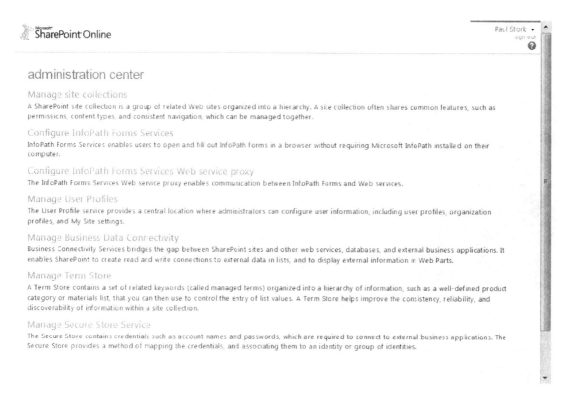

*Figure 2-2. The SharePoint Online administration center page*

## Additional Public Web Site Customizations

In addition to the site settings and service application customizations that are available in all on-premise installations of SharePoint, Microsoft has added additional control over the look and feel of the public web site. When an administrator is logged in to the public web site, an additional ribbon is visible, as pictured in Figure 2-3. This ribbon provides control over many of the aspects of both the master page and regular pages in the site. There are even things such as applying a page background or setting a fixed width to the master page that can only be done with a custom-developed master page in on-premise environments. By using this ribbon, administrators can create a compelling Internet presence environment that is so different from a standard SharePoint look and feel that most users will never know it's running on SharePoint.

■ **Note** This custom design ribbon is only available for pages in the top-level site of the one public web site collection. It is not available for use on the private site collections or subsites of the public web site created in SharePoint Online.

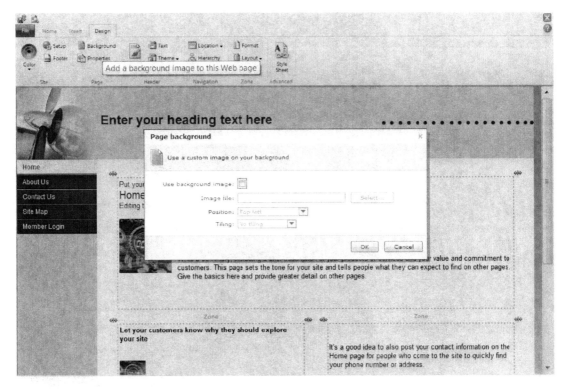

**Figure 2-3.** *Applying a page background to the public web site*

This custom ribbon has the following four tabs:

- *File:* Controls saving and publishing the page.

- *Home:* Similar to the Format Text tab available when editing a WIKI page, you use it to create new pages and format text.

- *Insert:* Adds controls that you can use to add things as simple as an image or as complex as slideshows, embedded video, or maps to the page.

- *Design:* Customizes the color, style, layout, background, and navigation.

There are other ways to accomplish many of the customizations available in this ribbon. For example, you can apply an overall color change to a site by selecting or creating a theme in the Site Settings page. However, some of these enhancements can only be accomplished elsewhere in SharePoint Online using SharePoint Designer or custom-developed code.

## When the Browser Is Not Enough

Although you can make a lot of changes using only the web browser user interface (UI), these changes are often insufficient. Many companies will need to move beyond the capabilities of the browser UI to reach the level of customization they want in SharePoint Online. When the customizations possible using the browser UI fall short of what you envision, the next step is to move to SharePoint Designer 2010.

▪ **Note** Chapter 4 will provide additional details about customizing SharePoint Online using only the browser.

## Customization Through Declarative Solutions and Client-Side Coding with SharePoint Designer

Customizing a site with SharePoint Designer 2010 (SPD) provides an almost identical experience whether you are accessing an on-premise or SharePoint Online environment. The main difference between the two environments will be that you cannot use SPD to connect to external data when customizing a SharePoint Online environment. In spite of this difference, you will probably use SPD more frequently when customizing SharePoint Online than you have in on-premise installations because of the development limitations of SharePoint Online. For example, SPD is the only way to create a workflow for SharePoint Online. SPD provides extensive capabilities to change the look and feel, and extend the functionality of your SharePoint Online site. Using SPD, you'll be able to customize SharePoint Online sites in the following ways:

- Create or apply a theme to change fonts and colors.

- Create and deploy custom master pages.

- Create or edit Cascading Style Sheets (CSS).

- Create or edit new pages or publishing page layouts.

- Build declarative workflows.

- Customize how users view and interact with content.

- Provide access to external data through Business Connectivity Services (BCS).

- Add client-side code to a page.

▪ **Note** Chapter 5 will provide additional details about how to customize SharePoint Online with SharePoint Designer 2010.

## Changing the Look and Feel

SPD has always been one of the preferred tools for prototyping the branding of your SharePoint site, and that won't change because you move to SharePoint Online. Figure 2-4 shows a typical master page being edited in SPD. In addition to its editing capabilities, SPD can do even more to change the look and feel of your site.

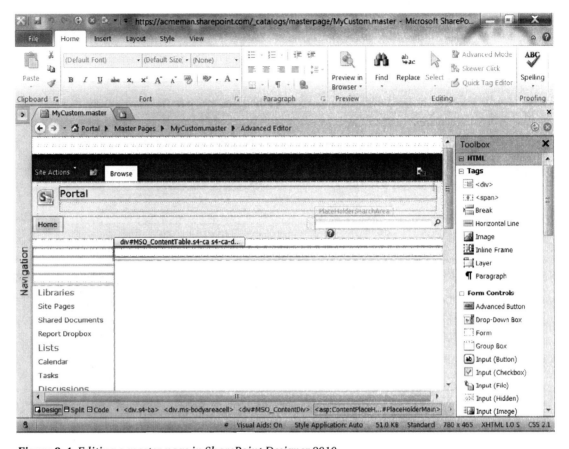

***Figure 2-4.*** *Editing a master page in SharePoint Designer 2010*

## Applying and Creating Themes

Many corporate intranets require only a minimum of branding. Using SPD, you have the same access to themes that you have when using the web browser UI. In fact, selecting the Change site theme link on the summary page for a SharePoint Online site will launch your browser and take you to the Site Theme page under Site Settings in your SharePoint Online site. From here you can select one of the built-in themes, create your own custom theme, and preview what your site will look like.

## Customizing Master Pages

Using SPD, you can easily create or modify a master page. By implementing a custom master, you can insert your company logo, add a standardized footer, modify how navigation is displayed, and much more. The result will be a consistent look and feel for every page in your site. After your master page and CSS customizations are complete, you can apply them to all the pages in your site using buttons on the ribbon.

### Creating Publishing Page Layouts and New Web Part Pages

If your site is using SharePoint's publishing features, then SPD is also the easiest place to create new page layouts. After you've chosen a publishing content type to base your layout on, you can add field controls to the layout to display information on that page. Using publishing and page layouts, you can delegate the creation of content pages in your site to multiple people and still guarantee a consistent look and feel across all the pages.

You can also use SPD to make changes to existing pages in your site or create new nonpublishing pages. Master pages often supply default content to be displayed on the page, but through SPD you can override that default content and change the way a specific page displays. For example, you can easily remove the quick-launch navigation supplied by the master from the left side of the page. This kind of fine-tuned control often removes the need for multiple master pages. You can also easily add your own static content or Web Parts to the page.

### Editing Cascading Style Sheets

SharePoint 2007 used mostly HyperText Markup Language (HTML) tables to control placement of elements on a rendered page. But SharePoint 2010 has concentrated on doing most of this placement through the use of CSS <div> and <span> tags. As a result, SharePoint has an extensive set of CSS files that contain the classes used to control how content is displayed and formatted on a page. SPD provides an easy way to override the built-in CSS files for your site. When you choose to edit a specific CSS class in SharePoint, SPD will automatically make a copy of the built-in CSS file and store it in the content database of your site. Using this copy, you can override the existing CSS classes or create your own custom classes to control how your site is displayed.

## Creating Workflows

One of the most common focuses for wanting to do development in a SharePoint site is to change the way information is processed by your company. Creating controlled, repeatable business processes is the role of workflows in SharePoint. In an on-premise SharePoint installation, you can choose to build workflows in either SPD or Visual Studio. However, due to limitations on custom code in SharePoint Online, you can create workflows only in SPD.

Figure 2-5 shows the creation of a declarative workflow. SPD declarative workflows can even be created in a local on-premise development environment and then uploaded to SharePoint Online as a WSP sandbox solution. You can also extend the set of actions available in SPD by creating custom actions in Visual Studio 2010.

---

### WHAT ARE SANDBOXED SOLUTIONS?

Sandbox solutions are a new feature introduced in SharePoint 2010. They make it possible to upload code to a SharePoint environment without needing access to the server file system. Sandboxed solutions can be deployed by a site collection administrator—or by a user who has the Full Control permission level at the root of the site collection—into the solution gallery for a site collection. Sandboxed solutions have limited access to the server object model and run in a security-restricted context that provides isolation and monitoring of the sandboxed solution's code.

---

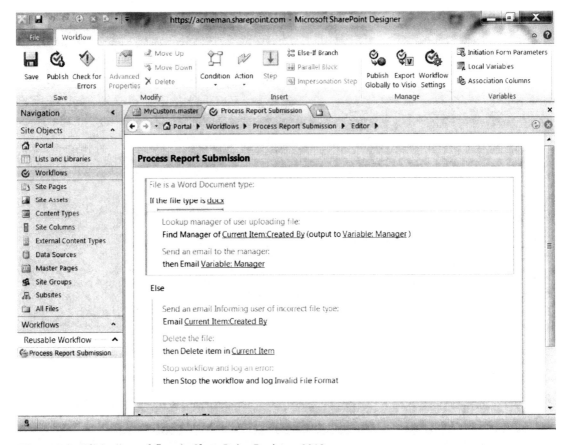

*Figure 2-5. Editing a workflow in SharePoint Designer 2010*

---

■ **Note** Chapter 8 will provide a more detailed discussion of declarative SPD workflows.

---

## Building Dynamic User Interfaces

You can also control how users interact with content through Web Parts using SPD. By default, SharePoint 2010 uses an Extensible Stylesheet Language Transformation (XSLT)–based Web Part to display the contents of lists and libraries. In SPD, you can directly apply conditional formatting, sorting, filtering, and paging to the Web Part. Or you can modify the XSLT used to format the display of content in the Web Part. In addition to customizing the existing XSLT List View Web Part, you can also insert your own Data View or Data Form Web Parts on the page. Using these tools, you can create sophisticated dashboards that highlight critical content for your users.

You can also customize how individual content entries are added, edited, or displayed. Using InfoPath 2010 you can replace existing ASPX (Active Server Page Extended) pages used to create, display, or edit content entries with InfoPath forms.

## Accessing External Data with Business Connectivity Services

Most organizations discover that it isn't feasible to store all their information inside SharePoint. There are a variety of reasons for this. Typically, organizations may find that the following content would not be appropriate to store in SharePoint:

- Files, such as videos, that are too big to upload

- Information stored in third-party line of business applications

- Content that is best stored in a relational database

However, organizations still want to be able to browse or search for all their content, whether it's in SharePoint or not. Using SPD, you can create external content types and external lists that surface data from external data sources. These external lists can even provide full create, read, update, and delete (CRUD) access to this external data. In an on-premise installation, this is often accomplished by surfacing content in external lists through Business Connectivity Services (BCS).

When Office 365 was originally released, BCS was not supported. Microsoft added support for BCS in late October 2011. Although this is a welcome addition, it should be noted that this is more limited than BCS in an on-premise SharePoint farm. On-premise BCS models can connect directly to SQL databases, via .NET class, or through WCF. In SharePoint Online, you can access external data only through WCF endpoints. Despite these limitations, the addition of BCS support opens new opportunities for managing all your information in a SharePoint Online environment.

## Creating Pages with Client-Side Code

One of the frequently overlooked capabilities available in SPD is the insertion of client-side code into a page. SharePoint 2010 added a rich client object model implementation that allows the creation of client-side code using either .NET managed code, Silverlight, or JavaScript. Later in this chapter, we'll discuss deploying client object model code from Visual Studio, but you can also embed this kind of code directly on a page using SPD. More traditional JavaScript or jQuery code can also be embedded on a page. This is often the easiest way to get small snippets of code deployed to specific pages in your environment.

---

⬛ **Note** Server-side code cannot be embedded into SharePoint pages through SPD because of restrictions imposed by the PageParserPath settings in the `Web.config` file. These settings cannot be modified in SharePoint Online.

---

## Limitations Using SPD with SharePoint Online

Although SPD is a powerful tool, there are several limitations that you should be aware of when using SPD to customize SharePoint Online. One of the primary limitations is that SPD is scoped at the web site level. You can only open and edit individual sites in SPD. So when editing a site in SPD, you are unable to apply changes to an entire site collection. For example, if you create a custom master page, you can apply it only to the site you are currently editing. To apply the same master page to subsites using SPD, you would have to open each subsite and apply the master page. However, if the publishing features are enabled, you can apply a master page to an entire web site hierarchy using the user interface. This same limitation exists when working with on-premise sites in SPD.

## Packaging Solutions for Deployment

When customizing sites using SPD, you will frequently work directly on the production site in Office 365. However, sometimes it's better to test your customizations on a local on-premise development environment before you deploy them to Office 365. SPD includes the capability to package many of the customizations you develop as sandbox solutions that can then be deployed to the solution gallery of an Office 365 site collection. Workflows can be saved directly to a sandbox solution template, or you can customize a site and save the whole site as a template. When saving a whole site, you can determine what is saved in the .wsp file. It can contain the entire contents of your site, including views, forms, workflows, and Web Parts. You can also save individual components, such as a list, a view, or a workflow.

# Customization Through Visual Studio 2010

SharePoint Online is based on a multitenant environment. As a result of this shared environment, support for custom code solutions is more limited than in an on-premise SharePoint installation. Using Visual Studio 2010, you can create projects that will be deployed only as sandbox solutions. Deploying custom code to the sandbox user code service restricts the operations that your code can perform and also includes a monitoring environment that keeps your code from adversely impacting other sites on the server. Farm solutions developed in Visual Studio 2010 cannot be deployed to SharePoint Online.

## Using Sandboxed Solutions

Sandbox solutions normally involve custom code that is deployed and run at the site collection level in SharePoint. Where farm solutions in an on-premise environment must be deployed by a farm administrator, sandbox solutions can be uploaded and activated by any site collection administrator. Figure 2-6 shows a site collection administrator uploading and activating a sandbox solution. Sandbox solutions are uploaded to a solutions gallery in the top-level site of the site collection. When activated, they run in an environment that restricts their functionality. For example, sandbox solutions cannot run with elevated privileges or access external data. Monitoring is also conducted to ensure that a solution does not negatively impact the stability of the rest of the environment. Because of the shared environment that underlies SharePoint, online sandbox solutions are the only way to upload and run custom code.

■ **Note**  You should install the Visual Studio Power Tools for SharePoint to properly error check compilation of sandboxed solutions for Office 365.

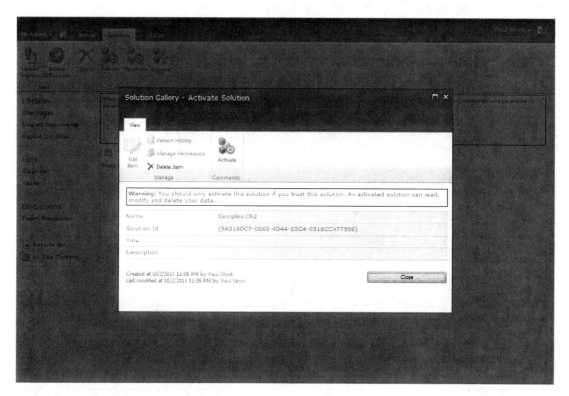

*Figure 2-6. Activating a sandbox solution*

■ **Note**  Chapter 7 will provide more coverage of sandbox solution development for SharePoint Online.

## Client Object Model

SharePoint 2010 introduced a robust client object model that can be leveraged using .NET managed code, Silverlight, or ECMAScript (JavaScript/jQuery). SharePoint Online's requirement that server-side code only be deployed using sandbox solutions, and the limitations imposed by that deployment, will lead to an increased reliance on client code. The client object model APIs provide a subset of the features available in the server object model, but are relatively full featured when manipulating objects at the site-collection level or below. Client-side code is also one of the primary workarounds for calling XML web services to interact with data that is stored in external systems.

---

**Note** Chapter 9 will discuss SharePoint's client object model in more detail.

---

# Customization Limitations

As we have seen, SharePoint Online supports many of the same customization and development options that are available in a SharePoint 2010 on-premise deployment. However, there are some limitations that need to be considered when developing for SharePoint Online. There are a variety of reasons for these limitations, but many of them are imposed because SharePoint Online is based on the multitenant environment. This imposes several limitations, including the following:

- Can only access objects stored within the site collection

- Cannot modify files in the server file system

- No deployment of managed code assemblies to the Global Assembly Cache (GAC)

- Cannot deploy Farm-level solutions

- Cannot create SharePoint timer jobs

- Only a subset of shared service applications are provided

There are workarounds for several of these limitations that will be discussed in later chapters. These workarounds frequently use client-side code in place of a managed code assembly deployed on the server.

## Sandboxed Solution Limitations

Not all of the SharePoint 2010 project templates available in Visual Studio 2010 can be deployed using sandbox solutions. Table 2-1 lists the project types that can be deployed to the sandbox and those that cannot.

*Table 2-1. Sandbox-Supported and Sandbox-Unsupported Project Types*

| Supported | Unsupported |
|---|---|
| Empty Projects | Visual Web Part |
| List Definition | Sequential Workflow |
| Event Receiver | State Machine Workflow |
| Content Type & Site Column | Business Connectivity Model |
| Module | Site Definition |
| | Import Reusable Workflow |

---

▨ **Note** Installing the Visual Studio Power Tools for SharePoint will add a Visual Web Part project that can be added using a sandbox solution.

---

## Missing Shared Service Applications

Because of SharePoint Online's multitenant environment, there are only a limited subset of the shared service applications that are available in an on-premise environment. Lack of support for several of these service applications imposes significant limitations on custom development in SharePoint Online. SharePoint Online currently does not include support for the following service applications:

- PerformancePoint Service Application

- Secure Store Service

- Web Analytics Service Application

- Word Automation Services

# Summary

In this chapter, we provided an overview of the different approaches available for customizing and extending SharePoint Online in Office 365. In later chapters, we'll examine each of these approaches in greater detail. Table 2-2 summarizes the points discussed. Now let's turn our attention to building an environment that we can use to develop customizations for our Office 365 environments.

*Table 2-2. Development Capabilities of SharePoint Online vs. SharePoint On-Premise*

| Feature | SharePoint Online | SharePoint Server 2010 (On-Premise) |
|---|---|---|
| Browser configuration | Full access to site settings<br>Access to a limited number of shared service applications<br>Custom ribbon for customizing public web site | Full access to site settings<br>Able to deploy farm solutions<br>Create and configure all service applications |
| SharePoint Designer customization | Create rich data visualizations<br>Manage business processes through workflow<br>Create and deploy custom branding<br>Implement client-side code | Create rich data visualizations<br>Manage business processes through workflow<br>Create and deploy custom branding |
| Visual Studio 2010 | Sandbox solutions only<br>Silverlight, .NET Framework managed code, or JavaScript client-side code<br>InfoPath forms with sandbox code | Farm or sandbox solutions<br>Silverlight, .NET Framework managed code, or JavaScript client-side code<br>InfoPath forms with compiled code<br>XML web services<br>REST API |

**CHAPTER 3**

▣ ▣ ▣

# Setting up a Development Environment for SharePoint Online

## Introduction

To be able to customize your SharePoint Online environment for Office 365, you first need to set up a development environment locally. Some of the changes to your online environment can be made directly to the SharePoint Site Collections and pages in your online environment without the need for a local development environment. However, there are other customizations that can be deployed to your SharePoint Office 365 Site Collections only by way of a specialized packaged solution file. These solution files can be constructed using Visual Studio 2010 (and later editions). A local environment helps avoid the necessity of direct production changes without the ability to experiment and refine solutions.

### Goals

The primary goal in setting up a development environment for SharePoint Online and Office 365 is to have a place to work on customizations that is not your primary production environment. The online offerings of Office 365 do not provide a common development and testing environment as part of the core offerings, so a different approach is needed to be able to make ongoing modifications that will not affect your end users.

Other goals that are related to this can include initiating a repeatable environment and process for all the software developers in your organization to be able to develop, test and deploy solutions and customizations for SharePoint Online and on your corporate Office 365 instance. Also a goal could be to provide management and end users the ability to preview, give feedback on, and approve solutions being developed before they are deployed to Office 365. Still another goal could be compliance with any internal corporate procedures and processes in place related to software development.

### Hardware and Software Requirements

#### Hardware Requirements

Table 3.1 shows the hardware requirements for SharePoint Server 2010.

*Table 3-1. SharePoint Server 2010 Hardware Requirements*

| Component | Minimum Requirement |
|-----------|---------------------|
| Processor | 64-bit, 4 cores. |
| RAM | 4 GB for developer or evaluation use. |
| | 8 GB for production use in a single server or multiple server farm. |
| Hard disk | 80 GB for system drive. |
| | You must have sufficient space for the base installation and sufficient space for diagnostics such as logging, debugging, creating memory dumps, and so on. For production use, you also need additional free disk space for day-to-day operations. Maintain twice as much free space as you have RAM for production environments. |
| | For more information, see "Capacity management and sizing for SharePoint Server 2010" (`http://technet.microsoft.com/en-us/library/cc261700.aspx`). |

SharePoint 2010 is a product that is built based on a 64-bit code base. As such, SharePoint 2010 can be installed on operating systems that are 64-bit. For the purposes of Office 365 customizations, it is not necessary to install a local development SharePoint environment as a full-featured SharePoint 2010 Server install on one of the 2008 Server products. It is sufficient to work with a Windows 7 x64 operating system and a simplified SharePoint 2010 Server installation there. The scripting option shown later in this chapter—the SharePoint 2010 Easy Setup Script—offers two options for installing SharePoint 2010 on Windows 7 environments through a PowerShell-scripted environment.

For a virtualized hardware environment it is important to keep in mind that some processors do not support 64-bit virtualization.

## Software Requirements

The key point to remember regarding software requirements for SharePoint 2010 is that SharePoint 2010 is an x64 application. It is built upon a 64-bit base, so it can be installed only on 64-bit operating systems. This is different from SharePoint 2007. The exact details behind all the operating systems supported can be found, including the latest information at the SharePoint Technet sites at `http://technet.microsoft.com/en-us/library/cc262485.aspx`. A shortened version of that list is as follows:

- Windows 2008 Server R2

- Windows 2008 Server (with patches)

- Windows 7 x64 (with patches)

- Windows Vista x64 (with patches)

The server products are useful for server installations, but it is fine to use Windows 7 x64 for your development environment.

# Virtual Machine Options

If you are accustomed to standard ASP.NET or other .NET development environments, you might not be used to working in a virtual machine (VM). SharePoint can be set up in any supported environment on a VM, just as it can on physical hardware.

To run VMs on your local Windows 7 (or other OS) environments, you will need some type of hypervisor (virtualization) software. For SharePoint development, there are a few choices available.

---

⬛ **Note** The hypervisor software (as well as your hardware) *must* support 64-bit operating systems.

---

## Hypervisor Software

Hypervisor software is software that specializes in running a full virtual machine within software on another machine. Virtual hard drives (.vhd files for HyperV or .vmdx files for VMWare) are used as operating system drives, and machine settings are stored within VMs. There are several options on the market for this type of software.

VMWare Workstation is a full-featured hypervisor option for running VMs. You can learn more about the software, licensing, and purchasing options at http://www.vmware.com/

VirtualBox is a free option available at https://www.virtualbox.org/. It is the only option of its kind released under the GNU GPL (version 2), so a core portion of it is guaranteed to remain free. It is a fully featured hypervisor or virtualization product and works well for SharePoint 2010 and Office 365 development.

Hyper-V is a hypervisor that Microsoft provides and is available as a role on the 2008 Server R2 products. It is also available as a free operating system (OS) from Microsoft. The OS is Microsoft HyperV Server 2008 R2. It can be obtained from Microsoft Downloads at
http://www.microsoft.com/download/en/details.aspx?displaylang=en&id=3512

For x86 environments (such as running a hypervisor on a laptop Windows 7 OS), VMWare Workstation and VirtualBox are the only products supported. HyperV Server or Windows Server 2008 R2 can be run on a laptop or desktop environment, but many convenience options such as Power Saver options on laptops will be missing.

VMWare and VirtualBox are great solutions for mobile or demo environments on laptops or desktops running Windows 7. Standalone server hardware or an old desktop that is upgraded to have enough hardware is a great environment for running Windows 2008 Server R2 or HyperV Server 2008 R2.

---

⬛ **Note** At some point not too far from the intended publication date of this book, Windows 8 and Windows 8 Server environments will become available with more-advanced virtualization options. Be sure to check on those options before settling on a path for your development environments.

---

## Advantages and Disadvantages of Virtual Machines

There are advantages and disadvantages of using VMs as opposed to setting up your development environment on your main local hardware.

### Advantages

- **Snapshots**: Easier to reset virtual environments.

- **Scalability**: You can store a VM for each client, project, or customer you work for to keep it contained.

- **Mobility**: You can copy and move VMs to and from more permanent storage solutions as necessary. Included in this advantage is the ability to pull up an old VM to look at something you worked on years ago.

- **Templates**: You can save VM configurations as templates and run sysprep on them to remove individual machine SIDs. This makes copying and spinning up a new VM much faster.

### Disadvantages

- **More work**: It is more work to install another OS on a VM. Some of that can be alleviated with templates and other tools (such as SystemCenter Virtual Machine Manager and some of VMWare's Labmanager products, which are more expensive).

- **Storage**: It takes more disk space.

- **Time**: Copying around all those VMs consumes a lot of time that you could avoid with a simple hardware SharePoint environment.

- **Snapshots**: It takes a lot of discipline to maintain and record snapshots diligently. Restore might not take you to exactly where you want to go. Sometimes many snapshots can degrade an OS; we've had to take a machine out of and rejoin domains at times because of this problem.

We like the best of both worlds: we maintain a local SharePoint environment that is simple for doing quick walkthroughs and code tests, but do the bulk of the customization and development work in VMs.

## Visual Studio 2010 Setup

To develop solutions for SharePoint 2010 (including Office 365) with Visual Studio, your development environment must meet the requirements outlined in this section.

## Version

Visual Studio 2010 Professional or higher is required in order to get the SharePoint 2010 development templates. You must also enable either the Visual C# or Visual Basic feature, or both, when installing Visual Studio.

## Visual Studio 2010 SharePoint Power Tools

One important add-on to Visual Studio for Office 365 development is the Visual Studio 2010 SharePoint Power Tools found at `http://bit.ly/jdeGVF`. These tools include a template for building Visual web parts in a sandboxed solution. The advantage is that you can use the built-in Visual Designer in Visual Studio to help build customizations.

## Visual Studio Extensions

One of the most useful extensions to Visual Studio 2010 for doing SharePoint 2010 development is the CKS Development toolkit (found at `http://cksdev.codeplex.com`). This is the Codeplex center for development surrounding the tools. However, the actual installation extensions are distributed through the Visual Studio Gallery at `http://bit.ly/eLft1J`.

## Resources

The one other resource that is recommended for download for getting started with SharePoint 2010 online development is the product SDK – that is available at `http://msdn.microsoft.com/en-us/library/ee557253.aspx`. This has rich code and platform examples to help you be able to get a head start on SharePoint development.

Another great online resource is the SharePoint 2010 Online Developer Resource Center at `http://msdn.microsoft.com/en-us/sharepoint/gg153540`.

# SharePoint 2010 Local Setup

Two separate versions of SharePoint 2010 are available for local setup: SharePoint Server (SPS) 2010 and SharePoint Foundation (SPF) 2010. While SPF is sufficient for the majority of customizations you will want to create, if you are trying to access Term Stores such as the ones in your Office 365 E1-E4 plans, you may wish to install SPS. If you are developing against an Office 365 P1 plan, SPF is sufficient.

## Office 365 SharePoint Unique Points

Office 365 offers an environment that is somewhat unique when compared with SharePoint on-premise installations. The overall look and feel of SharePoint's express team site is different (see Figure 3-1).

*Figure 3-1. Office 365 team site*

There are many other unique points to Office 365 as we start drilling down into development techniques. Other chapters in the book will start to highlight them as we develop the concepts further.

# SharePoint 2010 Easy Setup Script (for Setting Up a Dev Environment)

One of the tools that has been provided by members of Microsoft's product teams (the Metro SharePoint Productivity Team) is a PowerShell-based setup script that makes setting up a development environment on Windows 7 for SharePoint 2010 much simpler.

This Easy Setup script can be downloaded from `http://www.microsoft.com/download/en/details.aspx?id=23415`. Extracting the downloaded .zip files to the default download location unzips it to C:\SharePoint2010EasySetup. The files appear as shown in Figure 3-2.

| Name | Date modified | Type | Size |
|------|---------------|------|------|
| Assets | 10/20/2010 3:19 PM | File folder | |
| images | 10/20/2010 3:19 PM | File folder | |
| Labs | 10/20/2010 3:19 PM | File folder | |
| Presentations | 10/20/2010 3:19 PM | File folder | |
| styles | 10/20/2010 3:19 PM | File folder | |
| Videos | 10/20/2010 3:19 PM | File folder | |
| Default | 10/20/2010 3:19 PM | HTML Document | |
| Demo | 10/20/2010 3:19 PM | HTML Document | |
| EasySetupLab | 10/20/2010 3:19 PM | HTML Document | |
| Eula | 10/20/2010 3:19 PM | HTML Document | |
| Lab | 10/20/2010 3:19 PM | HTML Document | |

*Figure 3-2. Installed SharePoint EasyScript files*

The EasyScript files consist of HTML files, a Microsoft PowerPoint presentation, a lab file written up in Microsoft Word, and a series of PowerShell scripts for installation. All these are packaged up into an HTML based learning package that is similar to the Microsoft Online Learning Labs.

One of the reference files that shows up in the Easy Setup Lab is the *SharePoint 2010 Professional Developer Evaluation Guide and Walkthroughs,* which can be found at http://www.microsoft.com/download/en/details.aspx?displaylang=en&id=7204.

While this evaluation guide is very useful, it is more focused toward standard SharePoint development. There is a more pertinent evaluation guide titled *SharePoint Online for Office 365: Developer Guide* that can be found at http://www.microsoft.com/download/en/details.aspx?id=17069.

This guide at the time of writing is the beta version of the guide. The contents are more directly focused on SharePoint Online development, so should be referenced in place of the standard guide.

## Prerequisites

Before kicking off the Easy Setup Script, we need to determine whether we will choose to install SharePoint directly on the Windows 7 box or if we want to set it up on a bootable VHD.

---

■ **Note** A bootable VHD will provide an additional option on bootup of Windows 7 to allow you to select the Easy Script SharePoint environment to boot to rather than your current OS. This can be effective for isolating your development environment but is less convenient than having everything on your Windows 7 work environment.

---

## Running Easy Setup Script

After downloading the SharePoint 2010 Easy Setup Script, we can get started by opening up the Default.htm file and navigating through the Easy Setup labs. Start with the "Getting Started With Sharepoint Development" lab, which will help you download and set up your SharePoint environment.

Browse to the Labs directory – Easy Setup Lab – Source – found at
C:\SharePoint2010EasySetup\Labs\EasySetup\Source. Click the Run.bat file; the output is shown in
Figure 3-3.

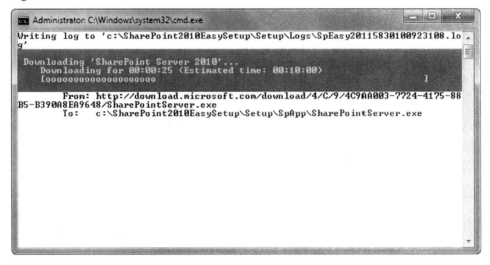

***Figure 3-3.*** *Start of SharePoint Easy Setup batch script: run.bat*

In the default running of the script, all the necessary software will download to the Setup directories
of your SharePoint2010EasySetup folders.

Included are all the following (trial editions):

- SharePoint 2010 Server

- SharePoint 2010 Prerequisites

    - Filter Pack

    - Chart Controls for .NET 3.5

    - Sql Server 2008 Analysis Services

    - Windows Identity Framework

    - Sql Server 2008 Native Client

    - Synch Framework

- Visual Studio 2010 Ultimate Edition Trial

- Silverlight 4 Tools for Visual Studio

- Expression Studio 4 Ultimate Trial

- Open XML SDK

- Visual Studio 2010 SDK

- Visual Studio SharePoint Power Tools

- Office 2010 Professional Plus Trial (includes InfoPath 2010)

- SharePoint Designer 2010

- Visio 2010 Trial

Next, the setup script asks if you want to install on this host or on a new VHD (see Figure 3-4).

*Figure 3-4. Install on this host or VHD*

The script proceeds to install the prerequisites and set up SharePoint 2010 (see Figure 3-5).

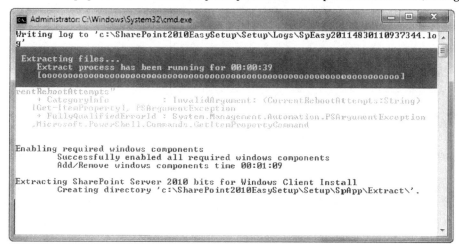

*Figure 3-5. Installing prerequisites and SharePoint 2010*

After the script completes running, you should be able to browse to the default URL for your computer and pick a template, as Figure 3-6 shows.

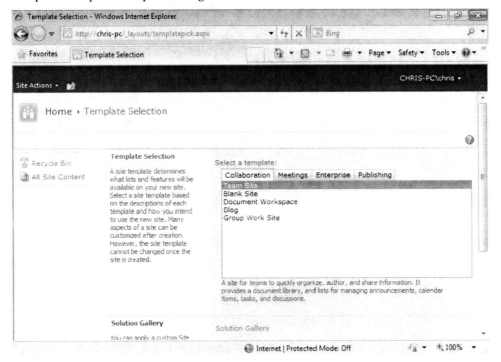

***Figure 3-6.*** *Select template*

Then you should be able to browse to your local team site, as shown in Figure 3-7.

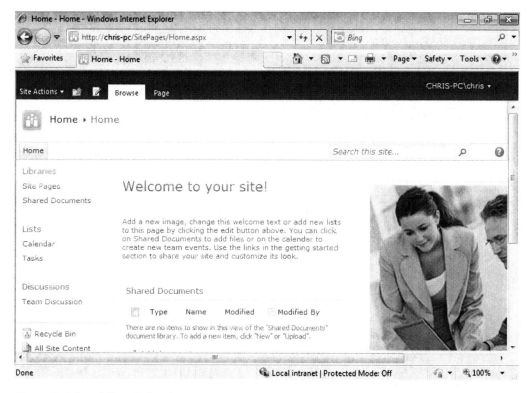

**Figure 3-7.** *Local SharePoint site*

# SharePoint 2010 Setup on Windows 7

For installations outside of using EasyScript, the MSDN article entitled "Setting Up the Development Environment for SharePoint 2010 on Windows Vista, Windows 7, and Windows Server 2008,"which is found at http://msdn.microsoft.com/en-us/library/ee554869(office.14).aspx, is an excellent resource. It highlights specific steps for installing SharePoint 2010 on Windows 7.

The difference in setting up SharePoint 2010 on Windows 7 as opposed to a Windows Server product is that the automated Prerequisites Installer that is available on the server products is not available on Windows 7 (or Vista*).

---

■ **Note** We are obligated to mention Vista as an option because it is officially supported and is mentioned in the MSDN and TechNet articles. However, no .NET developer is likely at the time of this writing to be doing development work on a machine with Vista installed on it. As a result, we focus mainly on Windows 7 in this chapter.

---

For Windows 7 installs, you need to run the Prerequisites Installer yourself. The Easy Setup Script provides an automated way to do that. Also, resources are available to automate the download of prerequisites. One source is the Technet Gallery at `http://bit.ly/kBjdbG` or search for "Download SharePoint 2010 Pre-Requisites". This is the script portion of the Codeplex project AutoSPInstaller (`http://autospinstaller.codeplex.com/`). The advantage is that you can do prerequisites installations in environments in which your computer cannot reach the Internet.

If you follow the standard setup steps shown in the article, you should have a SharePoint 2010 environment ready to start customizing.

## Sandboxed/User Code Service Setup

One final thing that you need to ensure before starting to deploy sandboxed or user code solutions in your local environment is that the service that supports them needs to be turned on in your SharePoint environment. The **Microsoft SharePoint Foundation Sandboxed Code Service** is a Windows Service that is started and stopped in SharePoint through Central Administration.

We will enable the Microsoft SharePoint Foundation Sandboxed Code Service through Central Administration. The following steps outline the process:

1. On the Start menu, click All Programs, click Microsoft SharePoint 2010 Products, and then click SharePoint 2010 Central Administration.

2. In the System Settings section, click Manage Services on Server.

3. In the list, next to the **Microsoft SharePoint Foundation Sandboxed Code Service**, verify that the service is started or click **Start** to start the service.

If you are testing in a multiserver environment, the Sandboxed Code Service must be started on at least one of the web front-end (WFE) servers. Starting it on multiple WFE servers will allow for load balancing of sandboxed solutions.

When this service is running, you can deploy sandboxed solutions to your local environment as well as attach your Visual Studio debugger to them.

## Duplicating Your Office 365 Environment

For a local development environment, it is desirable to duplicate as many settings as you can from your Office 365 SharePoint environment. This would include a representation of users and permissions, although you won't be able to exactly duplicate these locally. You also won't be able to duplicate exactly the same sandboxed or user code solution filters as there are in the Office 365 environment. However, a close approximation on your local settings will help you to develop your solutions in an efficient manner, without needing to rework things that could be avoided due to disparate settings between your on-premise development environment build and your Office 365 environment. Aside from duplicating settings as closely as you can, another approach that's often used is to create a fresh site collection in your Office 365 environment that serves as a test-bed for testing your customizations. You can delete the site collection when you're done testing to free up resources. Of course, this approach assumes that you have an Office 365 for Enterprises plan that allows you to have multiple site collections.

# SharePoint Designer 2010 Setup

Another tool commonly used for customizing SharePoint Online is SharePoint Designer (SPD) 2010. SPD can be used for customizing pages, master pages, and workflows.

# Installation

SPD 2010 can be downloaded and installed for free by visiting http://bit.ly/jWplOw. This is the 32-bit version, which is best for most development environments.

---

■ **Note** The 32-bit version corresponds to the 32-bit version of Microsoft Office 2010. If you have installed the 64-bit version of Microsoft Office 2010, also install the 64-bit version of SharePoint Designer 2010. The 32-bit versions of Microsoft Office work a little bit better with respect to the social media plug-ins available and some synchronization tools. Even though SharePoint 2010 is 64-bit, and you have a 64-bit SharePoint 2010 install on your local Windows 7 environment, use the Microsoft Office 2010 32-bit version and SPD 32-bit version for best results.

---

The download and installation of SPD 2010 is pretty straightforward. Follow the installation wizard to successfully install SPD.

## Connecting SharePoint Designer to SharePoint

To connect to SharePoint, open SPD 2010, as in Figure 3-8.

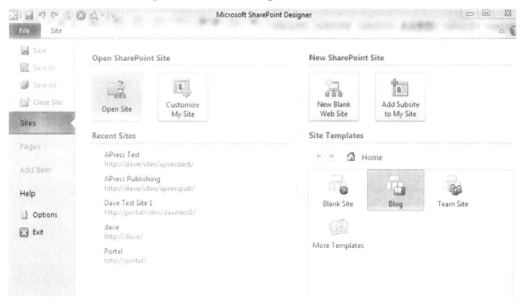

*Figure 3-8. SharePoint Designer initial screen*

In Figure 3-8, several of the Recent Sites selections represent the URLs of local SharePoint Site Collections that we have connected to recently with SPD.

To connect to a new site in Office 365, click "Open Site" and type in the URL of your Office 365 team site, as in Figure 3-9.

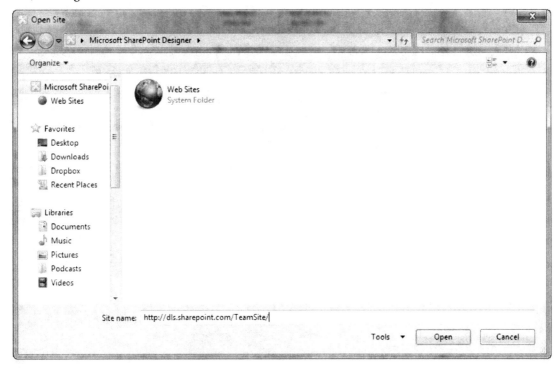

***Figure 3-9.*** *Open team site in SPD*

If the site is local, you will connect directly to it.

# Connecting to Office 365

To connect to Office 365, enter the URL of your Office 365 team site, as shown in Figure 3-9. This will connect you to the remote team site on Office 365 instead of to one of your local SharePoint sites.

After you click the "Open" button, you may be presented a credentials screen like the one shown in Figure 3-10.

**Figure 3-10.** *Credentials screen from SPD 2010*

Credentials for your Office 365 account must be entered to allow SPD access to your Office 365 team site. After you enter your credentials successfully, you will see your Office 365 team site properties screen in SPD as shown in Figure 3-11.

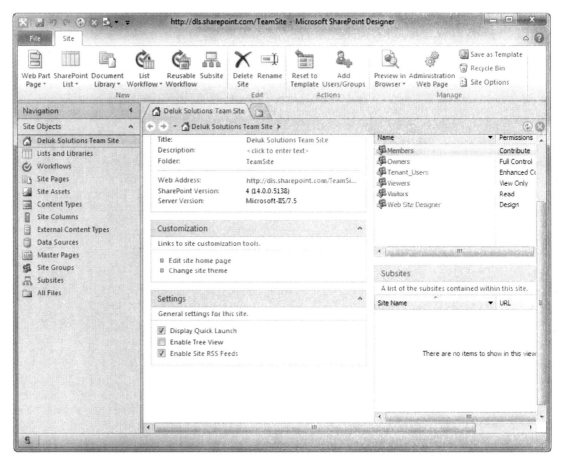

***Figure 3-11.** SPD 2010 open to Office 365 team site*

# Setting Up a Good HTML Editor

Some SharePoint customizations for Office 365 can involve a good HTML editor. Easy Scripts installs a trial version of Expression Studio Ultimate edition, which includes Expression Web 4. While SharePoint Designer 2010 has some capabilities with respect to editing and producing HTML, there are some areas in which you might want to utilize another good HTML editor to shore up how things will look prior to plugging them into your final page design. Many HTML editors (either on the market as products or free versions) will have tools for quickly crafting CSS, JavaScript, and HTML together. You can prototype designs in another editor and then plug them into SPD 2010 in your development environment for final checking.

# Team Development

One of the biggest questions that arises when starting to set up environments for customizing Office 365 is how to work together with a team of other developers who also are making changes to the environment. Some core tenets of team development for Office 365 include each developer maintaining his or her own local development environment, and then having a common development and/or testing environment in which all changes can be tested before rolling them to production.

# Common Virtual Hard Drive Images

One great way to work with all developers having their own SharePoint 2010 local environments is to set up all the prerequisite software to prepare one developer machine and then sysprep the machine image to be able to clone to other developers' environments. Full SharePoint development images will require at least two virtual machines (VMs): one for the domain controller to contain Active Directory and another for the SharePoint environment. To be able to fit both machines on a USB drive, you will need a 64 GB drive to hold them. You may be able to squeeze a basic development image on a 32 GB drive, but a 64 GB drive will definitely provide enough room to include other software on your development images.

The problem of standardizing on and providing common development environments for your SharePoint development teams is a very common one. Solving it by providing a standard development environment on a sysprepped USB drive or download folder will save many setup hours for a developer and development teams.

# Environments

## Local Development Environment

The local development environment is the one that we have been setting up in this chapter to this point. It offers debugger attach capabilities and a quick turnaround for testing. This is the primary starting point for Office 365 development.

## Centralized Test Environment

While it is ideal to have a local test environment to test all your SharePoint changes and customizations against, it is recommended that before you deploy your changes to your production Office 365 or SharePoint Online site, you should perform a final verification of the functionality of what you are deploying in an environment that closely mirrors your Office 365 platform.

There are a couple of possibilities that are available with respect to setting up an online centralized test environment.

### Test Office 365 Site Collection

A simple solution is to simply set up a separate site collection within your Office 365 SharePoint account to use as a testing environment. To do this, log on to Office 365 as an Administrator and select "Manage" under SharePoint Online (see Figure 3-12).

> ■ **Note** The Admin features shown are part of the enterprise-level Office 365 plans (E1 to E4). If you have a P1 plan, it allows a total of only one Site Collection, so it is not possible to add a new one for test purposes.

*Figure 3-12. Manage SharePoint Online*

From the SharePoint Online screen, select "Manage Site Collections," as shown in Figure 3-13.

*Figure 3-13. Manage site collections*

Add a new site collection, as shown in Figure 3-14. Ensure that you select the "Private Site Collection" option in the drop-down menu as opposed to a public website.

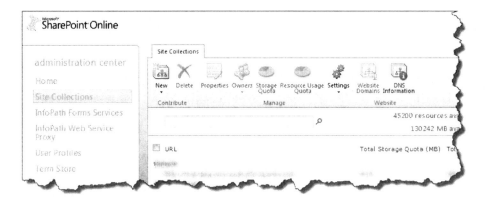

*Figure 3-14. New site collection*

The New Private Site Collection option displays the pop-up window shown in Figure 3-15.

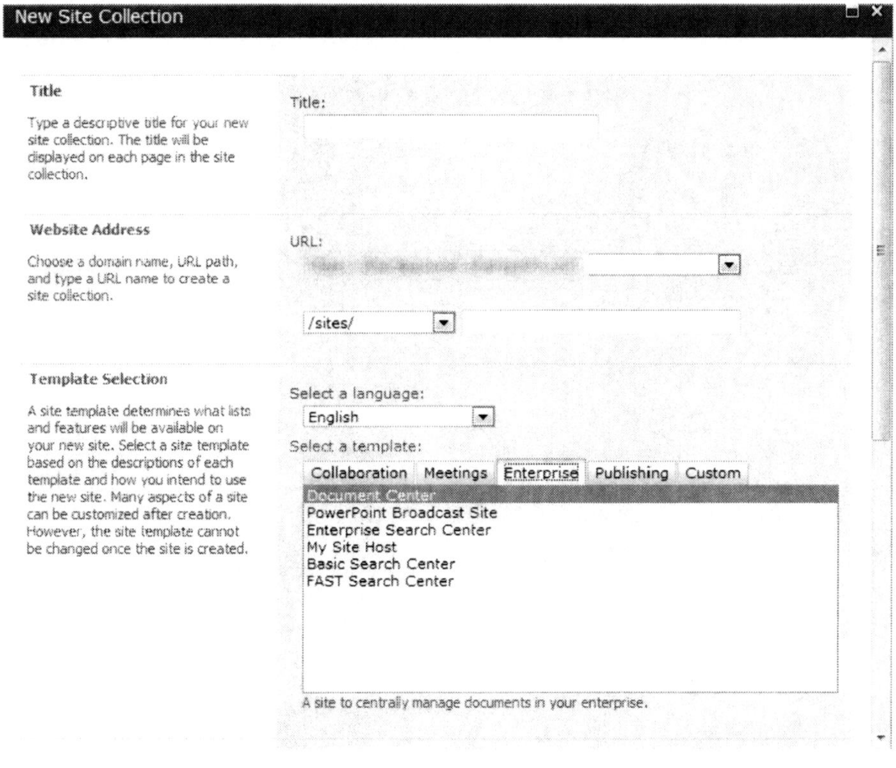

*Figure 3-15. New Site Collection window*

Depending on the Office 365 plan that you purchased, you can select from a number of site templates including the standard Collaboration templates as well as Meeting, Publishing, and Enterprise templates. Provide a title and a URL for the website address.

Next, scroll down to see the rest of the screen (see Figure 3-16).

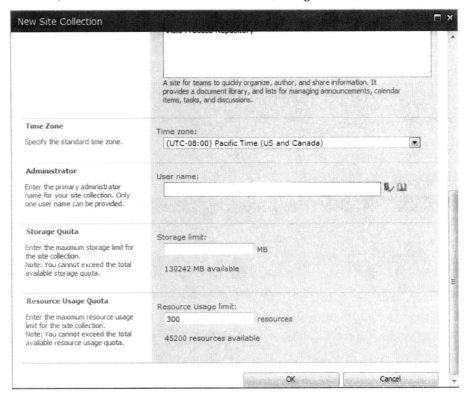

*Figure 3-16. New Site Collection window 2*

Select a primary administrator from your online users. You can also add other administrators later and grant access to the site collection directly through the site collection permissions. The storage quota is a limit on the overall storage for the site collection.

The Resource Usage quota is a site collection metric compiled by SharePoint Online. The main purpose of resource quotas is to limit the risk that custom code may negatively affect the site collection.

Now you are ready to deploy customizations to a site collection that mirrors your production environment.

## Test Office 365 Account

One possibility for a centralized test environment is to purchase a separate Office 365 account that has only one (or a limited number) of accounts set up as test accounts. This would completely separate the test environment from any production environment, including different access URLs and credentials.

The cost of this solution would simply be the monthly cost of the individual test user licenses involved in the separate account. One thing to consider with this option is to ensure that the type of plan you use for your test account matches your production account. (Example: A P1 test account and an E3 production account might not match up well.)

---

■ **Note** The process for adding test site collections to a new account is the same as for a new site collection in your production account. This option could be a possibility for small businesses who have P1 plans for Office 365 because each P1 plan only offers one site collection.

---

# Change Control

One critical thing to consider when starting to do customizations to the Office 365 environment is to instantiate some form of a change control process for ensuring quality in the environment. Because sandboxed solutions are already somewhat controlled, it can be tempting to bypass all the diligent processes that your company already has in place for deploying code to production in other environments. This is not a good practice to adopt!

On the contrary, the same discipline that you have for your other development environments should carry directly over to SharePoint Online. Three critical concepts to put in practice are source control, binary control, and a process.

## Source Control

Source control is a core fundamental of software development. For SharePoint 2010 Online and Office 365, you should be using a source control system to maintain your codebase and customizations. There are many options available, including the ALM product offering from Microsoft that includes Team Foundation Server, or TFS. One advantage of using TFS is that it has a high level of integration with SharePoint, and SharePoint site collections house many TFS features.

What you use for source control is not as important as the fact that you *do* use source control.

## Binary Control

One question that commonly comes up is what should be stored in a source control system versus what should be compiled and deployed every time. SharePoint solutions deploy as packaged .wsp files. It is a decision for each development team whether or not they want to store .wsp files directly in source control or depend on the repeatable process in the test builds that produce a high enough quality result to not to have to store .wsp files in source control.

## Process

Equally as important as using source control is to hone a process for SharePoint Online development. Build, test locally, test in a common dev/test site collection, obtain user approval through user acceptance testing UAT, and then deploy to production. This a very quick and high level depiction of a process for deploying customizations.

# Summary

This chapter walked you through the process of setting up a local development environment to use when customizing SharePoint Online. We covered the requirements for installing SharePoint locally and discussed some of the advantages and disadvantages of using virtual machines over actual physical hardware. For those who want to use a Windows 7–based development environment, we talked about the Easy Setup PowerShell script Microsoft provides for installing SharePoint and its prerequisites on Windows 7. We also talked about tools you'll want to install for development work, approaches for making your local environment "match" your production environment, and some best practices related to change control.

This chapter delved into setting up a development environment for Office 365 and SharePoint Online. Now you are ready to dive into customizing your Office 365 environment.

# CHAPTER 4

# Basic Customization Using Only a Browser

As discussed in Chapter 2, there are three approaches you can take when customizing SharePoint Online. In this chapter, we'll be focusing on the easiest of those approaches: customizing SharePoint Online using only your web browser. The other two approaches—customizing it with SharePoint Designer and customizing it with Visual Studio—will be covered in Chapters 5 and 7, respectively.

Before proceeding further, it's important to understand that customization using only a browser is the least flexible approach. You're limited to only what you do through the SharePoint Online web interface. However, it's also the easiest approach to master and can cover a fairly broad set of scenarios without the need for more advanced tools or skills.

In this chapter we'll cover the following topics:

- When to Use the Browser

- Customizing Your Site's Look and Feel

- Customizing Site Structure and Pages

- Publishing-Enabled Sites

- Customizing the Simple Public-Facing Website

---

**Note** Remember to ensure you have the correct permissions on an object (site, list, page, and so on) before attempting to customize it.

---

## When to Use the Browser

SharePoint Designer and Visual Studio are both powerful tools for customizing SharePoint Online. So when does it make sense to stick with using only a browser? Here are a couple of questions that can help you decide.

## How Broad Are the Customizations?

Browser-based customizations are best suited for smaller, one-time, *ad hoc* scenarios. For example, you want to change the theme of a single subsite in your site collection. That's a simple, one-time customization that can easily be made in a browser. There's no compelling reason to pull out SharePoint Designer or Visual Studio for such a simple change.

But what if you have 30 subsites in your site collection, and you want to create an instance of the same custom list in every one of them? You could do it using only the browser, but it would be a painfully tedious (and error-prone) process. In that case, using Visual Studio to create and deploy a custom list definition would probably make a lot more sense.

## Who Will be Doing the Work?

As with many things in SharePoint, the skillset of the person (or people) doing the work is a big factor when choosing an approach. Anyone with the appropriate permissions and some basic training can customize SharePoint Online using a browser. No technical background or development skills are required.

Using SharePoint Designer or Visual Studio, on the other hand, requires a more technical skillset and some deeper knowledge about SharePoint as a platform.

# Customizing Your Site's Look and Feel

Let's begin by talking about how to customize the look and feel of your SharePoint Online site. Everything we do in this section will be done from the Site Settings page (Figure 4-1), which can be accessed by clicking the Site Settings link on the Site Actions menu. In particular, we'll be focusing on the *Look and Feel* section of that page.

---

■ **Note** This section assumes you're customizing an internal site, not the simple public-facing website you get with SharePoint Online. Customization of the public-facing site is discussed later in this chapter. Also, if you're working in a publishing-enabled site, see the "Publishing-Enabled Sites" section near the end of this chapter.

---

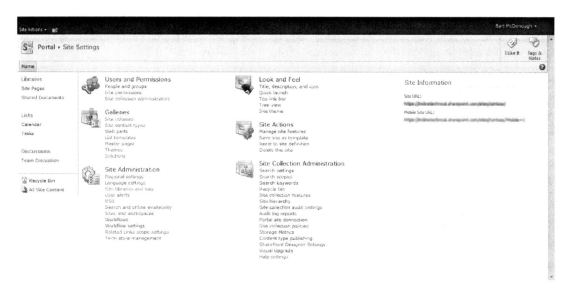

*Figure 4-1. The Site Settings page in a SharePoint Online site*

# Title, Description, and Icon

The first link in the *Look and Feel* section lets you customize your site's title, description, and icon. When you click that link, you'll be presented with the page shown in Figure 4-2.

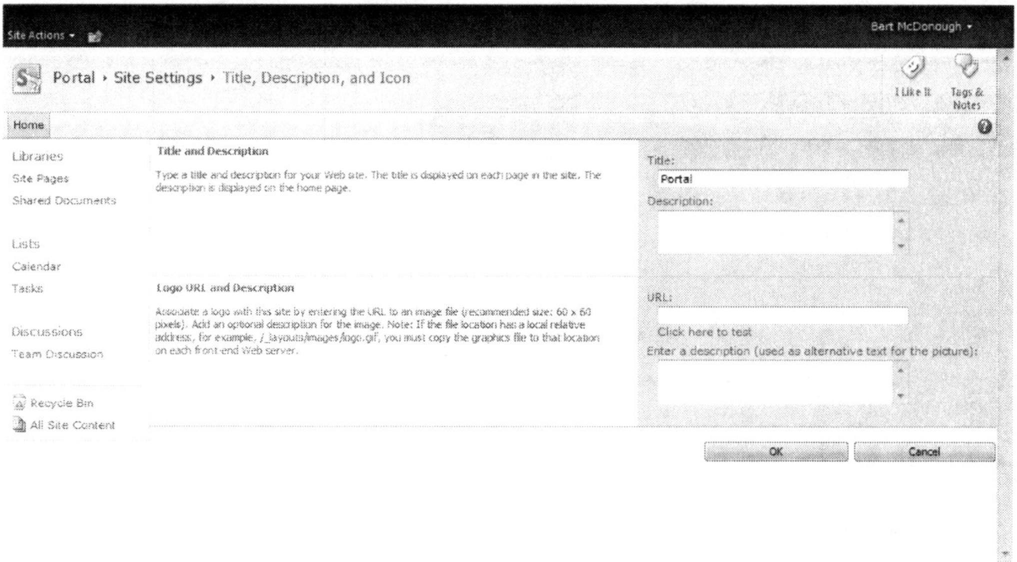

*Figure 4-2. The Title, Description, and Icon page*

If you're working in a subsite rather than in the top-level site (site collection), there's an additional *Web Site Address* field at the bottom of the page (see Figure 4-3). This additional field lets you change the last part of the URL for the site (for example, from "Human Resources" to "HR").

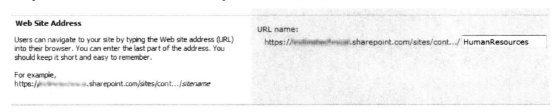

*Figure 4-3. Web Site Address field on Title, Description, and Icon page*

To change your site's title, type a new title in the *Title* field. The site title is displayed in the upper-left part of the page and is the first link in the breadcrumb navigation trail. The site in Figure 4-2 is titled "Portal."

To change your site's description, type your desired description in the *Description* field. Note that even though the text to the left of the *Description* field says the description is displayed on the site home page, it may appear on other pages as well. For example, wiki pages in the Site Pages library will typically display the site description even if they're not the site home page.

To change your site's icon, enter the URL of a new icon in the *URL* field. Optionally, you can enter a description as well. The icon description isn't visible on the page but can aid visually impaired users in navigating your site if that's a requirement.

Also, even though the text to the left of the *URL* field mentions the "_layouts" directory, it's not likely you'll be referencing that directory because you don't have access to deploy custom files to it in SharePoint Online. Instead, consider storing your icon in a document library on your site (like the Site Assets library) and referencing it there.

Figure 4-4 shows how the upper-left part of a page might look when all three of these elements are customized.

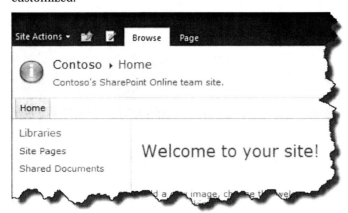

*Figure 4-4. Site home page with custom title, description, and icon*

■ **Tip** If you customize your site's icon, we recommend the new icon be appropriately sized to fit nicely on the page. SharePoint Online won't automatically scale or crop it for you. The icon shown in Figure 4-4 is 32x32 pixels in size.

## Quick Launch

The second link in the *Look and Feel* section of the Site Settings page lets you customize your Quick Launch menu. The Quick Launch menu is the menu that appears on the left side of your pages. In a brand new site created using the Team Site template, it will initially contain headings such as *Libraries*, *Lists*, and *Discussions*.

To customize the Quick Launch menu, begin by clicking the *Quick launch* link on the Site Settings page. You'll be presented with the page shown in Figure 4-5.

***Figure 4-5.*** *Quick Launch settings page*

To add a new heading, click the *New Heading* link at the top of the page. There are two values you'll need to specify: the *Web Address* and the *Description*. The web address is the URL that a user will navigate to if they click on your heading. The description is the actual text that appears on the Quick Launch menu.

Figure 4-6 shows a custom heading on the Quick Launch menu along with the settings used to create it.

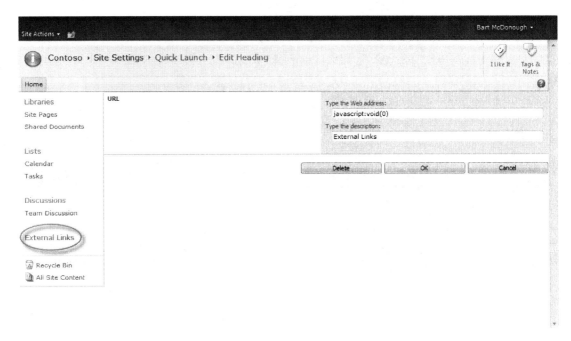

*Figure 4-6. Custom Quick Launch heading with settings*

One thing that probably stands out when you look at Figure 4-6 is the javascript:void(0) text that's in the *Web Address* field. Unfortunately, when creating a new heading, SharePoint Online doesn't give you a way to specify that you *don't* want the heading to be a link. And since the *Web Address* field is required, you can't just leave it blank, so you have to employ a work-around. A link with a URL of javascript:void(0) is effectively a "dummy link" because clicking it won't cause a web browser to navigate anywhere.

However, another approach that's more consistent with the other headings is to create a new page (perhaps called "External Links") that acts as a landing page for the heading. When the heading is clicked, users navigate to that page, and the same links will be listed there that are listed under the heading. We included the approach shown in Figure 4-6 simply to illustrate that there are multiple ways to solve the problem.

To add a new link, click *New Navigation Link* on the Quick Launch setting page. The page for adding a new link looks almost identical to the page for adding a new heading except for one extra field called *Heading*. This field allows you to select the heading under which your link will appear.

To edit or delete a heading or link, click its *Edit* icon as shown in Figure 4-7.

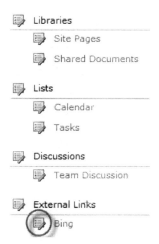

*Figure 4-7. Edit icon on Quick Launch settings page*

---

▪ **Note** Deleting a heading will also delete all the links beneath it.

---

Lastly, you can change the order of the headings and links on the Quick Launch menu as well. Just click the *Change Order* link on the Quick Launch settings page.

## Top Link Bar

The next link beneath *Quick launch* on the Site Settings page is *Top link bar*. Clicking this link will take you to the Top Link Bar settings page. This page works exactly the same way as the Quick Launch settings page, except there are no headings. Instead you can work only with links.

## Tree View

Clicking the *Tree view* link on the Site Settings page will take you to the page shown in Figure 4-8. The Tree View settings page allows you to enable or disable the site's Tree View as well as the Quick Launch menu. As shown in Figure 4-8, the Tree View (when enabled) appears under the Quick Launch menu on the left side of the page and is titled "Site Content."

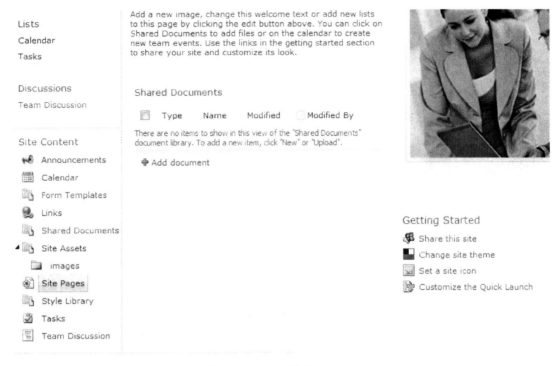

*Figure 4-8. SharePoint Online site with Tree View enabled*

One caveat to keep in mind is that disabling both the Tree View *and* the Quick Launch menu does *not* get rid of the shaded gray area on the left side of the page where they're located. Hiding that whole area requires making some Cascading Style Sheets (CSS) changes, which can be done on individual pages using a Content Editor Web Part (discussed later in this chapter). Also, even if the Quick Launch menu is disabled, some items (such as the *Recycle Bin* and *All Site Content* links) will continue to appear since they're technically outside of the Quick Launch menu.

## Site Theme

Clicking the *Site Theme* link on the Site Settings page will take you to the page shown in Figure 4-9, in which you can customize the theme of your site.

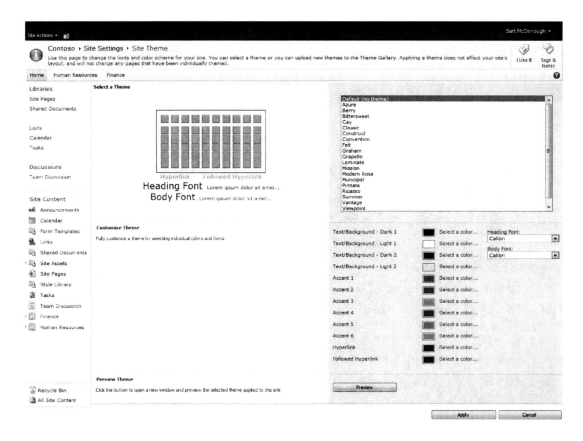

**Figure 4-9.** *Site Theme page on a SharePoint Online site*

---

■ **Note** If you're using SharePoint Online for professionals and small business (P plans), the page shown in Figure 4-9 will not contain the *Customize Theme* or *Preview Theme* sections. Those sections only appear in SharePoint Online for enterprises (E plans).

---

The Site Theme page lets you choose a different theme for your site (a *theme* is a set of coordinated colors and fonts). If your Office 365 plan is a P1 plan, you must choose from one of the preinstalled themes, and no further customization of the theme is possible.

However, if you're using an E1-E4 plan, you can customize the theme's colors and fonts in the *Customize Theme* section of the page. For each color listed in that section, SharePoint generates five additional shades of that color (for a total of six, ranging from lightest to darkest). The color chart in the upper-left part of the page will show you the full range of colors used by the theme.

If you're working in the top-level site of your site collection, you can also upload your own custom theme to the site's Theme Gallery. The theme will then be available for you to select on the Site Theme page. Creating your own custom theme for SharePoint Online is relatively easy. See http://bit.ly/qPSost for an explanation of how to do it.

# Customizing Site Structure and Pages

In this section we'll talk about how to customize the structural elements of your site. By "structural elements," we mean anything related to data or document storage (such as lists, columns, and content types).

## Lists and Libraries

It may not be intuitive to think of creating lists and libraries as "customizing" your site, but in fact that's exactly what it is. Any time you change the structure of your site to accommodate your particular data storage needs, you're customizing your site.

---

■ **Tip** When deciding whether to create a list or library, remember that libraries are for storing files (such as documents or pictures). Lists are for storing data (such as contacts or calendar events), but can be configured to allow file attachments on items if desired.

---

## Creating a List or Library

You can create a new list or library by opening the Site Actions menu and selecting the More Options… link. If your browser has the Silverlight plug-in installed (which we recommend for the best user experience), you'll see the dialog shown in Figure 4-10.

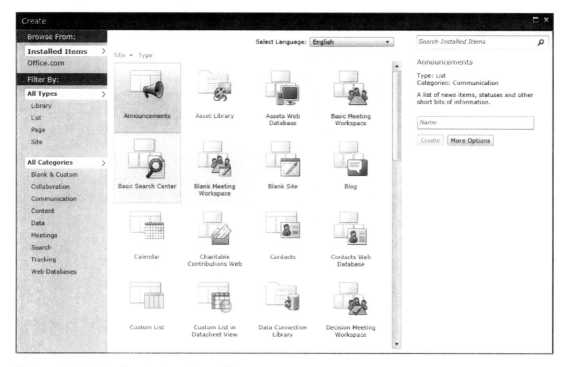

*Figure 4-10. Dialog for creating a list or library*

As you can see, this dialog doesn't just let you create lists and libraries. You can also use it to create pages, subsites, and other items. To create a list or library, we recommend you select *List* or *Library* under the "Filter by" section on the left. This will filter the items in the center of the dialog down to just lists or libraries (depending which filter you selected). Figure 4-11 shows how the dialog would look if you selected the *List* filter.

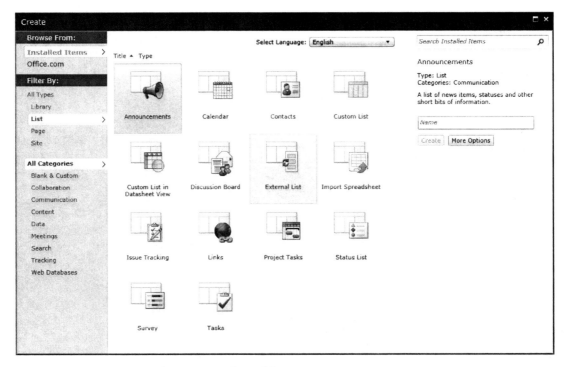

*Figure 4-11. Filtered dialog for creating a list or library*

The items you see listed on the dialog represent the different types of lists and libraries you can create. Clicking an item will show you a brief description of it on the right to help you decide whether it's the one you want. If desired, you can also click the *More Options* button on the right to specify more properties (other than just the name) for your list or library. However, you can also change those same properties after the list is created.

One recommendation is that when typing the name of your list or library on this dialog, enter it *without* spaces (e.g., "PolicyDocuments" instead of "Policy Documents"). After the list or library has been created, you can edit the name and insert spaces. The reason for this recommendation is the URL of a list or library is based on its initial name (when it first gets created). If the name contains spaces, the URL will have %20 inserted in place of each space, which makes for a messier URL. A messier URL isn't necessarily a big deal, but it is a bit of a pain when you're giving it out to people, doing any custom development against the list down the road, and so forth.

---

**Note** If you just want to create a document library and don't need to see the other list and library templates, you can select *New Document Library* from the Site Actions menu.

---

## Editing a List or Library

To edit a list or library, navigate to one of its views (for example, its "All Items" view). A new group of ribbon tabs will appear and will be titled either "List Tools" or "Library Tools" (depending on whether you're looking at a list or library). Click the *List* or *Library* tab. On the right side of the ribbon under that tab is the *Settings* group. Click the *Library Settings* or *List Settings* button in that group (see Figure 4-12) to edit the list or library.

*Figure 4-12. Library Settings button on the ribbon*

From the list or library settings page, you can customize many different aspects of the list or library. You can change its title, specify whether it appears on the Quick Launch menu, enable versioning, allow attachments, change permissions, and change a variety of other settings, too.

## Deleting a List or Library

To delete a list or library, first go to its settings page, as described in the preceding section ("Editing a List or Library"). In the middle of the page, under the *Permissions and Management* heading, you'll see a link titled "Delete this document library" or "Delete this list." Click that link to delete the list or library.

## List Columns and Content Types

The settings page for your list or library allows you to manage columns and content types to help meet your data storage needs.

To manage columns, look at the *Columns* section of the settings page (shown in Figure 4-13).

Columns

A column stores information about each document in the document library. The following columns are currently available in this document library:

| Column (click to edit) | Type | Required |
|---|---|---|
| Title | Single line of text | |
| Created By | Person or Group | |
| Modified By | Person or Group | |
| Checked Out To | Person or Group | |

Create column
Add from existing site columns
Column ordering
Indexed columns

*Figure 4-13. Columns section of the List/Library settings page*

From here you can create new list columns, edit existing ones by clicking their name, re-order columns, or index columns (indexing columns can help improve performance on large lists—see `http://bit.ly/uBg8YW` for more information). You can also use columns to link lists together that contain related data. For more information on linking lists, see `http://bit.ly/tnsh8u`.

To manage content types, you first must ensure that the list allows management of content types. To do that, click the *Advanced settings* link under the *General Settings* heading on the settings page. Make sure that the *Allow management of content types* setting is set to "Yes." Otherwise, you won't be able to manage content types on the list or library.

If management of content types is allowed, a new section called *Content Types* will appear on the settings page above the *Columns* section (see Figure 4-14).

### Content Types

This document library is configured to allow multiple content types. Use content types to specify the information you want to display about an item, in addition to its policies, workflows, or other behavior. The following content types are currently available in this library:

| Content Type | Visible on New Button | Default Content Type |
| --- | --- | --- |
| Document | ✔ | ✔ |

Add from existing site content types

Change new button order and default content type

*Figure 4-14. Content Types section of the List/Library settings page*

You can use the links in this section to add content types, edit existing ones by clicking their name, or control how content types are displayed on the *New* menu for the list or library (used when creating new items).

## List Views

*List views* are pages that let you view list items in SharePoint Online. An example is the page you see when you navigate to the Shared Documents list on a team site. That page is the "All Items" view of the library and lets you view all documents in the library.

You can customize these views to a fairly high degree just using your browser. There are two ways you can do it. The first way is to use the *List* or *Library* tab that appears on the ribbon when you're looking at a list view. The second is to go to the list or library settings page and work with the *Views* section at the bottom of the page. Both ways allow you to create, modify, and delete list views. You can also designate a specific list view as the "default view" that users see when they navigate to the list's URL (e.g., http://www.contoso.com/Shared%20Documents).

When creating a view, the first thing you must choose is the view format. There are a variety of choices, including a Standard View, Calendar View, Datasheet View, and Gantt View. Depending on the type of view you're working with, you'll have different configuration options for sorting, filtering, grouping, scope, and so on. If your permissions allow it, you'll also have the option of making the view private (visible to you only) or public (visible to everyone).

For more information about working with views, see `http://bit.ly/rVN7hq` (SharePoint Online for enterprises) or `http://bit.ly/uEDDRf` (SharePoint Online for professionals and small business).

## List Templates

One nice feature of SharePoint Online is the ability to create and use custom list templates. A *list template* allows you to save a specific list configuration and then create new lists (from the template) that are configured exactly the same way. Similar to how "Announcements" and "Discussion Board" are two templates that come with SharePoint Online, you can create your own custom templates that appear in the dialog for creating lists and libraries.

To create a list template, navigate to the settings page for a list or library. In the middle of the page under the *Permissions and Management* heading, you'll see a "Save list as template" or "Save document library as template" link. Clicking that link will take you to the page shown in Figure 4-15.

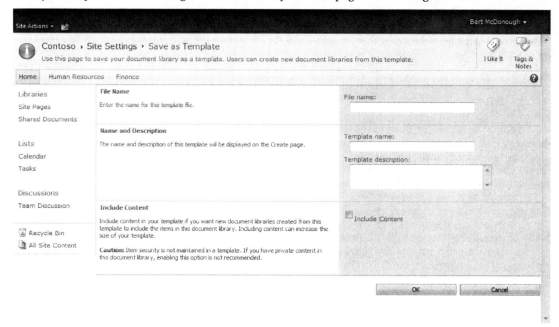

*Figure 4-15. Save as Template page in SharePoint Online*

When saved, the list template will be stored as a file (with an .stp extension) in the List Templates Gallery of the top-level site in your site collection. The name you specify in the *Template name* field will be the name used in the dialog for creating a new list or library (refer to Figure 4-10).

Once saved to the List Template Gallery, the list template is available for use anywhere in your site collection. However, you can also upload the template to a different site collection and use it there as well. (Just be aware that if your list contains lookup columns or other column types that reference specific items in your site, those columns may not work properly in the new site collection unless they are reconfigured.)

To move a list template to a new site collection, start by navigating to the Site Settings page of the top-level site in the site collection in which you saved the template. Under the *Galleries* heading, click the *List templates* link to view the List Templates Gallery. Download and save the template file you just created.

Next, navigate to the List Templates Gallery of the target site collection where you want to use the template. Upload the template file you saved earlier to the gallery. Now the list template is available for use in that site collection as well.

# Site Pages

Creating and editing pages in SharePoint Online is pretty straightforward. Creating a new page is as simple as selecting New Page from the Site Actions menu and giving it a name. As indicated on the new page dialog window, the new page will be added to the Site Pages library on your site.

---

**Note** The information in this section pertains to pages that you create and edit in a site *without* publishing features enabled. See the "Publishing-Enabled Sites" section near the end of this chapter for information on working with pages in publishing-enabled sites.

---

To edit a page, first navigate to the page. Once there, click the *Edit* button under the *Page* tab on the ribbon (or click the edit icon to the right of the Site Actions menu). Once in edit mode, the *Editing Tools* ribbon tab group will appear to aid you in editing the page. One tab–the *Format Text* tab–focuses on editing and formatting text on the page (including raw HTML if you so desire). The other tab—the *Insert* tab–focuses on adding new elements to the page (images, links, web parts, list views, and so on).

You can also change the layout of a page by using the *Text Layout* button under the *Format Text* tab. Note that you must select one of the prebuilt layouts. You cannot create your own custom page layout using a browser. If none of the built-in page layouts meets your needs, consider using SharePoint Designer to create a custom page that's laid out the way you desire.

For more information on Site Pages, see http://bit.ly/skTfB5 (SharePoint Online for enterprises) or http://bit.ly/sYA66A (SharePoint Online for professionals and small business).

## Content Editor Web Part

The *Content Editor Web Part* is a simple web part that allows you to add markup directly to a SharePoint page. Despite its simple appearance, this web part is actually fairly powerful because it allows you to do more than just add text, images, links, and other visual elements to your page. You can also add JavaScript (ECMAScript) code and CSS markup within the web part, allowing you to make more powerful customizations and even call into the ECMAScript API of the Client Object Model (see Chapter 9).

Adding the web part to a page is simple. Simply switch the page to edit mode, click the *Insert* tab in the ribbon, click the *More Web Parts* button, and select *Content Editor* from the *Media and Content* category (see Figure 4-16).

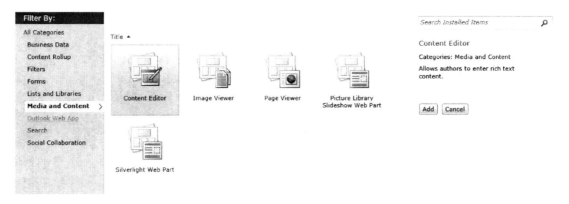

*Figure 4-16. Adding a Content Editor web part to a page*

Once on the page, open the web part's menu and select *Edit Web Part*. Now you have two options: add content directly to the web part or use the *Content Link* field to link to a file containing your content (markup).

Suppose we edit the web part and add the following markup to it (using the *HTML* button under the *Format Text* tab in the ribbon):

```
<style type="text/css">
    #s4-leftpanel {
        display: none;
    }
    .s4-ca {
        margin-left: 0;
    }
</style>
```

When we save our changes to the web part, the area containing the Quick Launch menu on the left side of the page disappears. So by adding a web part and this little bit of code, we effectively changed the layout of our page to make the main content stretch across the entire browser window. A layout like this might be good for a page in which secondary navigation isn't needed—such as a welcome or splash page.

If you like to use jQuery, you can also use a Content Editor Web Part to integrate jQuery into your page. Just upload the jQuery application programming interface (API) into a document library, add a Content Editor Web Part that references the library (using a `<script>` tag), and you're ready to use jQuery!

---

▓ **Tip** If all you're using your Content Editor Web Part for is JavaScript or CSS code, you'll probably want to set its *Chrome Type* property to "None." That way, the web part border and title won't render on the page.

---

## Site Columns

A *site column* is a data field that can be used by the lists, libraries, and content types on your site. Unlike a list column (a column created for a specific list), a site column is available across an entire site as well as its subsites. See http://bit.ly/uCEnTu for an overview of column types and options.

## Site Content Types

A *content type* represents a way to categorize or classify data in SharePoint Online. It is a reusable set of columns, workflows, behaviors, and other settings that can be applied to a document or list item. For example, all policy documents on your site could have a content type of "Policy Document" applied to them. This would ensure that they're all treated the same way and contain the same metadata (list item properties).

You can manage content types from the Site Settings page (which can be accessed by selecting Site Settings from the Site Actions menu). Under the *Galleries* heading on the Site Settings page, click the *Site content types* link. This will take you to the Site Content Types page where you can create, modify, or delete content types for your site. Site content types are available to the current site as well as its subsites.

For more information, see http://bit.ly/u9of2n (SharePoint Online for enterprises) or http://bit.ly/vhNvL7 (SharePoint Online for professionals and small business).

## Subsites

Using your browser, you can create *subsites* in your site collection by clicking New Site on the Site Actions menu.

When the dialog for creating a new site appears, you'll notice two tabs across the top: *Featured Items* and *Browse All*. By default, the *Featured Items* tab is selected when the dialog first appears, and the *Express Team Site* template is selected as the template for your subsite. (If you're using an Office 365 P1 plan, the Express Team Site template is the template from which your team site was created. It's easy to identify because the Quick Launch menu includes an "[+ Add New Page]" link.) To select a different template, select the *Browse All* tab.

The fields on the right side of the dialog allow you to specify the title and URL name (last part of the URL) for your subsite. Optionally, you can click the *More Options* button and specify other information, such as the subsite's description, permissions, and navigation settings.

## Site Templates

Similar to list templates, *site templates* allow you to save a site's configuration (properties, structure, features, and content) as a reusable template from which you can create other sites. The template is saved to the solution gallery of the top-level site (site collection) and appears on the new site dialog window when creating a new site.

To save a site as a template, go to the Site Settings page for the site. Click the *Save site as template* link under the *Site Actions* heading. For a detailed walk-through of the process and more information about site templates, see http://bit.ly/tVwaUo.

# Publishing-Enabled Sites

If you're using SharePoint Online for enterprises, you also have the option of working with *publishing-enabled sites* (*publishing sites* for short) and publishing pages. If your site isn't already publishing-enabled, see http://bit.ly/v5qqMe for an explanation of how to activate the publishing features in your site and/or site collection.

Also, if you haven't already done so, we suggest you look at http://bit.ly/svWlBM for an overview of working with and customizing publishing sites. Certain tasks, such as customizing navigation, are slightly different from when working with nonpublishing sites.

## Publishing Pages

Similar to how nonpublishing sites use site pages for displaying their content, publishing sites use publishing pages. The goal of *publishing pages* is to enforce a certain level of consistency across a site while still allowing nontechnical users to easily edit pages in a browser.

To create a new publishing page, you have a couple of options. One option is to use the Site Actions menu and select New Page. This will create a new publishing page (normally based on the Article Page content type) for your site and save it in the Pages library (as opposed to the Site Pages library, where site pages live). The other option is to navigate directly to the Pages library and use the *New Document* button on the ribbon (under the *Documents* tab). Opening the menu beneath that button will allow you to choose the exact type of publishing page (for example, Article Page or Welcome Page) you wish to create.

When editing a publishing page, you also have a couple of options. You can edit the page or you can edit its properties (metadata) by editing its list item properties in the Pages library.

To edit the page, navigate to the page and click the *Edit* button under the *Page* tab on the ribbon (or click the edit icon to the right of the Site Actions menu). This will check out the page to you (assuming that it isn't already checked out, and you haven't disabled that behavior) and put it in edit mode so you can make changes. Note that not all page properties may be visible and editable on the page when it's edited. Sometimes, editing a page's properties (through its list item) is the only way to change certain property values. For more information on editing page properties, see http://bit.ly/sYoVmf. For more information on the overall process of creating and editing publishing pages, see http://bit.ly/sCL5kd.

Depending on the way your Pages library is configured, pages may also need to be submitted for approval before they're published. If that's the case, you can submit a page for approval after editing it and wait for a user with appropriate permissions to approve or reject the page. If approved, a major version of the page is published. See http://bit.ly/vpkRon for an explanation of how to approve or reject pages that are pending approval.

## Customizing the Simple Public-Facing Website

If you're using SharePoint Online for professionals and small business, you automatically get a simple public-facing website as the top-level site in your site collection (the team site that you get is actually a subsite of that public-facing site).

However, if you're using SharePoint Online for enterprises, no public-facing site is created by default. Instead, you have the option of creating one if you desire (from the SharePoint Online administration center).

Either way, the public-facing website is intended to serve as a simple "brochure-ware" style website for your business. It's not intended to be data-driven or heavily customizable. It's important to understand this up front because if you don't, you'll be disappointed and frustrated by the customization experience (which differs from how site pages are customized).

We covered basic customization of the public-facing site in Chapter 2. For more detailed information and articles about customizing the public-facing site, see http://bit.ly/rMUe6W (SharePoint Online for enterprises) or http://bit.ly/kHZyYv (SharePoint Online for professionals and small business).

## Summary

This chapter discussed several ways to customize your SharePoint Online sites. We provided some guidelines on when it's appropriate to stick with browser-only customization. The next two chapters cover other approaches you can take to customize your site when browser-only customization isn't sufficient to meet your needs.

# CHAPTER 5

# Taking It to the Next Level with SharePoint Designer

You can do a lot to customize SharePoint online using just the web user interface (UI). But you inevitably run into the limitations when using just a web browser. To overcome these limitations, you need to move up to using SharePoint Designer (SPD) 2010. Development done in SPD is frequently called *customization* rather than *development* because the edits you make will be made using declarative statements instead of server-side compiled managed code assemblies. That's why development in SPD is frequently referred to as *no-code development* (even though you can still write code using HTML, XML, or client-side script).

This chapter takes a detailed look at how to use SPD as a development tool for customizing SharePoint Online. With SPD 2010, you can move beyond the basic customizations available in the UI to rapidly developing rich custom applications.

Okay, let's get started. In this chapter, we will cover the following topics:

- Using SPD to administer a SharePoint site

- Enhancing the display of data by customizing the XSLT List View or Data Form Web Parts

- Accessing external data using Business Connectivity Services (BCS)

- Customizing the look and feel of a SharePoint site

- Using SPD 2010

- Creating custom code with Visual Studio 2010

## Getting Started With SharePoint Designer 2010

One of the real advantages of using SPD 2010 as a development environment is that it's available as a free download from Microsoft. You can download either a 32-bit or 64-bit edition depending on your existing installation of Office 2010. If you haven't downloaded and installed SPD yet, you should do so before proceeding with this chapter. You can get it from these sources:

- **SPD 2010 32-bit**: `http://www.microsoft.com/download/en/details.aspx?id=16573`

- **SPD 2010 64-bit**: `http://www.microsoft.com/download/en/details.aspx?id=24309`

---

■ **Note** Although SPD 2007 can't be used to edit Office 365 SharePoint Online sites, SPD 2010 can be used to customize either on-premise or online SharePoint installations.

---

If you install SPD and still can't open your site, keep reading. The use of SPD might be disabled in your site collection. Controlling the use of SPD in your site collection is explained more fully in the next section.

## Controlling the Use of SPD 2010

One of the first things you need to do after installing SPD 2010 is to decide what users can do with it. By default, the use of SPD in SharePoint Online is very limited for anyone other than site collection administrators. Members of the Site Owners group or users with the Add and Customize Pages permission can open a site. But they can't edit a master page, create a publishing page layout, view files that arc hidden in the UI, or apply any customizations that aren't allowed using the UI. In other words, by default most users can't do anything with SPD that can't already be done in other ways. If you want to use SPD to customize your online site, you need to either be a site collection administrator or enable the full use of SPD through the SharePoint Designer Settings page shown in Figure 5-1. This page can be reached from a link in the Site Collection Administration section of the Site Settings page and is only available to site collection administrators.

---

■ **Note** Turning on the publishing features in your site collection will change the default settings and automatically enable all four options.

---

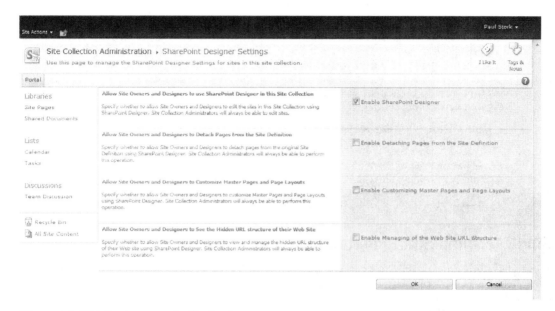

*Figure 5-1. SPD Settings page in Site Settings*

There are four settings available on the SharePoint Designer Settings page. Let's take a look at these options in order:

- **Enable SharePoint Designer**: This option controls whether sites in this site collection can be opened in SPD or not. Unless this option is enabled, none of the other options matter. Attempting to open a site when this option is disabled will display the error message shown in Figure 5-2.

*Figure 5-2. Error displayed when opening a site in which SPD use is disabled*

- **Enable Detaching Pages from the Site Definition**: Disabling this option will prevent users from performing actions that would effectively cause the page to become customized. If you are familiar with SPD 2007, you know that any time you made a change to a page using SPD, it would create a new version of the page and place it in the content database of that site, thereby causing the page to become a customized page. It would no longer reference the definition page located in the file system on the SharePoint Server.

- **Enable Customizing Master Pages and Page Layouts**: If this check box is disabled, users will not see the Master Pages or Page Layouts site object categories.

- **Enable Managing of the Web Site URL Structure**: Disabling this option will hide the All Files and Sub Sites site objects, keeping users from opening pages or subsites directly from the URL hierarchy of the site. Only pages stored in document libraries will be available for editing.

## Administering a SharePoint Site

Not everything you do with SPD 2010 is development. Many development efforts start with the creation of new sites or lists. Most of these sites or lists are unique and need to be created only once, so it might be easiest to create these in either the UI or using SPD. But even if you are working to create a site or list that will be reproduced in many places, you can often save time by prototyping the site using SPD and then transferring the completed design template to be deployed as a sandboxed solution. SPD provides an excellent tool for this kind of early prototyping development.

---

**Note**  Chapter 7 provides more coverage of sandboxed solutions.

---

### Building New Websites

Because of its multitenant-based design, new SharePoint Online site collections can't be created using SPD 2010. They must be created in the SharePoint Online administration center, as pictured in Figure 5-3.

---

**Note**  The Office 365 Small Business and Professional plans support only one public and one private site collection.

---

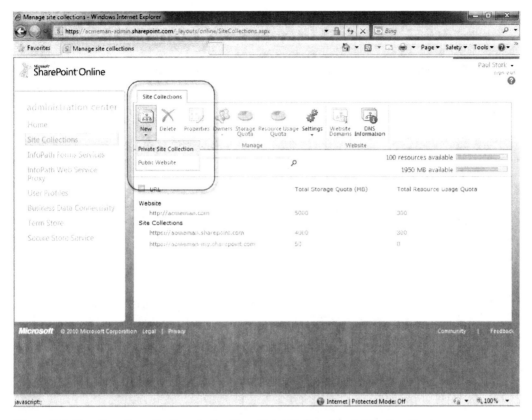

*Figure 5-3. Creating site collections in the SharePoint Online Administration Center*

But creating a new subsite using SPD is relatively easy. You'll be asked what template you want to use and where in the hierarchy of your site collection you want to place it. You can use either one of the default site templates or a custom template you created by saving a site as a template or deploying a site template using a sandboxed solution. Remember, just like an on-premise installation of SharePoint, you can't change the site template of a site after it is created, so make sure you know what kind of subsite you want before you create it.

## EXERCISE 5-1. CREATING A SHAREPOINT SUBSITE

In this exercise, we'll create a standard team site called "SPD Demo" that we will use to host practice exercises for the rest of this chapter.

1. Open the top-level site of your SharePoint Online private site collection in SPD. If you're not sure how to do this, review the steps in Chapter 3 on "Connecting SharePoint Designer to SharePoint."

2.  With the {*site collection name*} Site Object selected in the sidebar, you should see a page similar to the one in Figure 5-4. Click **New** in the Subsites section of the page.

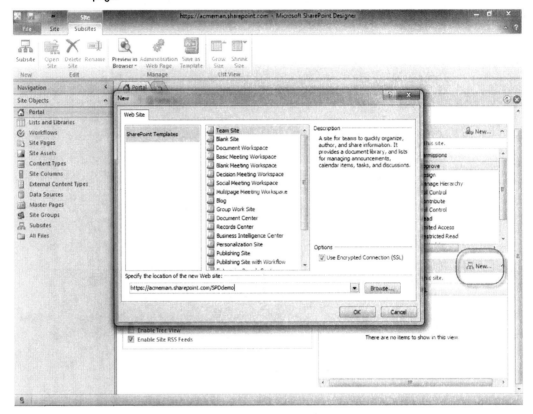

**Figure 5-4.** *SPD Settings page in Site Settings*

3.  Make sure the default Team Site template is selected and change the location in which your new subsite will be created to be http://{your top level url}/SPDdemo and click **OK**. Your new subsite will open in a second instance of SPD 2010.

4.  You weren't given a chance to name your new subsite, so SPD used the name of the template you selected. You can click the current name next to Title: in the Site Information section of the page to change the title. Change the name from Team Site to **SPD Demo**.

5.  It's also a good idea to provide a description for the new site by clicking the Description link <click to enter text>. Enter something like this: **This site is used for completing SPD Demos in Chapter 5.**

6. Notice that the tab for this page displays an asterisk by the name of the site. This means that the site has been edited, and the changes have not yet been saved.

7. Save your changes by right-clicking the page tab and selecting Save.

8. To look at your new site in the browser click the Preview in Browser button on the Site tab of the ribbon at the top of the page.

---

Once the subsite is created, you can use SPD to manage its settings or customize it in a variety of ways. The remainder of this chapter will focus on the different ways that a site can be customized using SPD. But before we move on to those topics, let's examine a few more important management tasks you can complete with SPD. Most of these administrative topics are outside the development focus of this book. But we will take time to look at two tasks that are critical to many developers: managing security and saving a customized site as a template.

# Managing Security

By default, a new subsite created in SPD 2010 will inherit security from the parent site where it was created. Using the SPD interface you can break this security inheritance, create new SharePoint groups, add new SharePoint users, and assign or adjust their permissions.

---

■ **Note** Before a user can be assigned permissions to a SharePoint Online site, they must be assigned a user subscription license (USL) in the Office 365 administration site. External users with a LiveID can also be invited to collaborate on a site collection. These external users are assigned a partner access license (PAL). At the time of this writing, Enterprise plan sites include 50 free PAL licenses.

---

## Breaking Inheritance

By default, security is inherited throughout the SharePoint Online hierarchy to all subsites, lists, libraries, documents, and items. To customize the permissions for any object in SharePoint Online, the first step is to break this security inheritance. To break the inheritance of permissions on the subsite you created in the previous exercise, click the Stop Inheriting button in the Permissions section of the site summary page, as shown in Figure 5-5.

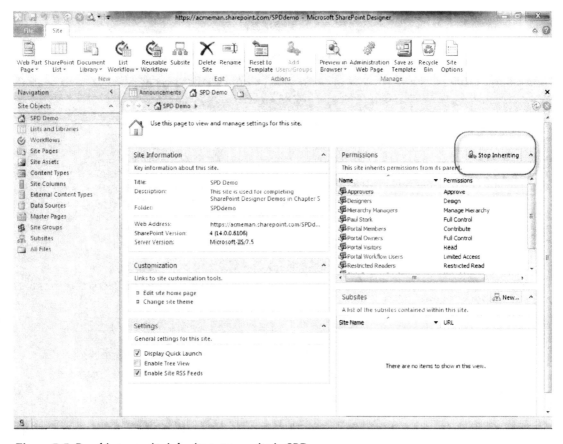

**Figure 5-5.** *Breaking security inheritance on a site in SPD*

## Creating Groups

Although you can assign permissions directly to a user, it isn't considered a best practice because long term maintenance of security based on individual users is difficult to maintain. Even if you want to assign permissions to a single user now, there is no guarantee that you won't want to broaden that assignment to include additional users later. Assigning permissions to a group makes the process of adding users or reassigning permissions to a different user easier to maintain.

---

■ **Note** SharePoint group membership is shared across an entire site collection. Never change membership of a group in a subsite unless the change should apply to the entire site collection.

---

---

**EXERCISE 5-2. CREATING SHAREPOINT GROUPS**

---

In this exercise, you will create a new SharePoint group.

1. Select Site Groups from the Site Objects list.

2. Click the New Group button in the Site Groups tab of the ribbon, as shown in Figure 5-6. Call the group **SPD Demo Group**, provide a suitable description, and enter your own name as the group owner. (As group owner, only you will able to manage the group's membership.) Click **OK**.

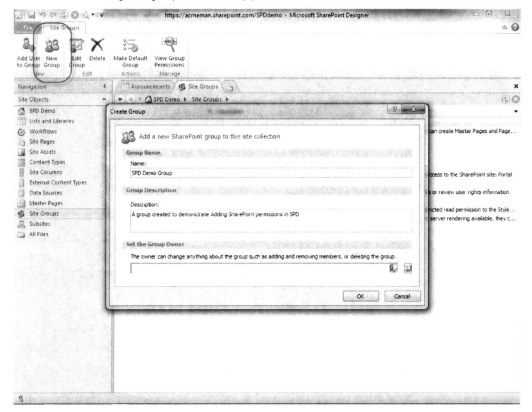

*Figure 5-6. Creating a new group in SPD 2010*

3. Once a group has been created, you can manage the membership of the group in the group summary page. Click the Add Users button and add another user to the group by typing the name or e-mail address in the resulting dialog box, as shown in Figure 5-7. Click **OK**.

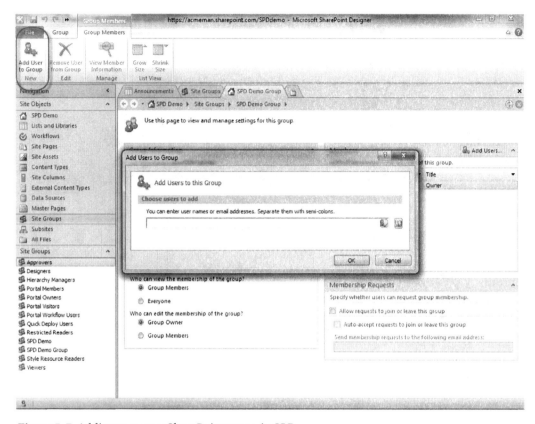

*Figure 5-7. Adding users to a SharePoint group in SPD*

## Setting Permissions

Permissions in SharePoint Online can be assigned either directly to users or to SharePoint groups like the one created in the previous exercise.

■ **Note** Users who are assigned a license in a Small Business and Professionals plan are automatically members of the Tenant_Users SharePoint group which is assigned the Enhanced Contribute permission level in the top-level site of the private site collection by default.

# EXERCISE 5-3. SETTING PERMISSIONS

In this exercise, you will modify permissions on the SharePoint group you created in the previous exercise.

1. Select the first item from the Site Objects list on the left side of the SPD interface. This displays the Site Summary page.

2. Click the New link in the title bar of the Permissions section of the Site Summary page, as shown in Figure 5-8. The same interface can also be used to add new users to the site.

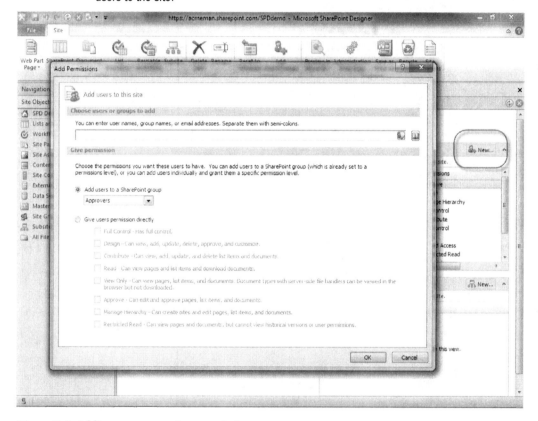

*Figure 5-8. Adding users or setting permissions on a group*

3. Enter the name of the SharePoint Group you created in the previous exercise: **SPD Demo Group.**

**Note** You can also use this interface to assign permissions directly to an Office 365 user or security group. Security groups are available only in the Enterprise-level plans.

4. To assign permissions to this group, you can assign a permission level to it. Select the **Give users permission directly** radio button.

5. Then select the **Design** and **Approve** check boxes to assign these permission levels to the group.

6. Click **OK**. You will see the group you added and the permission levels assigned to it in the Permissions section of the Site Summary page, as shown in Figure 5-9.

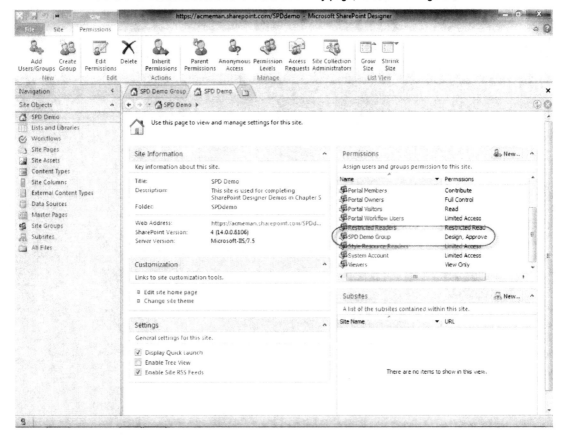

*Figure 5-9. Viewing permission levels assigned to groups and users*

## Other Security Tasks

Clicking one of the groups in the permission section of the Site Summary page will display a Site Permissions contextual tab in the ribbon. This tab contains buttons for a variety of other security-related tasks such as managing Anonymous Access, creating Permission Levels, or adding Site Collection Administrators. But these buttons are just links to the equivalent security pages in the SharePoint site, so we won't cover them here.

# Saving a Customized Subsite as a Template

One of the challenges that developers face when building customizations with SPD 2010 is that it is designed to makes changes directly in the SharePoint content databases. Because traditional source code isn't produced or compiled, it is difficult to develop in a local on-premise environment and then apply the changes to SharePoint Online. One way to overcome this challenge is by saving the customized site as a site template. The resulting WSP solution file can then be uploaded to the Solution Gallery in a SharePoint Online site collection and used to create new sites. You can also save customized lists, libraries, and workflows as templates.

## What Gets Saved in a Template

Saving a SharePoint site as a template saves the overall structure of the site. That includes the definition of all its lists, libraries, views, forms, pages, and workflows. You also have the option to include the contents stored in the site; for example, you might choose to include a set of sample events in a calendar, announcements in a list, or documents in a library. This capability is designed to provide sample content, not a fully populated site. The default template size, including all the content, is limited to 50MB. In an on-premise environment, this size can be increased, but there is no way to do that in SharePoint Online.

Unfortunately, not everything you customize using SPD is transferred in the solution file when you save the site as a template. For example, because permissions by default inherit from the parent site when a new site is created customized permissions, SharePoint users and groups are not included in the template. Another limitation is that sites with publishing features enabled can't be saved as a template at all. Table 5-1 summarizes what can and can't be saved when saving a site as a template.

*Table 5-1. What's Included in a Site Template*

| Included in WSP | Not Included in WSP |
| --- | --- |
| Lists | Customized permissions |
| Libraries | Running workflow instances |
| External lists | List item version history |
| Data source connections | Workflow tasks associated with running workflows |
| List views and data views | People/group field values |
| Custom forms | Taxonomy field values |

| | |
|---|---|
| Workflows | Publishing pages and publishing sites |
| Content types | My Sites |
| Custom actions | |
| Navigation | |
| Site pages | |
| Master pages | |
| Modules | |
| Web templates | |

In addition to uploading site templates to a solution gallery in SharePoint Online, you can also open them in Visual Studio 2010. This makes it easy to prototype something using SPD and then continue development in Visual Studio 2010.

## EXERCISE 5-4. SAVE A CUSTOMIZED SITE AS A TEMPLATE

In this exercise, you will save the subsite you created in a previous exercise as a site template.

1. If your SPD Demo site isn't already open, open it in SPD 2010.

2. Select the first item from the Site Objects list on the left side of the SPD interface. This displays the Site Summary page.

3. On the Site tab in the ribbon, click the Save as Template button. This opens your SharePoint subsite in a browser and takes you to the Save as Template page.

4. Provide a name, such as **SPDdemo**, for the WSP file in the File name field.

5. Type a display name, such as **SPD Demo Template,** for the template in the Template name field. You can also provide an optional longer description in the Template description field.

6. Select the Include Content check box to include the content of the site in the site template file. Remember that your template file can be only 50MB maximum.

7. Click OK to save the template to the site collection solutions gallery.

8. To download the solution from the solution gallery, click the user solution gallery link. You can then upload the solution to your SharePoint Online site and activate it to use the template when creating new subsites.

# Branding

One of the most common uses for SPD 2010 is implementing a consistent look and feel for your sites. This is commonly known as *branding*. As we've already seen, there are several areas where you can adjust the branding of your site using the UI. You can change the site logo or modify the color scheme and fonts by applying a theme. But what if you want to do more than change logos or modify the color scheme? What if you want to move things around, add a footer to the page, or replace the existing navigation? These kinds of tasks require modifying master pages, publishing page layouts, or overriding existing Cascading Style Sheets (CSS). To accomplish these kinds of tasks, you'll need direct access to the HTML or CSS code of the page. Although you could do this by downloading copies of these files, SPD provides a more convenient *what you see is what you get* (WYSIWYG) editor. Using SPD you can see the results of your edits immediately, making complex editing tasks easier.

---

■ **Note** By default, only SharePoint Online administrators can create or edit master pages and page layouts.

---

But these kinds of branding tasks aren't for everybody, so by default only SharePoint Online administrators can create or edit master pages and page layouts. As discussed in the "Managing Security" section in this chapter, you can also turn off everyone's ability to edit either master pages or any other page. These controls make it easy to limit when these kinds of branding changes can be made and by whom. Most organizations will work to get their branding in place for the top-level site of a site collection before it's made available to regular users and then lock it down. You can then re-enable editing of these features if changes need to be made in the future. You can also just lock down these features in your SharePoint online environment and prototype all your branding changes in an on-premise environment using SPD. Then package the files in the on-premise environment using a Visual Studio 2010 sandboxed solution (WSP), features, and event receivers to apply the changes in the SharePoint Online environment.

## Changing Fonts and Colors with a Theme

In Chapter 4, you learned how to change the default theme of a site to apply a unified color scheme and set of fonts. SharePoint Designer 2010 can also be used to change the default theme used by a site collection. But SPD doesn't add anything to this capability. The Change site theme link on the Site Summary page merely redirects user to the same browser-based page described in Chapter 4.

---

■ **Note** See Chapter 4 for additional information about using themes.

---

## Editing Pages

Using SPD 2010, you can create or customize standard web part pages, publish page layouts, and edit master pages. SharePoint WIKI pages can be created only in the UI, but they can be edited in SPD. Although each page type serves a different purpose, the page editing experience is essentially the same. Using SPD, you can edit the contents of a page either in a WYSIWYG view or by working directly with the

HTML code. You can also use SPD to change the master pages a site uses or designate a different default home page. The result is a site that is completely customized with your organization's unique look and feel.

---

■ **Note** Application pages (pages with URLs containing /_layouts/) reside in the SharePoint farm's physical file system and cannot be edited in SPD.

---

## Normal and Advanced Edit Modes

When you open a page for editing in SPD, it will default to the normal edit mode. When using this editing mode, you will be prevented from making any changes that would detach the page from its default site definition. Using the normal edit mode, you are essentially limited to doing the same things that you can do in the browser. For example, you can add web parts to a web part zone, but you can't add them directly to the page or add a new web part zone.

To really customize your site, you'll need to use the advanced edit mode. This editing mode gives you full access to change any HTML on the page and will always result in a customized page that is stored in the content database. Customized pages can present challenges when updates or service packs are applied because they are detached from the site definition and won't be updated if the site definition page is updated.

## Creating Publishing Layout Pages

If the publishing infrastructure site-collection feature and the publishing site feature have both been enabled in your top-level site, you can make use of publishing layout pages. These pages impose the same layout on multiple pages by dynamically loading a set of metadata into a layout template when rendering the page. Where a master page is used to standardize things like the header, navigation, and footer of multiple pages, a publishing page layout provides control over the look and feel associated with the main content section of a page.

When creating a new publishing page, a user will be prompted to choose from a predetermined list of available page layouts. Content is then added to the page by filling in controls on the page layout. The content is then saved as metadata attached to the page. HTML in the publishing page itself is not rendered. Instead, the metadata attached to the page is used to fill in the associated page layout and the HTML in the page layout is rendered. Because rendering of a publishing page layout is dependent on the metadata attached to the publishing page, the publishing page layout must know what metadata fields are available. This is done by connecting each publishing page layout to a specific content type. The content type defines the potential metadata fields available for display. The metadata fields available in a content type are defined through the use of site columns. So to create a new publishing page layout, you might need to create one or more site columns, a content type, and a publishing page layout. You can do all these tasks using SPD.

## Embedding Client-Side Code

As you'll see later in the book, the limitations imposed on deployment of server-side managed code assemblies make the use of client-side code an essential work-around in many cases. One of the easiest ways to deploy client-side code is to simply embed it into a master page or ASPX page with a Hypertext

Markup Language (HTML) <script> block. You can use the advanced edit mode in SPD to edit the HTML of a page directly and add client-side code to the page. You can also embed client-side code on the page by adding it to a Content Editor web part. Adding it in a web part can be done without requiring that the page be in advanced edit mode.

---

▪ **Note** Chapter 9 discusses the use of client-side code in more detail.

---

## EXERCISE 5-5. IMPLEMENTING A SIMPLE DYNAMIC MENU

In this exercise, we'll create a hyperlink–based menu system that could be used to navigate to other site–collection home pages. Client-side JavaScript will be used to highlight the current site in the menu. This code could be placed on a master page that is used in multiple site collections to provide cross–site collection navigation.

1.  If your SPD Demo site isn't already loaded, open it in SPD 2010.

2.  Select the Site Pages item from the Site Objects list on the left side of the SPD interface. This displays the contents of the Site Pages library.

---

▪ **Note** The Site Pages library is the default location used to store pages in most nonpublishing sites (like Team Sites).

---

3.  Click the Web Part Page button in the New section of the Pages tab of the ribbon, as shown in Figure 5-10. Select the Full Page, Vertical layout to create a new SharePoint page.

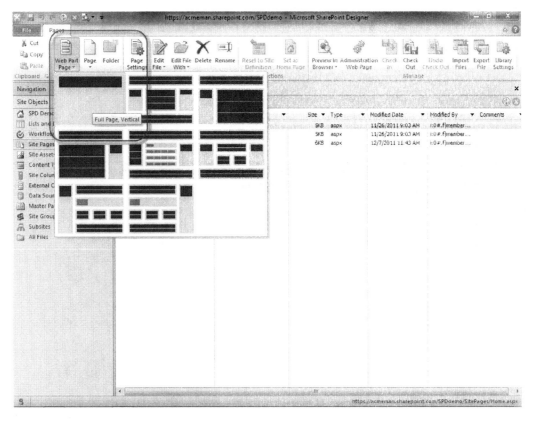

**Figure 5-10.** *Creating a new web part page*

4. Rename the page **MenuTest.aspx.**

5. Click the page to open the Page Summary of the page.

6. Click the Edit File button in the ribbon. This will open the page for editing.

7. Click the View tab on the ribbon and switch to the Split or Code view of the page to directly edit the HTML of the page. You will see that most of the HTML is highlighted in yellow, which signifies that you can't edit this code because you are in Normal Edit mode.

8. Click the Advanced Mode button in the Editing section of the Home tab to switch to Advanced Edit mode.

9. Insert the code from Listing 5-1 somewhere inside the PlaceHolderAdditionalPageHead *<asp:Content>* tag on the page. This is the CSS that will be used to style the menu entries.

***Listing 5-1.*** *CSS styles for dynamic menu*

```
<style type="text/css">
#SPSitesMenu1 li {
  padding:5px;
  }
#SPSitesMenu1 a {
  padding:5px;
  text-decoration:none;
}
.currentSPSite {background-color:blue; color:#fff !important;}
</style>
```

10. Insert the code from Listing 5-2 somewhere inside the PlaceHolderMain
    *<asp:Content>* tag on the page. Replace the *{SiteURL}* entries in the hyperlinks
    with page addresses from two different site collections in your SharePoint Online
    environment. If you are working in a profession and small–business licensed
    environment, use a page from your Public Web Site as the second address.

***Listing 5-2.*** *Dynamic menu code*

```
<div class="s4-pr s4-notdlg ">
  <ul id="SPSitesMenu1" >
    <li >
        <a href="http://{SiteURL}">Root Site</a>
    </li>
    <li >
        <a href="http://{SiteURL}" >SPD Demo Site</a>
    </li>
  </ul>
</div>

<script type="text/javascript">
  //** Set selected entry in menu **//
   _spBodyOnLoadFunctionNames.push("setMenu");

   function setMenu() {
    if (document.getElementById('SPSitesMenu1').getElementsByTagName('li')) {
      var link;
      for (var i = 0; (link =
document.getElementById('SPSitesMenu1').getElementsByTagName('a')[i]); i++) {
        if (link.href.indexOf(location.hostname) != -1) {
           var node = document.createAttribute('class');
           node.nodeValue = 'currentSPSite';

document.getElementById('SPSitesMenu1').getElementsByTagName('li')[i].getElementsByTagName('a'
)[0].setAttributeNode(node);
        }
      }
    }
```

```
    }
</script>
```

11. Right-click the tab labeled Menutext.aspx and select Save from the context menu. Accept the warning about customizing the page by clicking Yes in the dialog.

12. Repeat these steps for a page in a different site collection.

13. Once you've edited both pages click the Preview in Browser button in the Preview section of the ribbon. This will open the page in the browser. You should see a page similar to the one in Figure 5-11. The hyperlink referencing the current site should be highlighted.

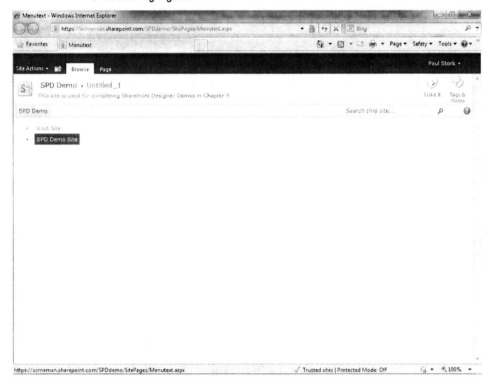

*Figure 5-11. Page with dynamic JavaScript–based hyperlink menu*

# Interacting with Data

One of the most common uses for SharePoint is to display information stored in lists and libraries. Simply create your list or library either from one of the preloaded types or from your own custom set of columns. Then add a web part to the page, and you can view the content you add to the list or library. You can even easily control which columns are displayed by editing the view.

But what if you want to improve the formatting of the content displayed in the web part? You might want to apply more extensive sorting and filtering than you can simply by editing the view. Or maybe you want to highlight specific fields or rows of content dynamically based on the value of the content. These kinds of tasks go beyond what can be accomplished through the UI and require more extensive customization.

In SharePoint Online, the web parts used to display content from lists and libraries are all based on Extensible Stylesheet Language Transformation (XSLT) code. One way to change the default display is to replace the Extensible Stylesheet Language (XSL) used by the web part with your own custom code. But in many cases, this is a time-consuming development task that might not be necessary. With SPD 2010, you can easily modify the XSL in these web parts to create dynamic UIs for your content without having to write custom code. Using just SPD you can create dashboards that highlight important information, design custom forms tailored to individual roles, and customize the available toolbars and Server ribbon commands associated with the data.

# Customizing List and Form Views

In SharePoint 2010, the contents of lists and libraries are displayed using XSLT–based web parts called List View or List Form web parts. List View web parts display items in a grid, while List Form web parts display the metadata fields of an individual item. List View web parts are the basis for the default page used to display a library and are also the default when adding a list or library to an existing page. List Form web parts are primarily used as the basis for the New, Edit, and View forms associated with a particular list, library, or content type.

XSLT List View web parts can be modified relatively easily using just the browser interface. This includes the ability to substitute completely custom XSL which can radically change the display of the content. But this requires an understanding of XSL coding. Using SPD, you can accomplish similar customizations more easily using commands in the ribbon. To customize an existing list view, just select the web part on the page in SPD. You will see a new set of contextual tabs that provide customizations for the web part. Table 5-2 highlights the various ways you can customize an XSLT–based List View web part in SPD.

***Table 5-2.*** *List View Web Part Customizations in SPD 2010*

| Customization | Explanation |
| --- | --- |
| Add or remove columns | You can add, remove, or arrange the order of columns in the view. |
| Filter data | You can filter the data in a list by showing only the items that meet a certain criteria. You are not limited to only two filters as you are in a regular view. |
| Sort and group | You can sort or group the data in a view. |
| Apply different view styles | You can select a different layout for the view from a predefined list of view styles. |
| Apply conditional formatting | You can modify how rows, columns, or cells are formatted or displayed based on conditions in the data being presented. |

| | |
|---|---|
| Create a formula column | You can create a calculated field that displays the result of a calculation based on other columns. |
| Change the paging | You can modify the paging settings to change the number of rows on a page or the total rows returned. |
| Display data from multiple sources | You can link two or more related data sources and display them in a single view. |
| Use asynchronous updates | You can enable the use of AJAX so that the view can be updated asynchronously without refreshing the entire page. |
| Add parameters | You can create and pass parameters to a view to allow for more user interaction with your view at runtime. |
| Use HTML, ASP.NET, and SharePoint controls | You can bind a variety of other controls to the data source to customize the formatting of your view. |

## Data View and Data Form Web Parts

Although XSLT List View web parts are the default for displaying lists and libraries in SharePoint Online, Data View and Data Form web parts are also still available. Customization of Data View and Data Form web parts in SPD is the same as it is for XSLT List View and List Form web parts. But the Data View and Data Form web parts can be used for any data source, while the List View and List Form web parts are available only for content displayed in the form of a SharePoint list. Table 5-3 summarizes when SharePoint uses each type of web part, what data sources they are used with, and some of the advantages/disadvantages associated with their use.

*Table 5-3. Web Part Usage, Advantages, and Disadvantages*

| Web Part | Data Sources | Advantages/Disadvantages |
|---|---|---|
| XSLT List View Web Part (XLV) | SharePoint lists | The default web part used to display SharePoint lists and libraries |
| | SharePoint libraries | Cannot be used with external data sources other than in the context of an external list |
| | External Lists | |
| XSLT List Form Web Part (XLF) | SharePoint lists | Used as the default form for viewing a single list or library item |
| | SharePoint libraries | Only customizable using code view in SPD |
| | External Lists | |
| Data Form Web Part (DFWP) | Any Data Source | The default web part used when creating a view from a data source in SPD |
| | | Can be used with any kind of data source |

## Implementing InfoPath Forms

By default, SharePoint Online displays content from lists and libraries with a set of four built-in ASPX forms that make use of either a List View or List Form web part. But these forms can be replaced by InfoPath-based forms. The forms will still be ASPX pages, but the pages will now contain an InfoPath Form Web Part (IPWP) in place of the XSLT List View or Form View web part. InfoPath 2010 can then be used to customize these web parts by adding rules, conditions, formatting, and branding. Once they are completed, you can use SPD to select them as the default form for the various list actions: adding, editing, or displaying list content. The InfoPath forms behind IPWPs can only be edited in InfoPath. When viewed in SPD they will display as shown in Figure 5-12.

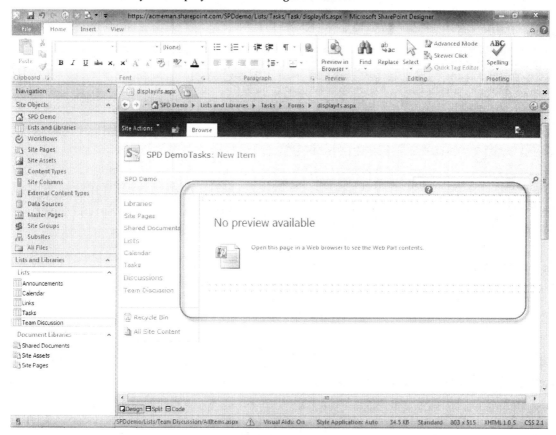

*Figure 5-12. InfoPath Form web part displayed in SPD 2010*

# Creating Custom Ribbon Actions

So far in this section, we have focused on customizing the display of content in SharePoint. But using SPD there are also some easy ways to add custom ribbon actions that are associated with specific lists and libraries in a site. There are three types of custom actions that can be added in the List or Library summary page in SPD:

- **Navigate to form:** Used to navigate to one of the existing List or Library forms to display, edit, or add an item. You can navigate to either a regular or InfoPath-based form.

- **Initiate a workflow:** Initiate one of the workflows associated with this particular list or library.

- **Navigate to a web URL:** Navigate to any other SharePoint or external URL.

# Interacting with External Data

One of the challenges that you will face when moving to Office 365 is that not all your data will be stored inside SharePoint Online. A lot of the data that your organization depends on will be stored in line-of-business (LoB) systems such as Customer Relationship Management (CRM) or Enterprise Resource Planning (ERP) systems. The information in these systems is stored externally to SharePoint, but it is often critical that you display the data inside SharePoint. In on-premise installations, this gap is often filled by SharePoint BCS. But BCS support was missing from the original rollout of Office 365. Limited support for BCS was added to SharePoint Online beginning with Service Update1 (SU1) that was applied in November 2011.

## Business Connectivity Services (BCS)

Microsoft Business Connectivity Services (BCS) provides support for reading and writing data stored in external systems from within Microsoft SharePoint 2010. In earlier versions of SharePoint, BCS was known as Business Data Connectivity (BDC). Using BCS developers can rapidly build solutions using SPD 2010. Using SPD you can define BCS models, connect to external data, and interact with that data inside SharePoint as though it were a SharePoint list.

### Business Data Catalog (BDC)

Business Data Catalog (BDC) was the name given to the service in Microsoft Office SharePoint Server 2007 designed to provide read-only access to external data systems. BCS provides richer integration, including full read/write access to external data in SharePoint 2010. Many of the concepts and artifacts available in BDC, like profile pages and BDC web parts, are now available in BCS. As a result, the terms *BCS* and *BDC* are often confused.

### Supported External Data Sources

In an on-premise SharePoint installation you can use SPD to configure three different types of connections in BCS. The three types of connections are a Windows Communication Foundation (WCF) service, a .NET class, or a Microsoft SQL database. The support added to SharePoint Online in SU1 includes only support for WCF service connections. Connecting directly to a SQL database might be supported in a future update. Support for .NET class connections will probably never be provided because SharePoint Online is limited to deploying .NET classes as sandboxed solutions.

---

■ **Note** BCS WCF support is not backward compatible with .NET 2.0 XML Web Services when using SPD 2010.

---

# The Secure Store Service

One of the challenges when building a BCS connection to a WCF data source in SharePoint Online is how to handle authentication. Most external data sources will not be using the same claims-based authentication as SharePoint Online. This is where the Secure Store Service (SSS) proves useful. The SSS provides a credential cache that maps the identities of SharePoint users, SharePoint groups, or security groups to credentials that are stored in an encrypted database. When the BDC model needs to use external credentials to access a data source, it passes the identity of the user to the SSS. The SSS then returns the external credentials that are mapped to that user or group and uses them in the WCF service call.

Credential mappings stored in the SSS are organized by target applications. Each target application is identified by a unique target application ID. The target application includes credential fields for a username and password, a group of users who can administer the application settings and a group representing the users or groups who can use the credentials. Each BDC model in BCS is configured to use credentials from a particular target application. The Secure Store service in an on-premise SharePoint installation can support multiple sets of credentials per target application, each mapped to a specific user or group. But in SharePoint Online there can be only one set of credentials per target application.

---

⊜ **Note** The Secure Store Service (SSS) in SharePoint Online only supports Group Restricted target applications. Individual and regular group credentials are not supported at this time.

---

> ### EXERCISE 5-6. CREATING GROUP CREDENTIALS IN THE SECURE STORE SERVICE

1. Navigate to the Administration Center for SharePoint Online and click the Secure Store Service link.

2. To create a Target Application click the New button on the ribbon.

3. In the Target Application ID text box, type **BCS** as the identifier for the new target application.

4. In the Display Name text box, type **BCS SPD Demo** as a longer and more descriptive identifier of the target application in the UI.

5. In the Contact Email box, type the e-mail address of your SharePoint Online user or any other Office 365 user who will be responsible for this external application. The user does not have to be an administrator.

6. Notice that you cannot change the Target Application Type drop-down. Only Group Restricted credentials are supported for Secure Store in SharePoint Online.

7. Accept all the defaults in the Credential Fields section. For a WCF service, you will normally be supplying a Windows User Name and Password.

8.  In the Target Application Administrators field, add yourself and any other users who will be able to manage the Target Application settings.

9.  In the Members field, add yourself and the other users or groups who will use the credentials stored in this target application to access the data represented by the BCS model.

10. Click OK to save the Target Application.

11. Once the Target Application has been saved, you can set the credentials that will be associated with it. Select the check box next to the BCS Target Application to select it. Then click the Set button on the ribbon.

12. In the Windows User Name text box, type the username.

13. In the Windows Password text box, type the password.

14. In the Confirm Windows Password text box, re-type the password that you entered in the last step.

15. Click OK to save the credentials.

# External Content Types

The *external content type* is one of the keys to BCS in SPD. Creating an external content type in SPD generates the BDC model that defines how to connect to the data through the WCF service. The BDC model also defines the data and how you will interact with the data in the external LoB system. Using an external content type, you can manage access to your external data. Once the external content type has been created, other users can use it to access the metadata and behaviors of a business entity such as customer or invoice without knowing the technical details of the underlying external system.

For example, you might want to let a user pick a customer from a list of customers in one web part and then filter invoices in another web part that are for that customer. You can create an external content type once and then reuse it in several places within your site collection. External content types provide a superset of entity capabilities by enabling solution designers to describe both the structure of the external system and how that data should behave within SharePoint applications and Office applications.

The first step in defining an external content type is to add a connection to an external data source through a WCF service. Once the connection has been defined, you can use the methods of the WCF service to define the operations that can be used to manipulate the external data. A list of the different types of external content type operations, their uses, and when they are required is in Table 5-4. Other types of operations might be supported in the WCF service, but they can't be added through SPD.

*Table 5-4. External Content Type Operations*

| Operation | Required | Use |
|---|---|---|
| Create | Not required | Creates a new record in the external data source |
| Update | Not required | Updates an existing record in the external data source |
| Delete | Not required | Deletes an item from the external data source |
| Read Item | Required for all external content types | Reads a single item from the external data source |
| Read List | Required to create an external list | Reads a list of items (zero or more) from the external data source |
| Association | Not required | Models a one-to-many relationship between two external content types |

■ **Note** Be careful when defining the create, edit, or delete operations. These operations might bypass business logic contained in the LoB application.

# Building Declarative workflows

If you want to automate business processes in SharePoint Online using workflows, you have to do it with SPD 2010. Workflows built using Visual Studio 2010 create managed code assemblies that must be deployed to the global assembly cache (GAC). Because access to the GAC is prohibited in SharePoint Online, you must build all your workflows declaratively using SPD.

Automating business processes through the use of declarative sequential workflows is one of SharePoint's core uses. You can use the workflow designer in SPD to build three different types of sequential workflows: List, Reusable, and Site Workflows. All of them can be deployed and used without limitations in SharePoint Online. These workflows can be used to structure and streamline the way you do things without requiring you to write code. Using the workflow designer in SPD, you can create sequences of actions and decision points that even include nested logic and substeps. You can even visualize your workflow design using the flowchart template tools in Microsoft Visio 2010.

■ **Note** Chapter 8 provides additional details about building declarative workflows for SharePoint Online using SPD 2010.

# Limitations

Although there are many good reasons to use SPD 2010 for customizing Office 365 SharePoint Online sites there are also a few limitations of which you should be aware. Knowing these limitations is crucial when choosing the best approach for a particular customization or development task.

## Some Customizations Must Be Developed in Production

Perhaps the most important limitation to recognize when using SPD is that you are frequently editing directly against your production SharePoint Online site. Although some SPD customizations, such as reusable workflows, can be exported as solution (WSP) files, many are portable only when included in a site template. Because site templates can only be used to deploy new sites; this limits the portability of SPD-developed customizations for existing sites. However, sandboxed solutions developed in Visual Studio 2010 can be debugged in a local SharePoint installation and then deployed to and activated in the solution gallery of your production SharePoint Online site.

## No Inline Server-Side Code

Another limitation when customizing a site with SPD is that you can't embed server-side code on the page. Inline code is disabled by default on any customized or uploaded web page in a SharePoint site. This exclusion is the result of the PageParserPaths setting in the web.config file. The PageParserPaths setting can be modified in an on-premise SharePoint environment to allow for inline code. But because SharePoint Online web.config files can't be modified, the default PageParserPath—and its exclusion of inline code—are always in effect for SharePoint Online sites. As a result, you can't embed inline server-side code in anything editable through SPD. Client-side code such as JQuery and JavaScript is not covered by this exclusion.

## Can't Reference Sandboxed Solution Managed Code

One of the major limitations facing developers in Office 365 is that all custom managed code must be deployed through sandboxed solutions. Because SPD prohibits the use of inline server-side code, one common work-around is to place that code in a compiled class library and reference it from the page using SPD. Unfortunately, managed code deployed through a sandboxed solution runs in its own thread and is not accessible by outside references. So you can't reference managed code in sandboxed solutions using SPD.

# Summary

In this chapter, we examined how SPD 2010 can be used to create declarative-based solutions that customize and extend SharePoint Online in Office 365. While many of these customizations are focused on the "look and feel" (branding) of your site, SPD can also be used to build declarative workflows or embed client-side code in a page. In Chapter 8, we'll expand on the topic of how to build declarative workflows, and other chapters will look at ways that artifacts developed in SPD, such as master pages, can be repackaged and applied to multiple sites or even to site collections.

# InfoPath and SharePoint Online

## Introduction

Microsoft InfoPath 2010 is a software product that is part of the Microsoft Office suite and is geared toward creating and using forms for gathering structured data. InfoPath is built around XML standards, and data gathered falls within XML guidelines. A key advantage of using InfoPath in a SharePoint Online environment includes presenting a better user interface than the built-in forms and web pages found in standard SharePoint lists and libraries. InfoPath forms can be used as substitutes for standard list and library forms, within workflows, and to provide a mashup of data collected from multiple data sources.

InfoPath is a client software product sold by Microsoft both on its own and as part of the Microsoft Office Professional Plus and higher Office package offerings. InfoPath consists of two programs: Microsoft InfoPath Designer 2010, and Microsoft InfoPath Filler 2010. Microsoft InfoPath Designer 2010 is the product that allows users to design and create form templates, which interact with SharePoint Online and Office 365. Microsoft InfoPath Filler 2010 is used for the local instance of InfoPath that does not interact with SharePoint or display in a browser. We will not cover functionality for Filler 2010 in this chapter.

## Goals

The goals for this chapter do not include providing an in-depth exploration of all of InfoPath's intricacies and features sets. Other books deal with that exclusively and that are dedicated completely to InfoPath. It is a recommendation that you investigate the full capabilities of InfoPath to augment this chapter with additional research information. The goals for this chapter include focusing on Office 365 and the SharePoint Online use of InfoPath. We do hope to provide enough of an introduction to InfoPath to get you up and running and being able to productively use InfoPath in an Office 365 SharePoint Online environment. We also hope to provide several clear use cases and examples that represent a full use pattern of InfoPath together with SharePoint Online.

## Hardware and Software Requirements

Prior to using InfoPath, you must plan for the proper hardware and software requirements for the product. These requirements will also hold true for other software related to InfoPath such as Microsoft Office Professional Plus 2010, SharePoint Designer, and Microsoft Visio 2010.

## Hardware Requirements

Because InfoPath 2010 is part of the Microsoft Office Professional Plus suite, the hardware requirements can be found at `http://office.microsoft.com/en-us/products/microsoft-office-2010-system-requirements-HA101810407.aspx` (`http://bit.ly/c0qAfe`). Table 6.1 lists the components and requirements.

*Table 6-1. Basic Hardware Requirements*

| Component | Requirement |
|---|---|
| **Computer and processor** | 500 Mhz processor |
| **Memory** | 256 MB RAM; 512 MB recommended for graphics features |
| **Display** | 1024 x 768 or higher-resolution monitor |
| **Operating System** | Windows XP (w/SP3) 32 bit; Windows 7; Windows Vista (w/SP1); Windows Server 2003 (w/SP2 and MSXML 6.0) 32 bit; Windows Server 2008 or later 32 or 64 bit OS. |

## Software Requirements

First, you must obtain a license for InfoPath, which you can do in a couple of ways:

- Purchase a license directly for InfoPath, either from Microsoft or a reseller. You can purchase a copy of InfoPath online from Microsoft directly here: `http://www.microsoftstore.com/store/msstore/en_US/pd/productID.216500500` (`http://bit.ly/tC8JLs`).

- Purchase an Office Professional Plus 2010 license online from Microsoft as part of a Volume License agreement. They are available for both small and larger businesses; details at `http://office.microsoft.com/en-us/buy/how-to-buy-office-2010-through-volume-licensing-HA101809925.aspx` – (`http://bit.ly/b7sdTF`).

- The Office 365 E3 and E4 subscription plans come with Office Professional Plus 2010. Once users are subscribed to an E3 or E4 plan, there is a Download button on the RH side when they log in. This Download form leads to the screen as shown in Figure 6-1.

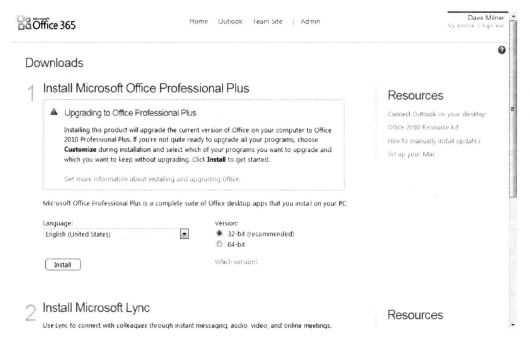

**Figure 6-1.** *Download Microsoft Office Professional Plus*

## Plans Required

To be able to take advantage of InfoPath and Office 365 together, you must have an Office 365 subscription that includes InfoPath Forms Services (such as the E3, E4, or SharePoint Online Plan 2 plans). For an idea of which plans offer InfoPath services, refer to the Microsoft SharePoint Online for Enterprise Services Description document available at `http://www.microsoft.com/download/en/details.aspx?id=13602`. Table 6-2 is an excerpt from that document.

**Table 6-2.** *InfoPath Features in SharePoint Online Descriptions*

| Feature | Partner Access Plan | SharePoint Online Kiosk 1 and Kiosk 2 | SharePoint Online E1 and E2 | SharePoint Online E3 and E4 | SharePoint Online Plan 1 | SharePoint Online Plan 2 |
|---------|--------------------|---------------------------------------|------------------------------|------------------------------|---------------------------|---------------------------|
| InfoPath Forms | Yes[1] | Yes[2] | No | Yes[1] | No | Yes[1] |

*Yes (1): Can view and upload Visio diagrams; view and build external lists; build and visit Access-based web pages; build and view embedded Excel graphs; and create/publish, fill in, and submit InfoPath forms.*
*Yes (2): Kiosk workers have read-only rights except they can edit web-based and InfoPath Forms only.*

## Optional Software

Along with the preceding hardware and software requirements, there are a few scenarios with InfoPath that will require other software as well. If you are going to use InfoPath forms to support custom workflows, you'll use SharePoint Designer 2010 to build your workflows. Visual Studio 2010 can be used as well to define custom actions for use in your workflows (SharePoint Online supports only declarative workflows, but custom actions are allowed if they're built and deployed as sandboxed solutions). Optionally, you can also use Microsoft Visio 2010 (Premium edition) to prototype workflows that can then be exported and fully implemented in SharePoint Designer.

## InfoPath Overview

InfoPath was first designed as a client software program released with Microsoft Office 2003. For the SharePoint solution provider, InfoPath is a fantastic way to rapidly develop rich user interface (UI) at the list and library level for interacting with SharePoint 2010 and Office 365.

## InfoPath Forms Services Overview

InfoPath Forms Services is a built-in feature and service of SharePoint Online and provides a browser-based experience for filling out InfoPath forms without the need for an InfoPath Filler 2010 license. To allow for this, forms based on browser-compatible form templates (.xsn files) can be opened in a web browser from computers that do not have InfoPath 2010 installed, but they will open in InfoPath 2010 when it is installed. Additionally, because the same form can be used in the browser or in the InfoPath editor, the form template design and management process is greatly simplified.

A browser-compatible form template created in the InfoPath 2010 Designer is rendered by a special control in SharePoint Online: the XmlFormView web part (see http://bit.ly/MjGtAz for information on this web part). This web part allows InfoPath forms to be viewed directly in a browser. Because web parts can be placed on a page in SharePoint in a free-form manner in conjunction with text, images, and other web parts, it is also possible to design a SharePoint page that has multiple InfoPath forms on one page.

## Office 365 Differences

Office 365 SharePoint online has some limitations surrounding InfoPath Forms Services as compared with an on-premise SharePoint 2010 installation. In an on-premise SharePoint installation, it is possible to add custom code in a managed .NET language (like C# or VB.NET) to an InfoPath form for more control over the form and elements than is available through InfoPath Designer directly. These special InfoPath forms are sometimes referred to as "InfoPath admin forms" because they must be deployed by an administrator with full trust rights and be stored and managed in a list of global form templates (that is, managed through the SharePoint Server Central Administration site). These InfoPath admin forms require being deployed as a full-trust solution in SharePoint 2010 as opposed to a sandboxed solution.

In SharePoint Online and Office 365 sites, it is not possible to deploy full-trust solutions. As a result, InfoPath forms that depend on custom code are not an option in Office 365. However, you can use the full features of InfoPath Designer to design form templates (.xsn files) and upload them to a SharePoint Online site to be stored in a Forms library.

## Data Connections

Another InfoPath-related difference between on-premise SharePoint 2010 and SharePoint Online is that there are practical restrictions to the data connection options that are available in SharePoint Online. Figure 6-2 shows the selections available on the Data Connection wizard in InfoPath Designer 2010.

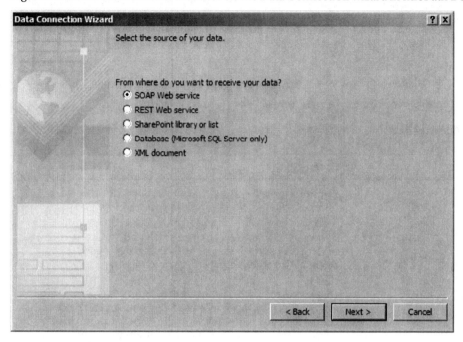

*Figure 6-2. Data Connection Wizard*

Data connections in general offer the ability to "mash up" data on a single form by including content from multiple sources. Typically, InfoPath forms will have a primary SharePoint library or list that they are reading data from and submitting data to. However, other data sources can be used for the form as well, such as populating drop-down controls with content from a separate data connection. Other types of examples are out in blog space such as the following:

- Mashing up Bing Maps interactively to an InfoPath form

- Connecting to User Profile web services in SharePoint to obtain current user information as well as groups

- Connecting to external REST or SOAP services.

In general, these data connections are not restricted from within InfoPath Designer. However, there are practical constraints involved when dealing with SharePoint Online. For example, care must be taken to ensure that the end point for the data connection is available to the Internet and that credentials are managed. Next, performance is a constraint because a nonresponsive data source connection could hinder the form from being rendered.

# InfoPath Controls

One of the areas that allows for great UI design in InfoPath is the area of InfoPath controls. Much like standard development controls used in ASP.NET development, InfoPath Designer offers the ability to utilize rich UI controls to interact with users. The controls are organized into three types: Input, Objects, and Containers. Input controls are primarily for obtaining feedback from the user, Object controls are controls with specific purposes, and Container controls are used to organize sections of your InfoPath template.

## Input Controls

Table 6-3 lists input controls you can use in your forms.

*Table 6-3. InfoPath Input Controls*

| Control | Description |
| --- | --- |
| Text Box | Commonly used control that allows users to enter unformatted text (for example, a street address). |
| Rich Text Box | Allows users to enter formatted text (bold, italic, underlined, and so on, and in a variety of sizes and colors). Also allows images, lists, and tables. |
| Drop-Down List | Displays a box with a list of choices from which a selection can be made by a user. The choices can come from a list you create, values in the form data source, or values from a data connection (for example, to an external web service). |
| Combo Box | Similar to a drop-down list except the box allows text input (so a user can type his/her own value in the box). |
| Check Box | Allows a user to indicate a yes/no or true/false selection by checking or unchecking a box. |
| Option Button | This type of control is sometimes called a "radio button" in other development tools. Usually several of these circular buttons are displayed at a time; they allow a user to select from a group of mutually exclusive options (i.e., selecting one unselects the others). |
| Date Picker | Allows a user to type a date in a box or click a button to display a calendar from which one can be selected. |
| Date and Time Picker | Similar to the Date Picker except also allows a user to specify a time. |

| Control | Description |
| --- | --- |
| Multiple-Selection List Box | Presents a scrollable list of choices with check boxes. Users can select one or more choices in the list and optionally add custom entries (depending how the form template is designed). |
| List Box | Presents a scrollable list of choices from which a single selection can be made. |
| Bulleted List | Allows users to add multiple text items into the form, and the items are formatted as a bulleted list (e.g., an Action Items list in a Meeting Agenda form). |
| Numbered List | Similar to a Bulleted List except items are formatted as a numbered list. |
| Plain List | Similar to a Bulleted or Numbered List except items aren't prefixed with a bullet or number. Instead items are simply listed one after another. |
| Person/Group Picker | Allows a user to type or select a user/group from a list. Users can also search through a directory for a user or group. |
| External Item Picker | Allows a user to type or select an item from an external system. |

## Objects

Table 6-4 lists objects (also known as *object controls*) that you can include in your forms. Object controls add specific capabilities to a form.

*Table 6-4. InfoPath Objects*

| Control | Description |
| --- | --- |
| Button | Adds interactivity to your form by executing an action when clicked. Buttons are used for actions such as submitting a form, switching views, and querying a database. |
| Picture Button | Similar to a Button control, except a picture can be used as the button (rather than the standard rectangular button that InfoPath draws). |

| Control | Description |
| --- | --- |
| Calculated Value | Displays the value of another control on the form or creates formulas (based on XPath expressions that you specify). |
| Vertical Label | Displays read-only text vertically on your form. |
| File Attachment | Allows a user to attach a single file to the form. To allow multiple attachments, more than one of these controls is needed (such as inserting this control within a repeating control). |
| Ink Picture | Allows users with a tablet PC to draw a picture using a stylus. |
| Hyperlink | Used for displaying web links. |
| Signature Line | Allows a user to digitally sign the form. |

## Container Controls

Table 6-5 lists container controls you can use in your forms.

*Table 6-5.* InfoPath Container Controls

| Control | Description |
| --- | --- |
| Section | Container for other controls (any control in the Controls gallery). |
| Optional Section | Similar to a Section control, except users can include whether to include it or not when filling out the form. |
| Repeating Section | Container for other controls that's useful for displaying repeated data (such as records from a database). |
| Repeating Table | Displays repeated information in a table. Each item is displayed as a row in the table. |
| Scrolling Region | Region with a defined size that displays a scrollbar for users to view content beyond its bounds. |
| Horizontal Region | Can be placed side by side so you can lay out content horizontally on your form. |

| Control | Description |
| --- | --- |
| Repeating Recursive Region | Contains other controls and can be inserted within it. Useful for creating an "outline" sort of structure. |
| Horizontal Repeating Table | Displays repeating information in a table. Each item is displayed as a column in the table. |
| Master/Detail | Used for organizing directly related pieces of information (such as related records in a database). A user can select a record from the "master" control, and the "detail" control will display its details. The master control is always a repeating table. The detail control can be a repeating table or repeating section. |
| Choice Group | Allows a user to replace the default section with another (such as a "Home Address" section with a "Work Address" section). |
| Repeating Choice Group | Displays two or more choice groups in a repeating fashion. This type of control is useful in scenarios such as when a user needs to add multiple emergency contacts to a form. |
| Choice Section | Inserts a section within a Choice Group. Users can replace the default section with a different one when filling out the form. |

# Where InfoPath is Used in Office 365

In Office 365, InfoPath is used in all the same ways that it is used in on-premise SharePoint 2010. InfoPath List forms, for instance, are a great way to customize and improve the visual quality of SharePoint list forms. InfoPath–based workflow forms can also be customized using InfoPath Designer (see the "Workflows and InfoPath" section later in this chapter). InfoPath can also be used to tie together multiple Lists or Libraries to produce a customized feature or application in SharePoint.

# Administering InfoPath in Office 365

Office 365 offers a browser–based administrative interface for managing InfoPath forms in Office 365. To navigate to the InfoPath settings in SharePoint online, select SharePoint management from your Admin panel, as shown in Figure 6-3.

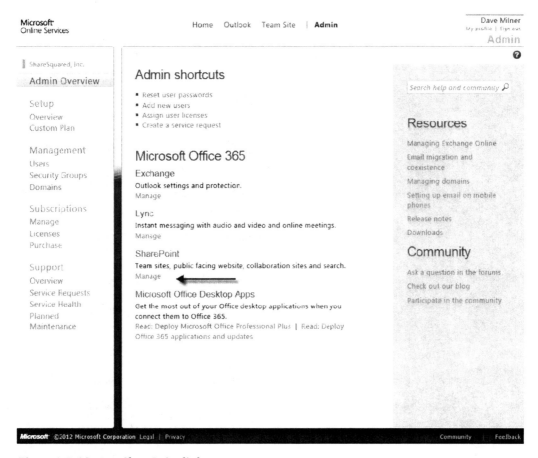

***Figure 6-3.*** *Manage SharePoint link*

From the next screen, select Configure InfoPath Forms Services on the SharePoint Online administration menu, as shown in Figure 6-4.

---

■ **Note** This option to manage SharePoint is available only in the Office 365 for Enterprises plans, not in the Office 365 for Professionals and Small Business plans.

---

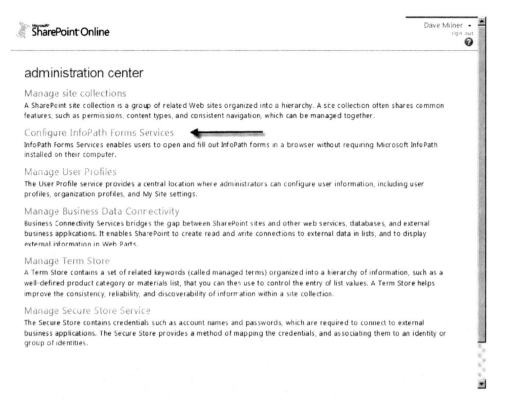

*Figure 6-4. Configure InfoPath Forms Services*

In the next management screen, shown in Figure 6-5, you will find all the settings around configuring InfoPath Forms Services.

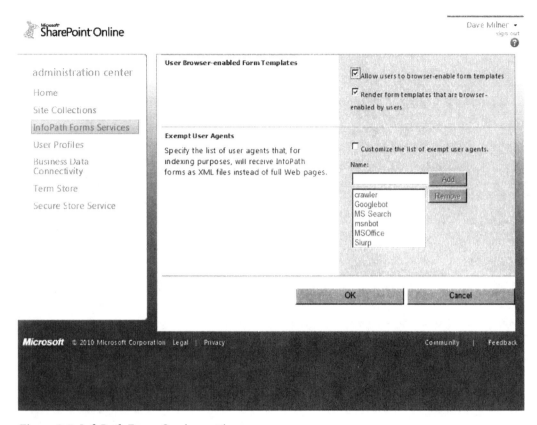

***Figure 6-5.*** *InfoPath Forms Services settings*

The primary settings of interest are in the "User Browser-enabled Form Templates" section. It is required that you check these two boxes to allow users to deploy browser-enabled form templates as well as have SharePoint render them in the browser.

## INFOPATH FORM TEMPLATES EXPLAINED

What exactly are InfoPath Form Templates? There's sometimes confusion in trying to nail this down. InfoPath Designer helps you develop an "InfoPath Form Template", which is a file (or group of files) with a .xsn extension (explained later in this chapter). These templates accept user input that is submitted to a single SharePoint list as an XML entry. Entries may be viewed with an InfoPath Form Template or consolidated in SharePoint to be tracked, viewed, and reported on through other means. These templates are stored in a library in SharePoint Online.

# Standard Lists and Libraries

One of the main areas for integrating InfoPath forms into SharePoint Online in Office 365 is replacing standard list and library forms with InfoPath forms. When you replace a standard form in a SharePoint list with an InfoPath form, the InfoPath Form View web part is used to display the form in the browser.

Launch InfoPath Designer and select the SharePoint List button, as shown in Figure 6-6.

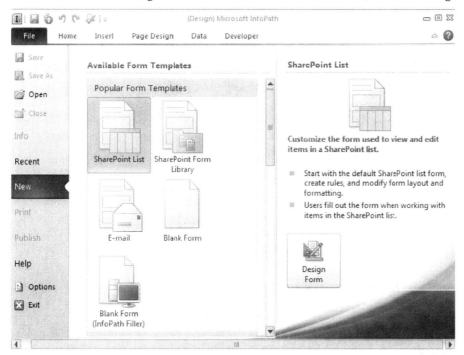

***Figure 6-6.*** *InfoPath Designer 2010 file tab (Backstage View)*

Selecting SharePoint List brings up the Data Connection Wizard. Here you can enter the URL of the SharePoint list you want to customize with an InfoPath form, as shown in Figure 6-7.

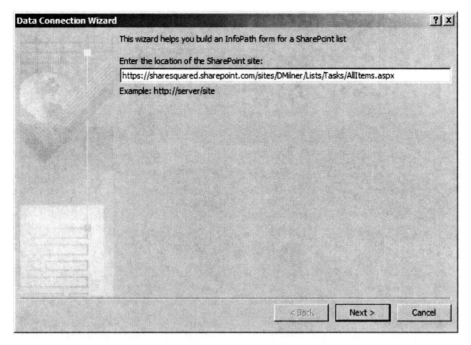

*Figure 6-7. Data Connection Wizard*

You will be prompted for your credentials when the wizard connects to your SharePoint Online site.

■ **Note** If your company has enabled the Single Sign-On features of Office 365 (that use AD FS 2.0 Identity federation), you will actually see a login prompt similar to one you see when logging on to a computer that's connected to the domain.

Next, you will be asked if you want to customize an existing SharePoint list or create a new list. Select the list you want to work with, as shown in Figure 6-8.

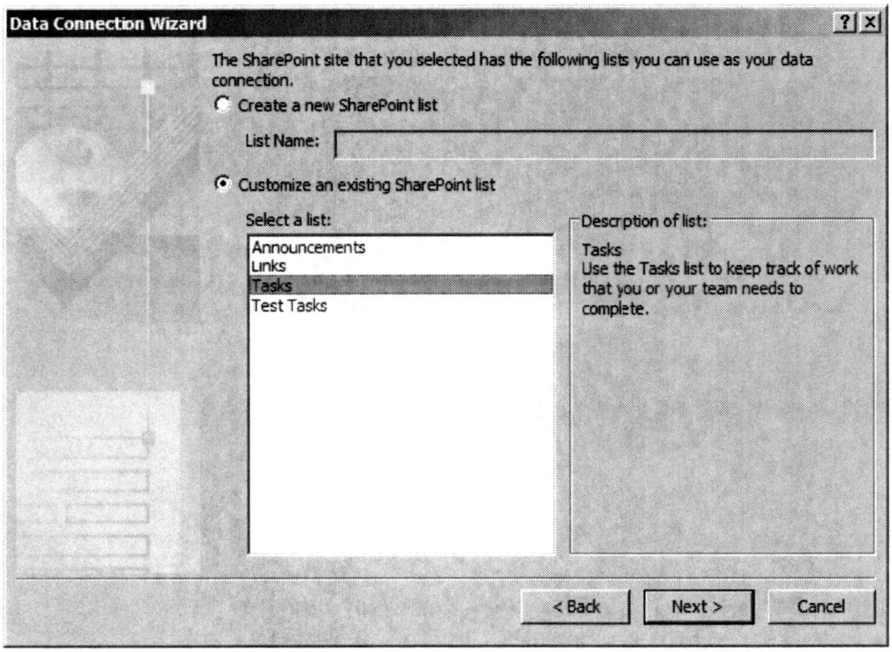

**Figure 6-8.** *Data Connection Wizard—Step 2*

For this example, we will select the built-in Task list that is installed by default with the Team Site template. Next, you will be asked if you want to design the form to handle multiple list items, or just a single list item. Selecting multiple list items will add repeating sections to your InfoPath form to allow handling multiple list items. This is shown in Figure 6-9:

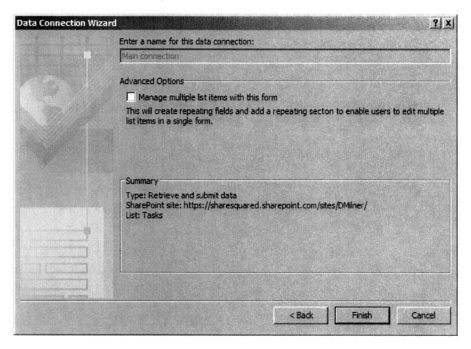

*Figure 6-9. Data Connection Wizard—Step 3*

On this last screen, click **Finish** to complete your InfoPath form selection process. The designer then loads with all the same fields that the Default View of the list has. For comparison, look at Figures 6-10 and 6-11 for the InfoPath and web-based list forms, respectively.

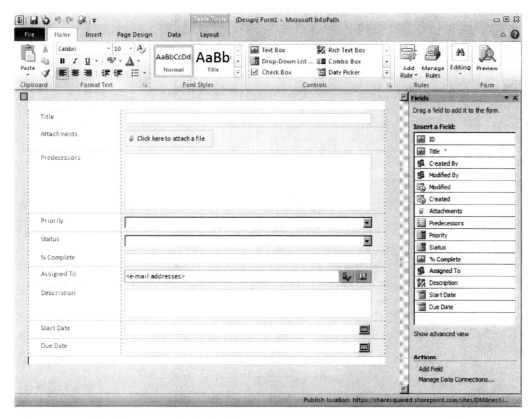

**Figure 6-10.** *InfoPath Designer for Tasks List*

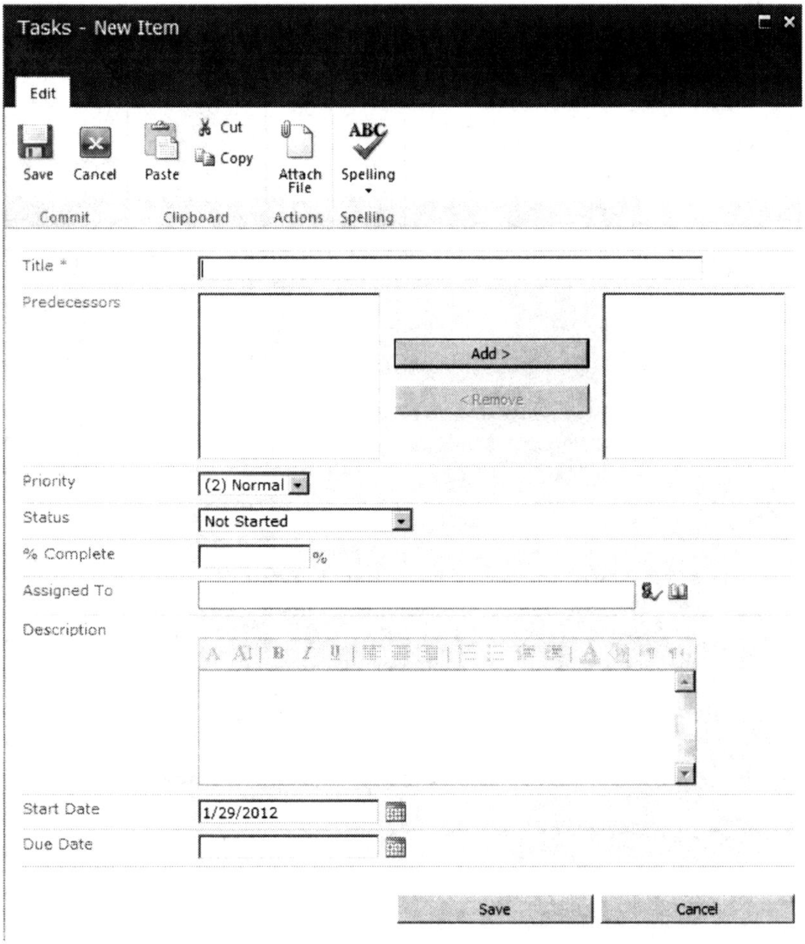

*Figure 6-11. Standard Modal Dialogue form for SharePoint List*

Notice the similarities and differences. And although you are starting to edit the InfoPath form, the changes to the List library will not be seen until you publish the InfoPath form to that library. In the interim period while you are working on the design of the form, you can save it locally. Saving the form will result in an .xsn file being saved on your local computer.

## XSN FILES EXPLAINED

The .xsn file that is created by InfoPath Designer is in reality a Windows Cabinet Archive (.cab) file, a file format that contains other files as its contents (similar to a ZIP file). InfoPath separates the design of the template from the data that the template gathers. You can examine the contents of an .xsn file by renaming it with a .cab extension and then opening it with Windows Explorer to view its contents. You can extract a .cab file using any number of available archiving and compression programs, such as 7-zip (http://7-zip.org/) or Windows Explorer (if you work in Windows 7). An example of what the InfoPath form XSN that we have been working on in this project looks like and what it contains can be seen in Figure 6-12.

| Name ^ | Date modified | Type | Size |
| --- | --- | --- | --- |
| builtincontrolsschema | 1/29/2012 8:21 PM | XML Schema File | 3 KB |
| choices | 1/29/2012 8:21 PM | XML Document | 1 KB |
| choices | 1/29/2012 8:21 PM | XML Schema File | 1 KB |
| dfschema | 1/29/2012 8:40 PM | XML Schema File | 6 KB |
| lookup1 | 1/29/2012 8:21 PM | XML Schema File | 2 KB |
| lookup1_cf | 1/29/2012 8:21 PM | XML Schema File | 2 KB |
| lookup1_item_controls | 1/29/2012 8:21 PM | XML Schema File | 3 KB |
| lookup1_item_type | 1/29/2012 8:21 PM | XML Schema File | 8 KB |
| lookup1_cf | 1/29/2012 8:21 PM | XML Schema File | 2 KB |
| manifest | 1/29/2012 8:40 PM | Microsoft InfoPath … | 14 KB |
| qfschema | 1/29/2012 8:21 PM | XML Schema File | 3 KB |
| rootschema | 1/29/2012 8:21 PM | XML Schema File | 2 KB |
| sampledata | 1/29/2012 8:40 PM | XML Document | 4 KB |
| template | 1/29/2012 8:40 PM | XML Document | 3 KB |
| typeschema | 1/29/2012 8:21 PM | XML Schema File | 8 KB |
| upgrade | 1/29/2012 8:40 PM | XSLT Stylesheet | 17 KB |
| view1 | 1/29/2012 8:40 PM | XSLT Stylesheet | 37 KB |

*Figure 6-12. Internal files in Tasks InfoPath Form .xsn file*

As you can see, there are 17 files that make up the .xsn file here for the task list. Many of them are XML documents, which contain information. There are also XML schema files, (.xsd) that define the contract for what the XML files can contain. There are a couple of XSLT stylesheets for visual transformations, and a special manifest.xsf file, which is the InfoPath form definition file.

Getting a picture of what is contained in an InfoPath XSN form is positive in that it is a good visual of how different portions of the form are constructed and how data is stored in parts. This can help when working with more-complex InfoPath forms such as InfoPath form library forms or some of the advanced data forms. In this form, there are a number of different lookup drop-down menus, fields, and controls that interact with other SharePoint–defined form data. These are generated automatically. If you are working with an *ad hoc* InfoPath library form, these fields will have to be created by you.

Once you are done with design efforts on your InfoPath form, you can perform a "quick publish" using the quick publish button, as seen in Figure 6-13.

*Figure 6-13. Quick publish button*

After it is published, you can view your newly designed Tasks InfoPath form on the New, View, and Edit Item actions of your Tasks list (see Figure 6-14).

*Figure 6-14. Modified Tasks form with InfoPath*

# Workflows and InfoPath

InfoPath forms can also come into play in the design of workflow forms in SharePoint Online. As long as your SharePoint Online subscription is one that includes InfoPath Forms Services (such as an E3 or SharePoint Online Plan 2 subscription), you can customize workflow forms with InfoPath. With plans that don't include InfoPath Forms Services, workflow forms are generated as normal web pages (.aspx files). You can customize them with a tool like SharePoint Designer, but not with InfoPath. The rest of this section assumes that you have a subscription that includes InfoPath Forms Services.

When designing workflows, an initiation form is often necessary to collect information from an end user. Workflow initiation forms are good candidates for customizing with InfoPath to present a better UI to the end user for starting (initiating) workflows.

---

■ **Note** Chapter 8 provides more information about creating workflows with SharePoint Designer for SharePoint Online.

---

Any of the forms that are used to collect user information can be modified in InfoPath after the creation of the workflow. As an example, Figure 6-15 shows a workflow that has two forms associated with it.

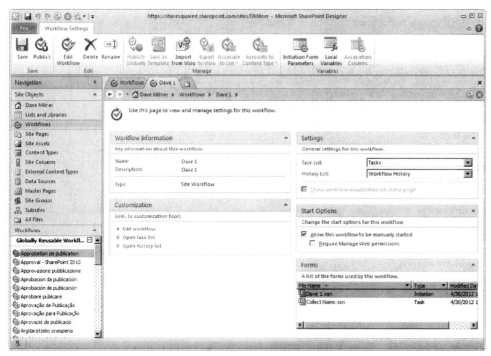

*Figure 6-15. Workflow forms*

Clicking either of these form names in the lower-right corner will open the form up in InfoPath Designer. These forms can be modified for better UI layout for interaction with end users.

## External Data and InfoPath

InfoPath provides the capability to create data connections to external sources. There are two types of external connections you can create: a connection to *submit* data and a connection to *receive* data.

If you create a connection to submit data, you can choose to submit data in the following ways:

- To a web service

- To a document library on a SharePoint site

- As an e-mail message

- To the environment that hosts your form, such as the ASP.NET page it resides within

If you create a connection to receive data, you can choose to receive data from these sources:

- A SOAP-based web service

- A REST-based web service

- A SharePoint list or library

- A database (e.g., a Microsoft Access database)

- An XML document

Depending on the type of connection you're creating (to submit or receive) and the type of source you choose (SharePoint list, database, and so on), the Data Connection Wizard will tailor the configuration options appropriately to help you configure the connection properly.

For more information on creating a data connection to *receive* data, please visit `http://bit.ly/KYZWKt`. For more information on creating a data connection to *submit* data, please visit `http://bit.ly/OeNCoS`.

## Summary

This chapter introduced InfoPath Designer 2010 and discussed the use of InfoPath forms in SharePoint Online. We also talked about administering InfoPath Forms Services and making sure the plan you're subscribed to supports Forms Services if you intend to use browser-based InfoPath forms within SharePoint. A walk-through of how to customize a SharePoint list form with InfoPath helped solidify the concepts in this chapter by putting them to practical use. Finally, we covered the use of InfoPath with workflow forms and the ability within InfoPath to create data connections to external sources (for receiving or submitting data).

# CHAPTER 7

## Custom Development with Visual Studio

So far in this book, we've discussed two customization tools for SharePoint Online: a web browser (see Chapter 4) and SharePoint Designer 2010 (see Chapter 5). But there's another tool—much more powerful and flexible than the first two—that will be the subject of this chapter: Visual Studio 2010.

If you have a background in software development and have developed solutions using the Microsoft .NET framework, you're probably no stranger to Visual Studio. It's the development tool of choice for most .NET developers and has an extensive array of features built in to aid you in developing for the Microsoft platform.

Up until the 2010 version, Visual Studio didn't have much to offer for SharePoint development (even with add-ons such as VSeWSS, the experience was pretty marginal), but thankfully those days are behind us now. Visual Studio 2010 introduces a wealth of new capabilities and templates that specifically target SharePoint development. While many of them were created with SharePoint 2010 in mind (rather than SharePoint Online), most of them still apply in the Office 365 world and will help us in developing custom solutions.

In this chapter, we'll cover the following topics:

- When to Use Visual Studio for customization
- Preparing Visual Studio for SharePoint Online development
- Creating a project
- Restrictions of the sandboxed environment
- Creating a feature and adding a feature receiver
- Creating a web part
- Creating a module to deploy files
- Creating an event receiver
- Creating a content type
- Creating a list definition
- Creating a custom action
- Packaging and deploying your solution

- Tips and recommendations

# When to Use Visual Studio for Customization

On the customization spectrum, Visual Studio is definitely at the advanced end. While a site administrator can customize SharePoint Online with a browser and a power user or web designer can customize SharePoint Online with SharePoint Designer 2010, the use of Visual Studio requires full-fledged software development skills. It also requires knowledge of SharePoint as a development platform (i.e., understanding that SharePoint is built on top of ASP.NET and knowing what its extension points are).

So when is it appropriate to make the jump to Visual Studio for your customizations? There's no one simple answer to this question, but here are some questions you can ask yourself that will help make that determination. Think of them as guidelines.

## Have You Exceeded What You Can Do in the Browser and SharePoint Designer?

This is an easy one. If the customization you want to make goes beyond what can be done in the browser or SharePoint Designer, Visual Studio is the only other choice. Of course, even that consideration assumes that the customization is possible in SharePoint Online in the first place. If the customization you want to make requires coding and deploying a custom timer job to the farm, for example, you're out of luck whether you've got Visual Studio or not (since that goes beyond the limits of what you're allowed to do in SharePoint Online).

## Who Will Be Doing the Work?

Visual Studio is definitely a tool aimed squarely at developers. Power users and designers generally aren't familiar with it and don't use it. If a developer or group of developers will be making customizations for SharePoint Online, Visual Studio will likely be the tool of choice. However, that's not to say developers may not also use other tools like SharePoint Designer to accomplish some of the customizations. It all comes down to what needs to be done and what the best tool is for the job. (For example, even developers will find SharePoint Designer useful for creating custom workflows for SharePoint Online.)

## How Reusable Do the Customizations Need to Be?

If you're developing customizations that will be used over and over again in SharePoint Online (for example, to be deployed to multiple sites or site collections that may even reside in multiple tenancies), Visual Studio is a great tool for packaging up those customizations and making them reusable. While you can certainly accomplish some of that without Visual Studio (e.g., creating a list template from a list and using it in multiple sites), Visual Studio offers more options and flexibility for creating truly reusable customizations that can even include custom code if desired.

# Preparing Visual Studio for SharePoint Online Development

## Setting Up Your Development Environment

Before you can use Visual Studio to customize SharePoint Online, you'll need a development environment you can develop and test against. If you don't already have a development environment set up, see Chapter 3 for instructions on how to do so.

## Extending Visual Studio

One extremely useful extension that will help you develop solutions for SharePoint Online is the *CKS Development Tools for Visual Studio* extension for Visual Studio 2010. The extension comes in two flavors (one targeting SharePoint 2010 *Foundation* and one targeting SharePoint 2010 *Server*) and is available from Microsoft's online Visual Studio Gallery.

To get the extension, open the Visual Studio extension gallery (either by clicking Tools > Extension Manager or by navigating to `visualstudiogallery.msdn.microsoft.com`) and search for "cks dev." Both flavors should come back in the search results. Download the one that matches the edition of SharePoint you're using in your development environment. The extension adds several new features and capabilities to Visual Studio, including:

- Several new project item templates (e.g., a *Custom Action* template for creating custom actions)

- Additional debugging and deployment options

- A "SharePoint" tab in the *Add References* dialog that lets you easily add SharePoint DLL references to your project without having to go browse the SharePoint root/hive folder and find them

- A Sandboxed Visual Web Part project item template

- Compile-time checking of sandboxed code to ensure that you're not using types or members that aren't allowed in sandboxed solutions

## Creating a Project

If you don't already have a project created for your customizations (for example, that you're grabbing from a source control system), that's the first thing you'll need to do.

To create a new SharePoint project, follow these steps:

1. Open the **File** menu in Visual Studio, and choose **New ➤ Project**.

2. On the New Project dialog, expand the **SharePoint** node on the left and choose **2010**. Select the Empty SharePoint Project template, give it a name, and click **OK**. See Figure 7-1 for an illustration of this step.

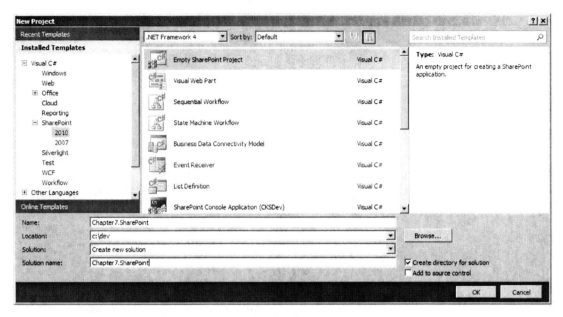

*Figure 7-1. Creating a new SharePoint project in Visual Studio 2010*

---

▪ **Tip** If you're creating a new solution and you think you may end up housing multiple projects, we recommend checking the *Create directory for solution* box, as shown in Figure 7-1. This will create a parent folder (which we've named "Chapter7.SharePoint") for the solution that can house all your projects.

---

3. Figure 7-2 shows the SharePoint Customization Wizard. Choose a local site for development/debugging and select the *Deploy as a sandboxed solution* option (which is the only valid choice when developing for SharePoint Online even though Visual Studio doesn't specifically call that out). Click the Finish button to create the project.

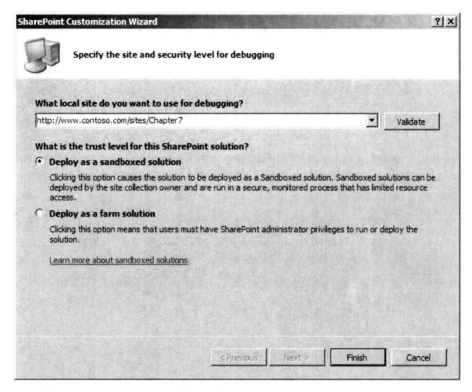

*Figure 7-2. SharePoint Customization Wizard*

# Restrictions of the Sandboxed Environment

Remember that *Deploy as sandboxed solution* option you selected when creating your SharePoint project? Before we go much further, it's important to understand the implications of operating in a sandboxed environment. In this section, we'll explore what a sandboxed solution is and what the sandboxed environment in SharePoint Online does and does *not* allow us to do.

## Sandboxed Solutions

A *sandboxed solution* is a solution (.wsp file) that is deployed to SharePoint Online and operates within the confines of the sandboxed environment. The *sandboxed environment* is a special environment (separate process) on the server farm in which custom code can execute but is subject to certain restrictions to prevent it doing any serious damage should something go wrong.

## Packaging and Installation

Just like farm solutions (the opposite of a sandboxed solution is a farm solution), sandboxed solutions are packaged into .wsp files. However, rather than being deployed to the farm's solution store, they are deployed to the **Solution Gallery** of a specific site collection by a site collection administrator. Just like other galleries in SharePoint sites (e.g., the Master Page gallery or the List Template gallery), the contents of this gallery live in the content database in which the site collection resides. For more information about deploying sandboxed solutions, see the "Deploy Your Solution to SharePoint Online" section later in this chapter.

## Restrictions

Sandboxed solutions are subject to a variety of restrictions compared with farm solutions. For instance, sandboxed solutions

- Cannot read from or write to the file system (except for reading/executing assemblies in the global assembly cache)

- Cannot call out to the network (for example, to access an external database)

- Cannot write to the registry

- Cannot call any assembly that's not deployed to the global assembly cache except for ones deployed as part of the sandboxed solution

- Can only access a subset of the server-side object model contained in Microsoft.SharePoint.dll

- Are restricted to the site collection in which they live (so you can't, for example, access a list in a different site collection)

- Are subject to the "split page rendering system" (explained in a moment)

- Are subject to resource usage limitations

- Are subject to a process called "validation" before they can be activated and used

- Are also subject to a few miscellaneous restrictions, including:

  - Cannot deploy a HideCustomAction element

  - Cannot deploy a CustomActionGroup element

  - Cannot register a control candidate for a delegate control

And this isn't even a complete list. There are a few other restrictions that we haven't specifically called out for the sake of brevity. For a complete list, we recommend you visit `http://bit.ly/ly9u5Y` ("Restrictions on Sandboxed Solutions in SharePoint 2010").

Also, not being able to read from or write to the file system introduces one big challenge: you cannot deploy files to the root (or "hive" folder) on the SharePoint farm like you can with farm solutions. That means no application pages, mobile pages, user controls, or visual web parts (using the normal Visual Web Part template that ships with Visual Studio, that is; the extension we mentioned earlier in this chapter works around that limitation). It also means no resource (.resx) files and no modifications to web.config. However, localization is still possible if that's a requirement for your solution. Visit `http://bit.ly/lgBOZp` for more information.

# Split Page Rendering System

Many of the restrictions in the preceding section are pretty self-explanatory. However, we believe one in particular deserves a little more explanation because it directly affects how you develop web parts in sandboxed solutions: the "split page" rendering system.

Here's a quick explanation of how the system works. When a SharePoint page is requested that includes a component from a sandboxed solution (e.g., a web part you deployed with your solution), SharePoint renders more than one page object (hence the "split" part of "split page"). One page is rendered in the normal ASP.NET worker process (w3wp.exe), and the other is rendered in the sandboxed worker process. When the page in the sandboxed process is fully rendered, it's merged in with the "real" page object in the ASP.NET process. If there is more than one sandboxed component on a page, each is rendered in its own page object that's later merged with the real one. That's all we're going to say about the technical details for now. The main thing you need to understand is how it affects development. In particular, there are certain properties of the Page object you have access to that are pointless to set because they won't get merged into the real Page object. A few examples include the following:

- ClientScriptManager (code in sandboxed solutions should not write to the ClientScript property—instead use a LiteralControl to render JavaScript to the page)

- ScriptManager

- Cache

- MasterPage (however, you can point to a different master page by setting the MasterPageFile property)

- HttpSessionState

That's all we're going to say about sandboxed solutions for now. If you're interested in knowing more of the technical details about how the sandboxed environment is architected, see http://bit.ly/aOQxzi.

We'll call out sandboxed solution considerations as appropriate throughout the remainder of this chapter.

# Creating a Feature and Adding a Feature Receiver

Since deploying customizations to SharePoint Online via solutions requires features (because you can't directly deploy elements to the SharePoint root folder on the farm), we're going to explain how to create a feature and associate custom code (called a *feature receiver*) if necessary.

## Creating a Feature

Follow these steps to create a feature in Visual Studio:

1. In the Solution Explorer window, right-click the *Features* node and select **Add Feature**. Visual Studio will create a feature (named *FeatureX*, where *X* is a number) and open the feature designer (see Figure 7-3).

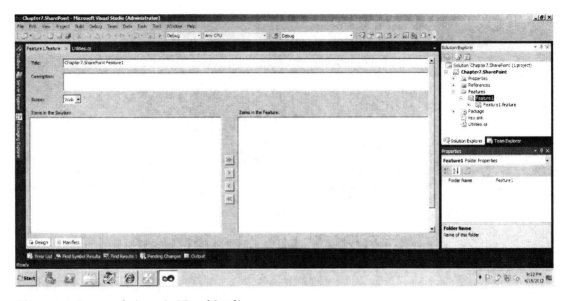

*Figure 7-3. Feature designer in Visual Studio*

2. Set the title, description, and scope (Site or Web) of your feature in the feature designer. If your project contains SharePoint elements that can be added to your feature, they will appear in the *Items in the Solution* section. Using the arrow buttons in the middle, you can move items to the *Items in the Feature* section, which adds them to the feature. While the feature designer is open, you can also set properties of the feature using the Properties window.

---

■ **Note** One slight annoyance of the feature designer is it doesn't provide an easy way to reorder the items in the right column. To reorder them, you must remove them and then re-add them in the desired order (or edit the feature XML directly, but doing so through Visual Studio disables the designer).

---

At the moment, the project we're showing in Figure 7-3 doesn't contain any SharePoint elements, so there's nothing readily available for us to add to our feature. That will change, however, as elements (lists, content types, and so on) are added to the project.

## Adding a Feature Receiver

A common task when creating features is to also create something called a *feature receiver*, which is a class containing "event handlers" that respond to various events associated with the feature's lifecycle.

To add a feature receiver in Visual Studio, right-click the feature in the Solution Explorer window and select **Add Event Receiver**.

After doing so, Visual Studio creates a class (named *FeatureName*EventReceiver) that inherits from SPEventReceiver. The class contains five overridden methods, all of which are initially commented out:

- FeatureActivated
- FeatureDeactivating
- FeatureInstalled
- FeatureUninstalling
- FeatureUpgrading

Uncommenting and implementing these methods allow you to respond to those particular events in the feature lifecycle (for example, the "activated" event if you uncomment and implement FeatureActivated). If you aren't sure which event you need to handle, see `http://bit.ly/HYcAnd` for an explanation of all of the events associated with a feature. In general, though, the "activated" and "deactivating" events are probably the most common ones you'll want to handle.

When would you need a feature receiver? There are plenty of times when they come in handy. Consider a simple example. Suppose you're doing a branding solution for a SharePoint Online site and your solution includes a custom master page that's deployed to the Master Page Gallery. When you deploy your solution and activate its features, you'll discover that although your master page was deployed, it was left in a pending (unapproved) state. With a feature receiver you can handle the "activated" event and add some code to approve the master page so it's immediately viewable by anyone who visits the site. You could even add code that sets it as the master page for the site when the feature is activated, saving an administrator the work of manually making that change.

# Creating a Web Part

One of the most common tasks you're likely to do when developing for SharePoint Online is to create custom web parts. Why? Well, aside from the normal reasons to create a web part (such as personalization), one big reason is you can't create and deploy custom controls in sandboxed solutions, so custom web parts are about as close as you can get to developing reusable "controls" you can use on multiple pages.

Let's get started. In the Solution Explorer window, right-click your project and select **Add ➤ New Item**. Select the *Web Part* SharePoint project item template on the Add New Item dialog, and click the **Add** button.

Right away, a couple of things happen:

- Visual Studio creates a web part SharePoint element and adds it to your project, as pictured in Figure 7-4.

*Figure 7-4. Web part element in a SharePoint project in Visual Studio*

- Visual Studio may create another feature (separate from any existing ones) and add your web part element to it. That's actually what happened in Figure 7-4. The project contained "Feature1," and adding the web part caused Visual Studio to create "Feature2." If the new feature isn't needed, just delete it and use an existing one (deleting the feature won't delete the web part).

---

■ **Note** The latest edition of the CKS Development extension for Visual Studio we mentioned earlier in this chapter offers a way to prevent Visual Studio from automatically adding new SharePoint project items to features (allowing you to control when they're added to a feature and which feature they're added to).

---

- Several files were created and placed under the web part element. You can see these in Figure 7-4. They include an Elements.xml file, a class file for your web part code, and an XML file with a ".webpart" extension.

Open the class (.cs) file, and you'll see something similar to Listing 7-1.

*Listing 7-1. Web Part class auto-generated by Visual Studio*

```
namespace Chapter7.SharePoint.WebPart1
{
[ToolboxItemAttribute(false)]
public class WebPart1 : WebPart
{
    protected override void CreateChildControls()
    {
    }
}
}
```

Notice the class inherits from the **System.Web.UI.WebControls.WebParts.WebPart** class (which is the standard ASP.NET base class for web parts, even outside of SharePoint).

Remember what we said earlier about sandboxed solutions only supporting a *subset* of the server-side object model from Microsoft.SharePoint.dll? This is one instance where it's important to remember that. If you try changing this class to inherit from a web part class that ships with SharePoint—like the Microsoft.SharePoint.WebPartPages.XsltListViewWebPart class, for example—you won't be able to do it. While that approach often works in SharePoint 2010 and is a common way to extend the functionality of SharePoint's built-in web parts, you can't do it in SharePoint Online. The namespaces that include the built-in web parts—including Microsoft.SharePoint.WebPartPages—are simply not available to us in sandboxed solutions.

Listing 7-2 shows the code for a simple web part. All this web part does is display a configurable number of months (mini-calendars) vertically on the page. If you wanted to get fancier, you could do something like add more code to this web part to query events lists in SharePoint Online and then link the dates on these calendars to those events.

*Listing 7-2. SimpleCalendarWebPart class*

```
using System;
using System.ComponentModel;
using System.Web.UI;
using System.Web.UI.WebControls;
using System.Web.UI.WebControls.WebParts;

namespace Chapter7.SharePoint.SimpleCalendarWebPart
{
    [ToolboxItemAttribute(false)]
    public class SimpleCalendarWebPart : WebPart
    {
        [WebBrowsable(true),
        Category("Calendar Settings"),
        WebDisplayName("Number of Months"),
        WebDescription("Number of months (1 or more) to display"),
        Personalizable(PersonalizationScope.Shared)]
        public int NumberOfMonths
        {
            get { return _numMonths; }
            set { _numMonths = Math.Max(1, value);  }
        }
        int _numMonths;

        protected override void CreateChildControls()
        {
            DateTime today = DateTime.Today;
            for (int i = 0; i < this.NumberOfMonths; ++i)
            {
                Calendar cal = new Calendar();
                cal.VisibleDate = today.AddMonths(i);
                cal.Style[HtmlTextWriterStyle.MarginBottom] = "10px";

                this.Controls.Add(cal);
            }
        }
    }
}
```

If we deploy this web part to SharePoint Online and add it to a page, it will look like the one pictured in Figure 7-5.

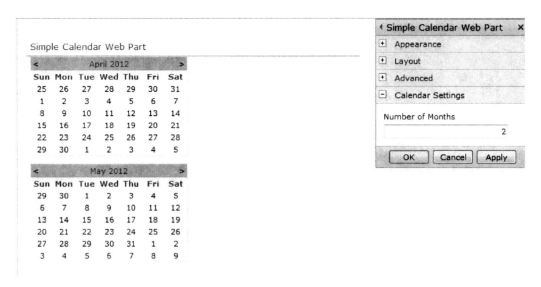

***Figure 7-5.*** *Simple Calendar Web Part on page in SharePoint Online*

As you can see in the figure, the web part properties pane automatically added a Number of Months property editor due to the attributes we added to our **NumberOfMonths** property in our web part class. We set this property to 2 in the browser and saved the changes, causing the web part to display two minicalendars on the page. (Incidentally, if you're interested in how the web part properties pane auto-generates property editors based on attributes, see this article that talks about the **System.Web.UI.WebControls.WebParts.PropertyGridEditorPart** class: http://bit.ly/II7jA2. The alternative, if you need more control, is to develop your own editor part class that inherits from **System.Web.UI.WebControls.WebParts.EditorPart**.)

## Creating a Module to Deploy Files

If your solution includes files you need to deploy to SharePoint Online (for example, CSS or JavaScript files), you'll need to create one or more *modules* to tell SharePoint where to provision those files within the site or site collection where your feature is activated.

To create a module, right-click your project in the Solution Explorer window and select **Add ➤ New Item**. Select the *Module* SharePoint project item template on the Add New Item dialog, and click the **Add** button.

When the project item for your module has been created, you'll see that Visual Studio has included two files beneath it: an Elements.xml file and a Sample.txt file. Delete the Sample.txt file. It's only there to demonstrate that adding files to the module will cause Visual Studio to automatically add them to Elements.xml (and likewise, deleting files from the module causes Visual Studio to automatically remove them from Elements.xml).

One key difference between modules in farm solutions and modules in sandboxed solutions (like we have to use for SharePoint Online) is the behavior of the **Type** attribute for a <File> tag in Elements.xml. If present, this attribute can be set to one of two values: *Ghostable* or *GhostableInLibrary*. Both values tell SharePoint the file can be cached on the web front-end server (rather than stored entirely in the content database). The only difference is that the latter attribute also creates a parent list item for the file if it's being deployed to a document library.

In farm solutions, the distinction between the two attribute values matters. However, it does *not* matter in sandboxed solutions. Even if you add **Type="Ghostable"** to a file in Elements.xml, SharePoint will *still* create a parent list item for the file if it's being deployed to a document library. This means the file will be visible as a list item in the library and able to be manipulated the same way as other files in the library.

## Creating an Event Receiver

*Event receivers* are classes that handle events associated with various objects in SharePoint. Visual Studio allows us to quickly create event receivers and deploy them to SharePoint Online.

To create an event receiver, right-click your project in the Solution Explorer window and select **Add ➤ New Item**. Select the *Event Receiver* SharePoint project item template on the Add New Item dialog, and click the **Add** button. This will bring up the SharePoint Customization Wizard, as shown in Figure 7-6.

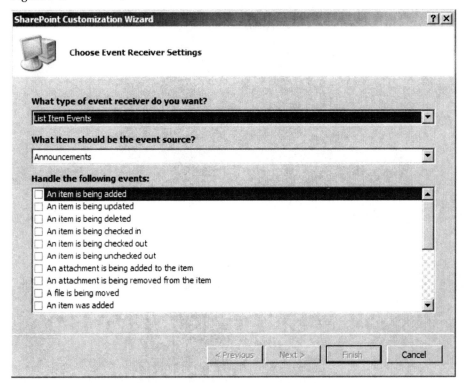

**Figure 7-6.** *SharePoint Customization Wizard for adding an event receiver*

As you can see in the figure, you have a variety of choices when creating an event receiver. First, you need to select which type of receiver you want. The choices include the following:

- List Events
- List Item Events

- List Email Events

- Web Events

- List Workflow Events

The event source can then be selected in the second drop-down menu if you choose *List Item Events, List Email Events,* or *List Workflow Events* in the first drop-down menu.

Finally, you can choose which specific events you want to handle. The list of events you can handle will vary depending on what type of event receiver you're creating. (For example, the events you can handle for a *List Item Events* receiver differ from what you can handle for a *Web Event Receiver.*)

For the sake of example, suppose you want to create a web (site) event receiver that automatically sets the master page of any newly created site to match that of the top-level site in the site collection.

On the dialog in Figure 7-6 you'd select *Web Events* for the type of event receiver and select *A site was provisioned* as the event you want to handle. This results in Visual Studio creating a class like the one in Listing 7-3.

*Listing 7-3. Empty Web event receiver class created by Visual Studio*

```
namespace Chapter7.SharePoint.WebReceiver
{
    /// <summary>
    /// Web Events
    /// </summary>
    public class WebReceiver : SPWebEventReceiver
    {
        /// <summary>
        /// A site was provisioned.
        /// </summary>
        public override void WebProvisioned(SPWebEventProperties properties)
        {
            base.WebProvisioned(properties);
        }
    }
}
```

As you can see in the listing, because we chose *A site was provisioned* as the event we wanted to handle on the dialog shown in Figure 7-6, Visual Studio has automatically overridden the **WebProvisioned** method for us.

To continue with our example, we can implement this method as shown in Listing 7-4.

*Listing 7-4. Implementation of the WebProvisioned method in a Web event receiver*

```
public override WebProvisioned(SPWebEventProperties properties)
{
    SPSite site = properties.Web.Site;
    SPWeb web = properties.Web;

    web.MasterUrl = site.RootWeb.MasterUrl;
    web.CustomMasterUrl = site.RootWeb.CustomMasterUrl;
    web.Update();
}
```

Now, assuming we include this event receiver in a Site-scoped feature, the **MasterUrl** and **CustomMasterUrl** properties of every newly created (provisioned) site will be set to match those of the top-level site in the site collection.

# Creating a Content Type

Next we'll discuss how to create a custom content type in Visual Studio to include in your solution—a fairly common scenario when customizing SharePoint Online.

Suppose we want to create a content type called "Custom Announcement" that inherits all the properties and functionality of the normal "Announcement" content type in SharePoint Online except for one important difference: our custom content type includes a "Show On Home Page" field that lets us determine whether the announcement should be automatically displayed on our site's home page in addition to where it would normally appear. This could be useful in a scenario in which we have an intranet site with a bunch of subsites (representing departments or divisions) and we want to put a web part on the home page that automatically rolls up and displays certain announcements from the various subsites.

To accomplish this, we'll need to do two things:

- Create a "Show On Home Page" field we can use in our content type

- Create the content type and include our custom field

To get started, we'll perform these steps:

1.  Right-click our project in the Solution Explorer window and select **Add ➤ New Item**.

2.  From the list of SharePoint 2010 project item templates, we'll select **Content Type** and name it *CustomAnnouncement*.

3.  Next the SharePoint Customization Wizard will appear and ask us which content type our new one should inherit from. We'll choose *Announcement* (the very first choice) and click **Finish**.

Visual Studio has now created a SharePoint project item (in the Solution Explorer window) for our content type and has created an Elements.xml file that looks similar to Listing 7-5.

*Listing 7-5. Elements.xml file for newly created content type*

```xml
<?xml version="1.0" encoding="utf-8"?>
<Elements xmlns="http://schemas.microsoft.com/sharepoint/">
  <!-- Parent ContentType: Announcement (0x0104) -->
  <ContentType ID="0x0104007ba7567139aa41ddb84c6b93eabee061"
               Name="Chapter7.SharePoint - CustomAnnouncement"
               Group="Custom Content Types"
               Description="My Content Type"
               Inherits="TRUE"
               Version="0">
    <FieldRefs>
    </FieldRefs>
  </ContentType>
</Elements>
```

Right away, there are few changes we can see we need to make:

- Change the value of the **Name** attribute in the <ContentType> tag. Normally the name is something similar to "[Company Name] [Content Type Name]" like "Contoso Announcement." Part of the reason for qualifying the name with a prefix (like a company name) is because SharePoint doesn't allow duplicate content type names within a site collection, so you should take steps in advance to ensure uniqueness.

- Change the value of the **Group** attribute in the <ContentType> tag. Generally speaking, the group name is usually something like "[Company Name] Content Types," e.g. "Contoso Content Types."

- Change the value of the **Description** attribute in the <ContentType> tag. This one is often overlooked but it's important. After all, if you use this content type in a list and make it available via the *New* button in a list view, this description is what shows up next to the content type name when that button is clicked.

- Add some fields inside of the <FieldRefs> tag. We'll be tackling this in a moment.

## Adding Fields to Your Content Type

Adding fields takes us into a little bit of a gray area (you knew gray areas existed in SharePoint, right?).

Don't get us wrong, the actual process of adding fields to the content type is very straightforward as we'll show in a moment. However, what's *not* as straightforward is where to put the field definitions (<Field> tags) in your project.

Here's some general guidance to help you. If the fields will only be used for a specific content type and aren't needed anywhere else in the project (e.g., list definitions or other content types), declaring the fields directly within the Elements.xml file for the content type is fine. In fact that's a pretty common practice.

However, if the fields will be used elsewhere, it's not a bad idea to put them in their own file (for the sake of "findability" and maintenance when working on the project down the road). Unfortunately there's no obvious way to do this in Visual Studio because "Field" isn't a SharePoint project item template we can pick from in the Add New Item dialog. However, there *is* a project item template called *Empty Element* we can use. Adding one of those to your project essentially creates an empty Elements.xml file that you can use for whatever you want. You can then put your field definitions in there. Just be careful that the Elements.xml file for your fields is included *before* the one for your content type (that uses the fields) in your feature manifest (XML). SharePoint takes a fairly unsophisticated approach to processing the feature manifest and essentially just goes in order. So if your field definitions appear *after* a content type that uses them, that will cause an error. (And remember that the feature designer in Visual Studio doesn't give you an easy way to reorder items in the feature manifest. You may need to remove items and then re-add them in the correct order.)

Suppose that we stick with the simple approach for now and define our custom field in the same file as our content type; we end up with an Elements.xml file that looks similar to Listing 7-6.

*Listing 7-6. Elements.xml file for content type that includes a field definition*

```
<?xml version="1.0" encoding="utf-8"?>
<Elements xmlns="http://schemas.microsoft.com/sharepoint/">
  <Field ID="{D67EBB56-A947-459D-8895-D7F18944D237}"
         Type="Boolean"
         Name="ContosoShowOnHomePage"
```

```
            DisplayName="Show On Home Page"
            Group="Contoso Fields"
            Description="Indicates whether item will be displayed on the site collection home
page.">
  </Field>

  <!-- Parent ContentType: Announcement (0x0104) -->
  <ContentType ID="0x0104007ba7567139aa41ddb84c6b93eabee061"
               Name="Contoso Announcement"
               Group="Contoso Content Types"
               Description="An announcement that can optionally be rolled up to the site
collection home page."
               Inherits="TRUE"
               Version="0">
    <FieldRefs>
      <FieldRef ID="{D67EBB56-A947-459D-8895-D7F18944D237}" Name="ContosoShowOnHomePage"
Required="FALSE" />
    </FieldRefs>
  </ContentType>
</Elements>
```

Now we've created a content type and a custom field to go with it. If we include the project item for this content type in a feature in our solution, they'll be availble for us to use in SharePoint Online when our solution is deployed.

# Creating a List Definition

*List definitions* let us define reusable list templates that users can choose when creating lists in SharePoint Online. A list definition contains all the details that define a particular type of list (such as which fields, content types, and views it has).

Follow these steps to create a list definition in Visual Studio:

1.  Right-click your project in the Solution Explorer window and select **Add ➤ New Item**.

2.  On the Add New Item dialog, you'll see there are *two* project item templates for list definitions: *List Definition* and *List Definition from Content Type*. If you choose the latter, the SharePoint Customization Wizard will appear and ask you which content type (from your Visual Studio project) you'd like to use for the list definition. Choose the former template for now so you can see what it's like to start from scratch.

3.  The SharePoint Customization Wizard will ask you three questions related to your list definition:

4.  What is its display name? (This is what a user will see when creating a list using your template.)

5.  What is its type? (What type of built-in list template in SharePoint is it based on?)

6. Do you want a list instance created along with your definition? (Selecting this will create an instance of the list in SharePoint Online when the feature containing the list definition is activated.)

7. Click **Finish** to complete the process.

When finished, Visual Studio will have created a list definition project item in your solution and will have added two files to it: *Elements.xml* and *Schema.xml*. (It will also have added a list instance project item beneath your list definition if you selected that option in the SharePoint Customization Wizard.)

Elements.xml contains a <ListTemplate> tag with details about your list definition. This is where you set its display name, description, and image (all common tasks when deploying a list definition to SharePoint Online).

Schema.xml contains the "guts" of the list definition. This is where fields and content types are defined (including which fields are required, hidden, and so on); and also where the views and forms associated with the list definition are defined.

If you're comfortable editing these files, you can now dive right in and start making your changes. Otherwise, if you need to brush up or haven't done it before, see http://bit.ly/HLUplb for information about the <ListTemplate> tag and Schema.xml file and how they can be changed to customize a list definition.

## Creating a Custom Action

Custom Actions give us a way to insert new functionality into existing menus and toolbars (including the ribbon) in SharePoint Online.

To demonstrate the concept, let's consider a real-world example. One of the first things many SharePoint Online administrators ask about is how to gather and report on web analytics data. Unbeknownst to many folks, SharePoint Online actually includes a fairly simple implementation of web analytics right out of the gate. If you need to get fancier you can (e.g., by integrating Google Analytics into your site), but sometimes the built-in analytics can be a great way to get started (or may even be enough depending on your needs). The only problem is they're not readily accessible in the SharePoint Online UI without some customization on your part.

Here's how you can do it:

1. Right-click your project in the Solution Explorer window and select **Add ➤ New Item**.

2. In the list of SharePoint 2010 project item templates, select *Empty Element*. This gives you a blank Elements.xml file you can edit.

3. Add a <CustomAction> tag like the one shown in Listing 7-7.

*Listing 7-7. Elements.xml file with custom action for web analytics link*

```
<CustomAction GroupId="SiteTasks" RequireSiteAdministrator="TRUE"
Id="Chapter7.SiteSettings.SiteTasks.WebAnalytics" Location="Microsoft.SharePoint.SiteSettings"
Sequence="105" Title="View Web Analytics">
    <UrlAction Url="_layouts/UsageDetails.aspx" />
</CustomAction>
```

When you're done, and your solution is deployed, your web analytics link will be visible on the Site Settings page for every site in your site collection (assuming you deploy this in a Site-scoped feature), as shown in Figure 7-7.

Site Actions
Manage site features
Save site as template
Reset to site definition
Delete this site
View Web Analytics

*Figure 7-7. View Web Analytics link added to Site Settings page with a custom action*

In farm solutions, you would also have the ability to hide existing menu and toolbar links (using a *HideCustomAction* element) and the ability to create new groups/headings (such as a "Custom Reports" heading on the Site Settings page under which our web analytics link could have gone), but those elements are unfortunately not available to us in sandboxed solutions. If you try to use them, they'll be ignored.

See http://bit.ly/bEWX15 for more information about the schema for custom actions. Remember that certain items mentioned in the documentation (such as *HideCustomAction* elements) are not available in sandboxed solutions.

# Packaging and Deploying Your Solution

When all your project elements have been created, it's time to get them packaged into features and into an overall solution (by which we mean a SharePoint solution package, or .wsp file, not a "solution" in the Visual Studio sense).

## Prepare Your Features

For the feature side of packaging, you're probably already part of the way or mostly done. Visual Studio automatically puts project's elements into features as they're created (unless you've turned that off with an extension that adds that capability), so you may just need to look them over and verify everything is in the correct feature. For example, you might have a feature called "Contoso Web Parts" that has a list definition in it simply because Visual Studio put it there. Double-click each feature in the Solution Explorer window and use the feature designer to ensure everything is where it should be. (Also, double-check the scope of your features, which should be *Site* or *Web* for SharePoint Online. Often, if you don't see an item in the feature designer that you expect to see, it's because Visual Studio is hiding it due to the feature's scope not matching the scope of the item.)

Make sure you also set titles and descriptions for your features so site administrators know what they're activating. (Images are nice, too, and can be set in the feature properties and show up next to the feature on the feature activation page in SharePoint).

## Preparing the Solution Package

Next, you can use the *package designer* to check the contents of the overall package ("package" is short for "SharePoint solution package"). To do so, find the node in the Solution Explorer window that's called **Package** and double-click it. You'll see the package designer shown in Figure 7-8.

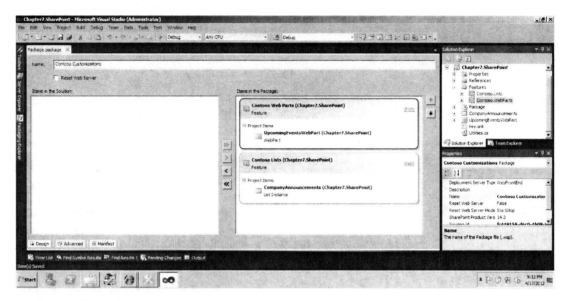

*Figure 7-8. The package designer in Visual Studio 2010*

The package designer lets you add features to the package as well as reorder them (unlike the feature designer, the package designer actually has a reordering capability built into it).

If you need to manually edit the package XML, you can do so by following these steps:

1. Click the **Manifest** tab at the bottom of the designer.

2. Expand the *Edit Options* panel at the bottom.

3. Click the Overwrite generated XML and edit manifest in the XML editor link at the bottom.

## Set Your Build Configuration

This may seem obvious, but in all the excitement of preparing features and packages, it often gets overlooked. If you're done testing, and this will be deployed to production (i.e. the live SharePoint Online site), make sure you change your project's build configuration to *Release* (rather than *Debug*).

## Deploy Your Solution to SharePoint Online

For this step, you'll need to navigate to the live site collection in SharePoint Online where your solution will be deployed. On the Site Settings page for the site collection, click the **Solutions** link under the *Galleries* heading (see Figure 7-9).

Galleries
Site columns
Site content types
Web parts
List templates
Master pages
Themes
Solutions

*Figure 7-9. The Solutions Gallery link on the Site Settings page*

Clicking the link will take you to the Solutions Gallery page. Click the **Solutions** tab in the ribbon to expose the *Upload Solution* button. Click that button to open the Upload dialog, as pictured in Figure 7-10.

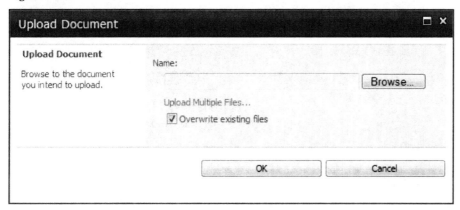

*Figure 7-10. Upload solution dialog window*

Once the solution is uploaded, you'll see the solution activation dialog shown in Figure 7-11. Click the **Activate** button to active your solution.

---

■ **Note** Activating your solution also *validates* it, which verifies that nothing in it violates the restrictions of the sandboxed environment. Also note that site-scoped features are automatically activated when the solution is activated. Web-scoped features are not.

---

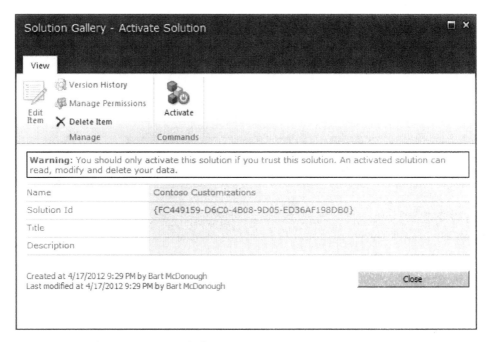

*Figure 7-11. Solution activation dialog*

# Tips and Recommendations

If you're new to developing custom solutions for SharePoint (whether for SharePoint 2010 or SharePoint Online), you're about to discover what phrases such as "open-ended" and "gray area" really mean. Developing for SharePoint is both a very rewarding and sometimes very frustrating experience. There's a lot you can do, but there are also a lot of ways you can accomplish almost every single task you set out to do, hence the importance of establishing patterns and best practices to assist you along the way.

Along that same line of thought, we've decided to list some tips and recommendations here that we hope you will find helpful and will make your life as a SharePoint developer a little more rewarding.

## Organize Your Projects in a Logical Manner

Project organization in Visual Studio is one of those "gray areas" in SharePoint development, and what ends up happening many times is developers just let things end up wherever Visual Studio puts them in the project, making maintenance more difficult down the road. Our recommendation is to structure things in a logical fashion, such as grouping related elements together. One example is if your project contains ten custom content types, you can create a "Content Types" folder and put all the content types in there. Then another developer can easily find your custom content types if doing maintenance on your project later.

## Don't Be Afraid to Change Namespaces

Just because Visual Studio generates a namespace for something in your project doesn't mean that it's the best namespace for you to use. Two examples that come immediately to mind are feature receivers and web parts. When creating these things, check the namespaces and change them if what Visual Studio generates doesn't make sense for your architecture and requirements.

Just be aware that if you change the namespace for a web part in its class file, you also need to update two other items:

- Update its type name in its .webpart file.

- Update any *Safe Control Entries* that reference it. To do so, view the web part project item's properties in the Properties window and edit the **Safe Control Entries** property. Fix the *Namespace* and *Type Name* attributes as required.

## Logging

Normally, in SharePoint development we'd recommend logging errors and trace messages to the Unified Logging Service (ULS) logs, but doing so isn't an option in SharePoint Online due to the sandboxed environment. However, there's still a work-around we can employ: using a list.

When you're creating custom solutions for SharePoint Online, consider adding a list instance (either through XML or through code) for a "logging" list of some kind. Put a few of the standard logging fields in there (category, message, details, and so on) and use it for logging in custom code. And of course, remember to ensure that the list is trimmed periodically to keep your storage allocation from getting eaten up by logging. (You can set a content expiration policy on the list, create a page in SharePoint where an administrator can clean it out, or do whatever else makes the most sense for your situation.)

Also remember that you can't call **SPSecurity.RunWithElevatedPrivileges()** in SharePoint Online, so you'll need to make sure every user has rights to create log entries in the list (because your logging code will always operate under the account of the current user).

## Summary

This chapter discussed when it might be appropriate to make the jump to Visual Studio for developing custom solutions for SharePoint Online (over using a web browser or SharePoint Designer). We also discussed the sandboxed environment in which our solutions operate and walked you through how to create some of the most common SharePoint elements in Visual Studio and add them to your solution. We then brought it all together by discussing how to deploy your customizations to SharePoint Online and offered a few development tips from our experience that will hopefully make your life a little easier.

**CHAPTER 8**

■ ■ ■

# SharePoint Designer Workflows

Workflows are one of the great features of SharePoint Online and are generally favored by power users (end users with some technical know-how) because of the ability to quickly automate business processes without the need for programming knowledge or IT involvement.

SharePoint Designer 2010 introduces a new workflow designer that makes the process of creating workflows intuitive and fairly painless. The process of creating a workflow has become less about "learning SharePoint Designer" and more about mapping out the logic for the workflow and making sure it accurately reflects the business process(es) you're trying to automate.

In this chapter, we'll cover the following topics:

- Introduction to Workflows in SharePoint Online

- A Quick Tour of SharePoint Designer

- Building and Deploying a Simple Workflow

- Integration with Microsoft Visio 2010

- Developing Custom Workflow Actions in Visual Studio

## Introduction to Workflows in SharePoint Online

Let's start by covering some workflow basics. If you're new to workflow development or could use a refresher on the topic, this section will quickly get you up to speed on key concepts that are critical to understanding the rest of this chapter.

### What Is a Workflow?

A *workflow* can be described in a very general sense as a series of tasks that produce an outcome. In the context of SharePoint Online, we can define a workflow more narrowly as *the automated movement of documents, items, or information through a sequence of actions or tasks that are related to a business process*. In other words, workflows allow us to apply automation to business processes.

---

■ **Note** The terms *workflow* and *business process* are often used interchangeably. In this chapter, we'll keep the two terms separate for the sake of clarity. When we say *workflow* we're talking specifically about automation applied to a business process in SharePoint Online.

---

Workflows in SharePoint Online have a beginning, an end, and a sequential flow of logic that progresses from start to finish. It's possible for workflows to execute tasks in parallel (using a structure called a *parallel block*), but they still ultimately progress sequentially from start to finish (an initial state to a final state).

## Modeling a Workflow

A workflow is typically modeled (visually represented) using a *flowchart*, which is a natural fit because it has a beginning point, an end point, and a flow of actions and conditions in between. SharePoint Online and SharePoint Designer are both aware of this and have built-in capabilities that let us view and work with our workflows as flowcharts. You'll learn more about those capabilities later in this chapter when we start building workflows.

## Types of Workflows

SharePoint Online supports three types of workflows:

- List
- Reusable
- Site

## List Workflows

A *list workflow* is one that is associated with a specific list (or library). Because it operates in the context of a specific list, it automatically has access to any custom fields that exist on that list. It cannot be associated with any other lists, however, so using it elsewhere means having to manually create another, separate instance of it. Therefore, a list workflow probably isn't the best choice if your workflow needs to operate on multiple lists or operate at the site level. (To be fair, there are some creative ways to "copy" list workflows from one list to another that you can find out on the Internet by searching on the topic. However, SharePoint Designer provides no built-in, supported way to do it.)

## Reusable Workflows

*Reusable workflows* are associated with a content type rather than a specific list. If they're published to the top-level site of a site collection, they're said to be "globally reusable" because they're available across the entire site collection.

Reusable workflows can also be exported from one site and then imported into another, providing a means to accomplish tasks such as migrating a workflow between environments (such as from test to production).

Because reusable workflows are associated with a content type rather than a specific list, the way we work with them in SharePoint Designer is a little different (especially if you choose to associate your workflow with *all* content types, which is one of the options when creating it).

A reusable workflow is a good choice if you're creating a workflow that will be used on multiple lists or in multiple sites.

## Site Workflows

A *site workflow* is exactly what the name implies: a workflow that operates on a site and not within the context of any list, library, or content type. One "side effect" of this difference in scope is that many of the actions available to the other workflow types are not available to site workflows because they don't apply when not working with list items.

Site workflows are a good choice when you need to create a workflow that doesn't operate in the context of a specific list, library, or content type.

# Workflow Building Blocks

The building blocks of a workflow are actions, conditions, and steps.

*Actions* are what actually do the "work" in a workflow. SharePoint Designer includes a set of built-in actions such as *Send an Email* and *Copy List Item* that you can use in your workflows.

*Conditions* control the flow of execution in a workflow by executing actions only when a given statement about something is true. For example, there's a condition called *Created by a Specific Person* that lets you execute a set of actions only when a list item was created by the person you specify.

*Steps* provide a way to logically organize a workflow into related sets of actions and conditions. Strictly speaking, you could put your entire workflow into a single step, but it's often more beneficial (in terms of readability and maintenance) to use multiple steps unless the workflow is extremely short.

SharePoint Designer provides a fairly robust set of built-in actions you can use in your workflows. However, if you need more, it's possible to build custom actions in Visual Studio 2010, deploy them to SharePoint Online, and then use them within SharePoint Designer. You'll learn more about that in the "Developing Custom Workflow Actions in Visual Studio" section later in this chapter.

# How Are Workflows Started?

Workflows are started (initiated) by *events*. There are three types of events that can start a workflow in SharePoint Online:

- An item is created

- An item is changed

- The workflow is manually started

Initiation of the workflow is automatic in the case of the first two events.

---

■ **Note** Site workflows cannot be started automatically because they're not tied to an item in a list or library. They must always be started manually.

---

The workflow settings page in SharePoint Designer provides a set of *start options* that let you configure how your workflow can be started. You'll learn more about the workflow settings page in the section titled "A Quick Tour of SharePoint Designer" coming up shortly in this chapter.

## Workflow Permissions

By default, the actions in a workflow execute with the permissions of the user who started the workflow (the workflow initiator). There is, however, a special type of step called an *impersonation step* that lets a workflow execute actions with the permissions of the workflow author. The workflow author is considered to be the last person who published the workflow. If a workflow is republished by a different user, the workflow author will not change for any in-process workflows; only for new instances that begin after the workflow was republished.

---

■ **Note** Impersonation steps can be added only to the root (outermost level) of a workflow. They cannot be nested within another step.

---

# A Quick Tour of SharePoint Designer

Now that we've covered some workflow basics, it's time to take you on a tour of the tool you'll use to build them: SharePoint Designer 2010. We're calling this a "quick" tour because we're focusing on the aspects of SharePoint Designer related to building and deploying workflows. SharePoint Designer is a powerful tool, however, and has a lot more capabilities for working with SharePoint Online than what's covered here.

---

### GET SHAREPOINT DESIGNER 2010

If you don't already have SharePoint Designer 2010, you can download it for free from Microsoft at http://bit.ly/bzi8wd. Make sure you download the correct format (32-bit or 64-bit) that matches the format of Microsoft Office you have installed. Otherwise, you'll get an error message at the end of the installation wizard and will have to start all over.

---

## Connecting to Your Site

There are two ways to connect SharePoint Designer to your SharePoint Online site.

### Method #1: Open SharePoint Designer from Your Site

For this method, begin by navigating to your SharePoint Online site in a browser. Once there, open the *Site Actions* menu and choose *Edit in SharePoint Designer*, as shown in Figure 8-1.

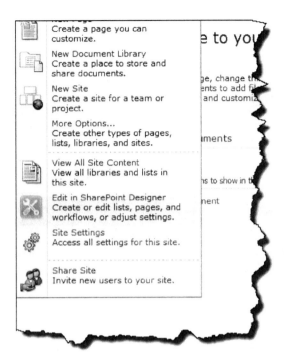

*Figure 8-1. Selecting* Edit in SharePoint Designer *option in Site Actions menu*

## Method #2: Open Your Site from SharePoint Designer

For this method, begin by launching SharePoint Designer 2010. The first screen you see will be SharePoint Designer's backstage view (*File* tab). If your site is listed in the *Recent Sites* list, you can simply click it to open it. Otherwise, click the **Open Site** button as shown in Figure 8-2.

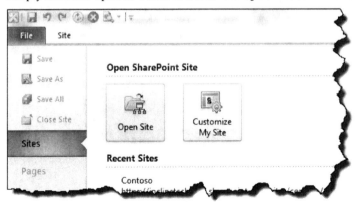

*Figure 8-2. The Open Site button in SharePoint Designer's backstage view*

When the Open Site dialog appears, enter the complete URL of your site and click the **Open** button to connect to it.

## Site Page

Once you've connected to your site, you'll be presented with the Site page in SharePoint Designer. The Site page lets you view and manage settings for your site and also displays a *Site* tab in the ribbon. In the Site tab's *New* group, you'll see two buttons related to workflow: a **List Workflow** button and a **Reusable Workflow** button, as shown in Figure 8-3.

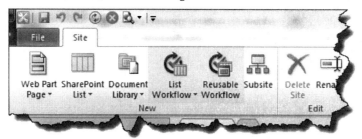

*Figure 8-3. Workflow buttons in Site tab of ribbon in SharePoint Designer*

Opening the drop-down menu beneath the **List Workflow** button will show you the lists and libraries in your site. Choosing one will begin the process of creating a list workflow for that particular list or library.

Notice the lack of a button in the ribbon for creating site workflows. Unfortunately, you can't create a site workflow from here. To do that you must use the *Workflows* page, which we discuss next.

# Workflows Page

To access the Workflows page, click the *Workflows* link in the Navigation pane, as shown in Figure 8-4.

*Figure 8-4. The Navigation pane with Workflows link selected*

The Workflow page contains a list of all workflows in the site as well as the *Workflows* ribbon tab for working with workflows. The Workflows page is pictured in Figure 8-5.

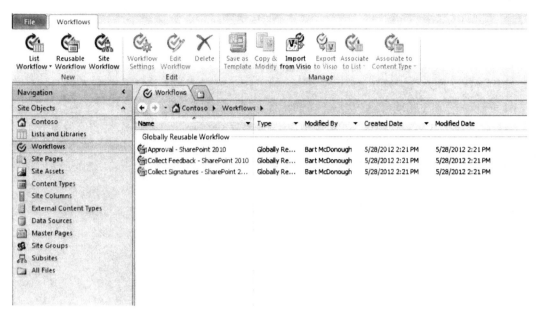

*Figure 8-5. The Workflows page in SharePoint Designer 2010*

First, let's look at the *New* group of the *Workflows* tab in the ribbon. Notice that unlike on the Site page, we now have a **Site Workflow** button we can use to create site workflows. The other two buttons for creating list and reusable workflows operate the same way as on the Site page.

---

⬛ **Note** Most of the buttons in the ribbon will show a help tip if you hover your mouse pointer over the button for a moment. This can be helpful if you're unsure of (or forgot) what a button does.

---

Table 8-1 explains what the other ribbon buttons do.

*Table 8-1. Ribbon Button Reference for the Workflows Ribbon Tab on the Workflows Page*

| Group | Button Name | Description |
|-------|-------------|-------------|
| Edit | Workflow Settings | Opens the workflow settings page for the selected workflow. |
| | Edit Workflow | Opens the workflow designer for editing the selected workflow. |
| | Delete | Deletes the selected workflow (prompts for confirmation first). |

| Group | Button Name | Description |
|-------|-------------|-------------|
| Manage | Save as Template | Saves the selected reusable workflow as a .wsp (SharePoint Solution Package) file so it can be deployed to another site collection. (This button can't be used for list or site workflows.) |
| | Copy & Modify | Copies a reusable workflow, prompts you for a name, and opens the workflow designer so you can edit the copy. (This button can't be used for list or site workflows.) |
| | Import from Visio | Create or update a workflow by importing a .vwi (Visio Workflow Interchange) file. |
| | Export to Visio | Exports the selected workflow as a .vwi file. (This button can't be used for site workflows.) |
| | Associate to List | Associates a reusable workflow with a list or library that you pick from the button's drop-down menu. (This button can't be used for list or site workflows.) |
| | Associate to Content Type | Associates a reusable workflow with a content type that you pick from the button's drop-down menu. (This button can't be used for list or site workflows.) |

■ **Note** The last two buttons in Table 8-1 will work only if the reusable workflow has been published. If it's been saved but not published, you'll get an error when the browser tries to bring up the workflow association page. It can be a bit confusing because there's no Publish button on this page. You'll need to visit the workflow settings page or edit the workflow to see the Publish button.

# Workflow Designer

The *workflow designer* is what you'll use to edit your workflows in SharePoint Designer. The workflow designer for a brand-new list workflow is pictured in Figure 8-6.

**Figure 8-6.** *Workflow designer in SharePoint Designer 2010*

As shown in the figure, new workflows are automatically given a default step called "Step 1."

---

■ **Tip** You can change the name of a step by clicking the step's title in the workflow designer. A text box will appear and allow you to edit the name.

---

When working in the workflow designer, a blinking cursor indicates where the next element (action, condition, and so on) in your workflow will be positioned. Did you notice the instruction *Start typing or use the Insert group in the Ribbon within Step 1* in Figure 8-6? This instruction is letting you know that there are two ways you can insert elements into your workflow:

1. Start typing. A search box will appear where the cursor was and will compile a list of suggested workflow elements as you type. You can press Enter to view the list of suggestions and choose one (assuming you have at least one match).

2. Use the *Insert* group in the ribbon. The buttons in this ribbon group allow you to insert all the standard elements into your workflow.

Besides inserting elements into your workflow, the ribbon in the workflow designer allows you to do other things as well, including:

- Saving and publishing your workflow

- Checking your workflow for errors (e.g., a required property of an action hasn't been assigned a value)

- Exporting your workflow to Microsoft Visio

- Managing settings for your workflow (such as how it can be started)

- Configuring parameters for your workflow's initiation form (a form that's displayed when the workflow is started)

- Defining local variables for your workflow

- Defining association columns for your workflow (*association columns* are columns that are automatically added to a list when your workflow is associated with that list; they're a way for you to ensure the columns your workflow requires are present)

Many elements—once inserted into your workflow—will allow you to configure their properties by clicking hyperlinks. Consider, for example, the *If value equals value* condition shown in Figure 8-7.

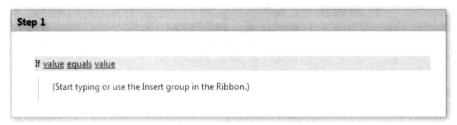

*Figure 8-7. Configurable workflow element with hyperlinks*

There are three hyperlinks in the condition shown in the Figure 8-7: *value*, *equals*, and *value*. The first and last hyperlinks are blue, indicating they represent properties that haven't yet been assigned values (properties with blue hyperlinks must be set before the workflow can function). The middle hyperlink is black, indicating it represents a property with an assigned value but that you can change the value by clicking it if you wish.

Clicking either *value* link will display a text box with a lookup button. The lookup button lets you set a value dynamically based on data the workflow knows about (such as the current list item for a list workflow). Clicking *equals* will display a drop-down menu of alternate conditions you can select if *equals* isn't the one you want.

Many other workflow elements are configured in exactly the same way: by clicking hyperlinks and setting property values. You can also hover over a workflow element to reveal the element's menu. When you open the menu, you get additional options for working with the element, as shown in Figure 8-8.

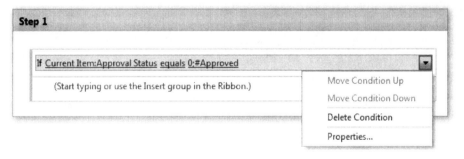

*Figure 8-8. Workflow element menu*

# Workflow Settings Page

The workflow settings page lets you configure settings for your workflow (see Figure 8-9).

***Figure 8-9.*** *Workflow settings page*

The workflow settings page can be reached a few different ways in SharePoint Designer:

- The **Workflow Settings** ribbon button on the Workflows page (that lists all workflows in the site)

- The **Workflow Settings** ribbon button in the workflow designer (when editing a workflow)

- By clicking the workflow name hyperlink on the Workflows page

You can perform all the following tasks from the workflow settings page:

- Configure general information (such as name and description) about your workflow

- Edit the workflow (clicking the **Edit Workflow** link will take you to the workflow designer)

- Configure start options, forms, and other general settings for your workflow

As long as we're on the subject of workflow settings, this is also a good time to discuss workflow visualization and workflow forms (because both appear on the settings page).

# Workflow Visualization

If you have a SharePoint Online plan that supports Visio Graphics Services (for example, the E3 plan) and have Microsoft Visio Premium installed on the computer from which your workflow is published, you can use *workflow visualization* in SharePoint Online.

---

■ **Note** Visio does not need to be installed on client computers that view workflow visualizations. It's only required to be on the computer from which the workflow is published.

---

You enable this feature from the workflow settings page by checking the *Show workflow visualization on status page* option in the **Settings** category. When workflow visualization is enabled, viewing the workflow status page in a browser will display a Visio workflow diagram indicating the current status of the workflow.

Other requirements for using workflow visualization include these:

- Make sure the *SharePoint Server Enterprise Site features* feature is activated at the site level and the *SharePoint Server Enterprise Site Collection features* feature is activated at the site collection level.

- Make sure Silverlight 3.0 or higher is installed in the client browser (because the Visio diagram is rendered using Silverlight). Technically, workflow visualization will still work without Silverlight, but a plain image will be rendered instead (so you'll lose zooming/panning capabilities you get with Silverlight).

---

■ **Note** When you republish a workflow after enabling visualization, instances of in-progress workflows will not be affected. Only new workflow instances will honor the visualization setting.

---

There are a couple of ways you can reach the status page for a list workflow from your browser:

- Select/view an item in the list and click the **Workflows** button in the ribbon. From the workflows page for the item, you can click the workflow name (it's a link) and view the workflow's status.

- When a workflow is associated with a list and has been run on at least one item, an extra column will appear in the list that's named after the workflow. The column contains an *In Progress* or *Complete* link that you can click to view the workflow's status on an item.

For site workflows, you can reach the workflow status page by selecting **View All Site Content** from the Site Actions menu and clicking **Site Workflows** at the top of the page (just as you would to initiate a site workflow). From there, you can click the link with the site workflow name and view its status.

## Workflow Forms

*Workflow forms* are used to initiate workflows and to collect information from users at various points throughout the workflow's execution.

SharePoint Designer 2010 allows you to create three types of workflow forms:

- **Initiation form**: This type of form is generated automatically by SharePoint Designer when a workflow is created. The default version of this form contains only two buttons: Start and Cancel. However, from the workflow designer, you can use the *Initiation Form Parameters* button in the ribbon to add extra fields and collect data from the user who initiates the workflow.

- **Custom task form**: A custom task form is just a list form that lets users interact with items in a workflow's Tasks list. Several of the standard workflow actions available in SharePoint Designer collect data from users by using tasks. Custom task forms give you more control over that process by specifying exactly what information gets collected.

- **Association form**: This type of form applies only to reusable workflows and is displayed when the workflow is associated with a list or content type. By default, a reusable workflow provides only the fields that are common to all list items (across content types). An association form lets you associate fields with a reusable workflow so those fields will be available when you design and run the workflow. To create association form parameters (fields), use the *Initiation Form Parameters* button in the ribbon just as you would for an initiation form. However, when you go to add a parameter, you'll notice an extra option that lets you specify whether it appears on the workflow's initiation form, association form, or both.

If your SharePoint Online subscription includes InfoPath Forms Services (e.g., the E3 plan), these forms will all be generated as InfoPath form templates (.xsn files). If you have InfoPath Designer 2010 installed on your computer, you can simply click the form link in SharePoint Designer (on the workflow settings page) to open the form in InfoPath and customize it. Otherwise, if your subscription does not include InfoPath Forms Services, the forms will be generated as ASP.NET web pages (.aspx files) and can be customized by opening them in SharePoint Designer and editing them like any other ASP.NET page.

# Building and Deploying a Simple Workflow

In this section, we'll walk you through the process of building a simple workflow and deploying it to SharePoint Online. Why a simple workflow and not a more complex one? The biggest reason is if you understand the basics, you can always create a more complicated workflow. It's just a matter of mapping out what your workflow needs to look like (for example, by using a flowchart diagram in Visio) and then choosing the appropriate actions and conditions to implement it. All the built-in actions and conditions are documented on Microsoft's help site for SharePoint Online (we provide links at the end of this section), so we're not going to rehash them here.

## What Our Workflow Will Do

Let us start by saying we're not going to demonstrate how to build an approval workflow. That topic has been heavily documented over the years, and you can find tons of examples of how to do it with a simple web search. And now that SharePoint Designer lets you copy and edit the built-in approval workflow that comes with SharePoint Online (assuming you have an enterprise-level plan like an E3 plan that includes that workflow), the process is even easier than it used to be. Instead, we're going to demonstrate how to create something we know many organizations want: a conditional alert based on the value of a column in a list.

The scenario is this: A department manager in a company requires weekly status reports on a project from the people who work in her department. The library in which the reports are submitted contains a column called *Overall Status* that can be set to three possible values: *Stellar, On Track*, and *At Risk*. The workflow will notify the department manager whenever a status report is submitted with its Overall Status column set to *At Risk*. For any other Overall Status value, she doesn't need a notification.

Because our workflow will operate in the context of a specific list, we'll be creating a list (nonreusable) workflow.

## The List

The list our workflow will use is a document library called *Status Reports*. It was created through the browser using the built-in Document Library list template. We then created a new choice column (marked as required) on the library called *Overall Status* and gave it the values mentioned in the last section. Versioning and content approval were not enabled, and a simple information management policy was created that moves status reports to the recycle bin once they become three months old (which isn't really relevant to our workflow but is included as a reminder to consider growth and retention when designing your lists).

## Workflow

Now we'll delve into the process of creating our workflow. First, we open SharePoint Designer and click the *Lists and Libraries* link in the navigation pane. On the Lists and Libraries page, we click the *Status Reports* link to navigate to the summary page for our library. We then locate the *Workflows* category in the lower-right portion of the screen and click the **New** button as shown in Figure 8-10.

*Figure 8-10. Creating a new workflow on the Status Reports library*

Next we'll see the Create List Workflow dialog and fill in the name and description of our workflow, as shown in Figure 8-11.

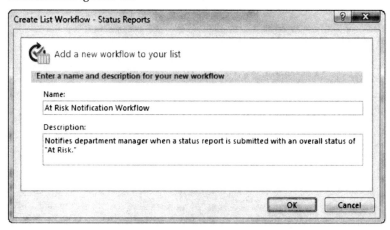

*Figure 8-11. Create List Workflow dialog with workflow name and description*

When we click **OK** on the dialog, we'll be taken straight to the workflow designer. All we'll see initially is an empty step called "Step 1." In this case, our workflow is short and doesn't need to be broken into multiple steps, so one step is fine. However, we'll rename Step 1 to "Notify if Report is At Risk" (by clicking the words "Step 1" in the step header and changing the value in the text box). Even with a single step, it's good to be descriptive.

Next, we'll click the **Condition** button in the Insert group of the ribbon and select *If current item field equals value*. Then we'll click the hyperlinks in the condition and set the values as shown in Figure 8-12.

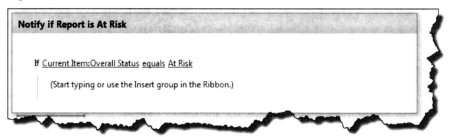

*Figure 8-12. Snapshot of workflow after configuring condition*

Once the condition is in place, we'll add an action within it (so that the action is executed only when the condition is true). To do so, we click inside the condition where the *Start typing...* message is and insert the *Lookup Manager of a User* action (it's in the Relational Actions category of the menu under the Actions button in the ribbon). The action, once inserted into the workflow, displays a hyperlink for the words *this user*. We click the hyperlink and see the Select Users dialog. We select **Workflow Lookup for a user...** and click the **Add** button, as shown in Figure 8-13.

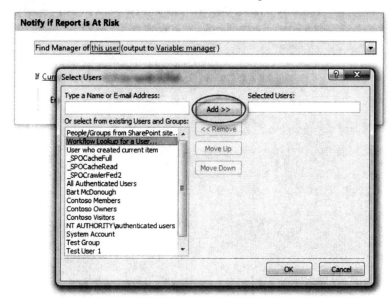

*Figure 8-13. The Select Users dialog for the Find Manager action*

Clicking Add brings up the Lookup for Person or Group dialog. For *Data source*, we select **Workflow Context**. For *Field from source*, we select **Current User**. For *Return field as*, we select **Login Name**. We click OK to close the dialog and click OK again on the Select Users dialog to close that one, too.

Next we'll insert the *Send an Email* action from the **Actions** button in the ribbon. When this action is inserted, it appears in the designer as *Email these users*, where *these users* is a hyperlink. What we want to do next is replace *these users* with the e-mail address of the department manager. In our case we know that all employees who use this site are members of the same department and report to the same manager. We also know that their managers are correctly mapped in Active Directory and that Active Directory is synchronized with Office 365 using the Directory Synchronization tool (http://bit.ly/xKJCw7). Therefore, there's an easy way we can get the e-mail address of the department manager, as we'll see in a moment.

To start configuring the e-mail action, we click the "these users" hyperlink and an e-mail message dialog appears with *To, CC, Subject*, and body fields. We click the book icon to the right of the *To* field, revealing the Select Users dialog again. We again select **Workflow Lookup for a User…** and click **Add** just like before. This time, however, we choose **Workflow Variables and Parameters** as the data source and select **Variable: manager** as the field from source. (Recall that our Find Manager action stored its result in a variable called *manager*, as seen at the top of Figure 8-13.) For the return type of the field, this time we choose *Email Address* and then click OK to close the dialog (and OK again to close the Select Users dialog).

We type a simple message into the e-mail body for now, as shown in Figure 8-14. To create the link to view the report, we used the hyperlink button in the toolbar (rightmost button) above the message body and selected *Current Item URL* from the *Workflow Context* data source.

*Figure 8-14. E-mail body for notification*

Finally, we enter "At risk status report" in the subject field and click OK to save the message. The final workflow is pictured in Figure 8-15.

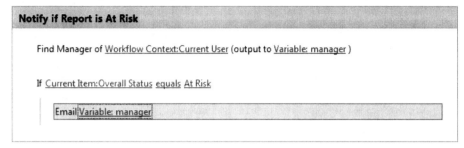

*Figure 8-15. Final workflow in workflow designer*

We're not quite done, though. We still need to tell SharePoint to start our workflow automatically whenever a status report is submitted. To do so, we click the **Workflow Settings** button in the ribbon. On the settings page, under *Start Options*, we uncheck the *Allow this workflow to be started manually* option and select *Start workflow when an item is created*. Now, whenever a status report is uploaded to the Status Reports list, our workflow will automatically run on that report.

## Deployment to SharePoint

To deploy the workflow, we save it (using the **Save** button in the ribbon) and then use the **Publish** button in the ribbon to publish it. That's it. Deployment is pretty easy when using SharePoint Designer.

Once you test it, if all works the way it should, you'll get an e-mail like the one shown in Figure 8-16.

**At risk status report**

Contoso <no-reply@sharepoint.com>

ⓘ This item will expire in 29 days. To keep this item longer apply a different Retention Policy.

Sent:    Sun 6/3/2012 10:13 PM

To:

A status report has been flagged as having an 'At Risk' status.

Click here to view the report.

*Figure 8-16. E-mail sent by notification workflow*

Finally, even though we didn't show it here, consider adding the *Log to History List* action in multiple places in your workflow and logging messages indicating where you are in the overall workflow execution. (For example, a message in the middle of our workflow might have said "Found manager. About to send e-mail.") That way, if something goes wrong, and your workflow doesn't fully execute (which happens frequently when you're first learning how to create workflows), you can view the messages when you look at the workflow status page in SharePoint. They'll help you narrow down where the problem is by seeing how far your workflow got before it failed.

## Resources

As promised in the beginning of this section, here are some resources that you can reference when building workflows in SharePoint Designer 2010:

- Workflow actions quick reference: `http://bit.ly/nnJWrr`

- Workflow conditions quick reference: `http://bit.ly/KparbA`

- Understanding approval workflows in SharePoint 2010: `http://bit.ly/LdXGds` (targets SharePoint Server 2010, not SharePoint Online, but most concepts will be the same if you have an enterprise-level SharePoint Online subscription)

# Integration with Microsoft Visio 2010

If you have Microsoft Visio 2010 Premium, you can design workflows in Visio, export them, and then import them into SharePoint Designer to put the finishing touches on them and deploy them to SharePoint.

After opening Visio, select the *Microsoft SharePoint Workflow* template from the **Flowchart** template category. Design your workflow using the template shapes by dragging and dropping them onto the drawing canvas like normal (remember to start and end the workflow with the *Start* and *End* shapes under the SharePoint Workflow Terminators shape group). When you are done, you can use the **Export** button under the Process tab in the ribbon to export your workflow as a .vwi (Visio Workflow Interchange) file. The .vwi file can then be imported into SharePoint Designer using the **Import from Visio** ribbon button that appears on the Workflows page and in the workflow designer.

The process works in reverse as well. Suppose you create a workflow in SharePoint Designer and want other team members (business analysts, perhaps) to review it before you publish it to SharePoint. You can use the **Export to Visio** button in SharePoint Designer (available on the Workflows page and in the workflow designer) to export the workflow as a .vwi file. You can then import the .vwi file into Visio (the import button in Visio is right next to the export button) to view the workflow as a flowchart diagram.

# Developing Custom Actions with Visual Studio

As good as the built-in workflow actions are in SharePoint Designer, you're likely to hit a situation sooner or later where you need one that isn't there. When that happens, you can develop your own custom action in Visual Studio 2010 and then deploy it to SharePoint Online as a sandboxed solution. Once deployed, the action will be available for you to use in the workflow designer in SharePoint Designer.

As the focus of this chapter is on creating workflows with SharePoint Designer, we're not going to delve into the details here of creating your own actions with Visual Studio. If you're interested in creating custom actions in Visual Studio, the following resources will help you:

- `http://bit.ly/Lr6bE3`: (MSDN article: "How to Create and Deploy Workflow Actions in Sandboxed Solutions")

- http://bit.ly/LXsOua: (Channel 9 video about creating custom workflow actions in Visual Studio and deploying them as sandboxed solutions)

See Chapter 7 for more information about creating custom solutions in Visual Studio 2010 for SharePoint Online.

## Summary

This chapter covered what workflows are and introduced you to the features in SharePoint Designer 2010 that are focused on creating and deploying them. We talked about the workflow designer and walked you through creating a sample workflow that creates a "conditional alert" on a status report document library. We also talked a little bit about how other tools, such as Microsoft Visio 2010 and Visual Studio 2010, can be brought into the mix to augment and streamline the workflow development process as needed.

■ ■ ■

# CHAPTER 9

# Intro to Client-Side Development

Let's face it. The client-side development experience in SharePoint 2007 wasn't exactly the best. While we had some web services we could work with, we really didn't have much else. If we needed more capabilities than what the web services provided, we were basically left with creating our own web service. Unfortunately, that left out a lot of developers who specialize in client-side technologies such as JavaScript and who weren't accustomed to web service development.

Thankfully, client-side development has received some much-needed attention, and SharePoint 2010 touts some significant improvements over its predecessor. The client-side development experience now targets a broader audience, includes out-of-the-box support for multiple user experiences, and offers us a better choice of application programming interfaces (APIs) to work with.

In this chapter, we'll cover the following topics:

- Why Go Client-Side?

- Client Application Landscape

- Client Application Models

- Accessing Data with Services

- The Client Object Model

## Why Go Client-Side?

We've had a robust server-side API in SharePoint for years, and we can already customize just about any aspect of SharePoint we want. So why is client-side development suddenly becoming so important? What's changed? And why should we care?

One big change is the subject of this book: SharePoint Online and Office 365. SharePoint Online represents a new paradigm in how SharePoint is offered and in how we develop solutions for it. We learned in Chapter 8 that if we want to develop for SharePoint Online, our only option is sandboxed solutions. Sandboxed solutions, as you might recall, don't give us access to the entire server-side API. Client-side development can help us get back some of what we've lost (and in some cases is our only option).

Of course, sandboxed solutions aren't the only reason to prefer client-side development. Other reasons include the need to access SharePoint data from outside of SharePoint or a desire to build richer user interfaces (UIs) with technologies like Silverlight and jQuery.

# Client Application Landscape

Before delving into the details of client-side development, let's focus for a moment on the big picture. It's helpful to think of client-side development as having two facets: the way we interact with the user (the user experience) and the way we get data to and from SharePoint. Collectively, we refer to these two facets as the *client application landscape*.

Figure 9-1 illustrates the client application landscape for SharePoint Online.

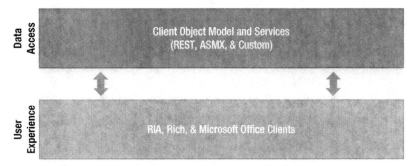

*Figure 9-1. Client application landscape for SharePoint Online*

---

■ **Note** The BCS Client Runtime Object Model isn't pictured in Figure 9-1 because it isn't available in SharePoint Online (even though it *is* available in SharePoint Server 2010 for client-side access to BCS).

---

On the data access side of the landscape, we have two new APIs that weren't available to us in SharePoint 2007: the REST API and something called the Client Object Model. Both will be discussed in more detail shortly.

Likewise, on the user experience side, we now have better out-of-the-box support for rich client applications. SharePoint Online includes a Silverlight web part for hosting Silverlight applications (XAP files) in the browser. Additionally, the new REST and Client Object Model APIs let us build rich client applications much more easily. By taking advantage of technologies such as WPF, Silverlight, and jQuery, we can now focus more on building compelling user interfaces and less on the mechanics of getting data in and out of SharePoint.

# Client Application Models

When we're doing client-side development for SharePoint Online, we have two application models available to us: the *in-browser* (rich Internet application [RIA]) application model and the *rich client* application model.

The in-browser application model is pictured in Figure 9-2.

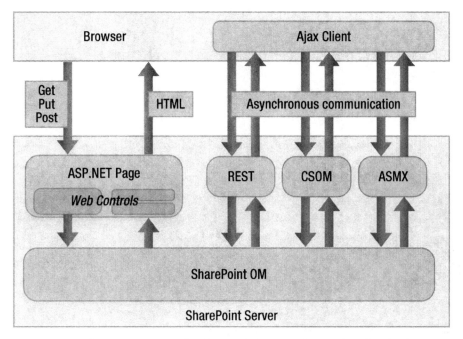

***Figure 9-2.*** *In-browser (RIA) application model (Source:* `http://bit.ly/Lh6Vkz`*)*

As you can see in the figure, one defining characteristic of in-browser applications (including Silverlight applications) is asynchronous communication with SharePoint. *Asynchronous communication* means that when the code makes a request of the server, it doesn't wait to receive a response because doing so could cause the browser to become unresponsive. Instead, it makes the request in the background and continues executing the rest of the code while the request is being made. Eventually, the code is notified that the request has completed and can take appropriate action. The trade-off with asynchronous communication is the UI is more responsive, but the code is a little more complicated to write (as you'll see later).

Now consider the rich client application model pictured in Figure 9-3.

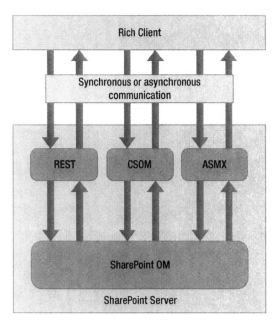

*Figure 9-3. Rich client application model (Source: http://bit.ly/Lh6Vkz)*

In this case, the application isn't limited to using only asynchronous communication with the server. If you're writing a Windows Presentation Foundation (WPF) application, for instance, you can use synchronous communication, in which you make a request of the server and then wait for a response before continuing. You could show a progress bar or other wait indicator while the request is being made and avoid the complexities of asynchronous communication. The UI may not be quite as responsive, but the code is also simpler to write.

# Accessing Data with Services

SharePoint Online includes two types of services you can use to access data: REST-ful services (or REST interfaces) and ASP.NET web services (also known as ASMX web services).

## Using the REST-ful Services

A *REST-ful service* is one that implements the *Representational State Transfer (REST)* design principles. A core concept of REST is the idea that *resources* (such as lists and list items in SharePoint) can be represented as HTTP resources addressable by remote uniform resource indentifiers (URIs). They can also be manipulated by create, retrieve, update, and delete (CRUD) operations that are mapped to the HTTP verbs *POST, GET, PUT,* and *DELETE,* respectively. You also get support for retrieving list information in several formats, including JSON, ATOM, and ATOMPub.

SharePoint Online exposes two REST-ful services. The first is a REST service for working with lists and libraries (and their contents).

To see which resources are available to you through this service, you can type a URL like this one into your browser (note that you must have logged into SharePoint Online first and be authenticated): http://contoso.sharepoint.com/_vti_bin/ListData.svc.

The results you see should look similar to Figure 9-4.

```xml
<?xml version="1.0" encoding="UTF-8" standalone="true"?>
<service xmlns="http://www.w3.org/2007/app" xmlns:app="http://www.w3.org/
  xml:base="https://              .sharepoint.com/_vti_bin/listdata.svc/">
  <workspace>
    <atom:title>Default</atom:title>
    <collection href="Announcements">
      <atom:title>Announcements</atom:title>
    </collection>
    <collection href="Attachments">
      <atom:title>Attachments</atom:title>
    </collection>
    <collection href="c_03f000b9c45844fe8cabdba4b9f226b9">
      <atom:title>c_03f000b9c45844fe8cabdba4b9f226b9</atom:title>
    </collection>
    <collection href="Calendar">
      <atom:title>Calendar</atom:title>
    </collection>
    <collection href="CalendarCategory">
      <atom:title>CalendarCategory</atom:title>
    </collection>
    <collection href="ContentTypePublishingErrorLog">
         tTypePubli   ngErr
```

*Figure 9-4. Results of calling the list data REST API*

You can then take one of the resources (such as the "Announcements" list in Figure 9-4), and enter a URL like this one:

`http://contoso.sharepoint.com/_vti_bin/ListData.svc/Announcements.`

Figure 9-5 shows the result of entering this URL into Internet Explorer.

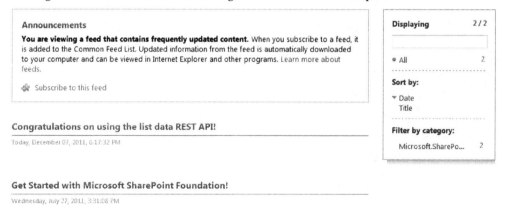

**Announcements**

**You are viewing a feed that contains frequently updated content.** When you subscribe to a feed, it is added to the Common Feed List. Updated information from the feed is automatically downloaded to your computer and can be viewed in Internet Explorer and other programs. Learn more about feeds.

Subscribe to this feed

| Displaying | 2/2 |
| --- | --- |

● All  2

**Sort by:**
▼ Date
  Title

**Filter by category:**
Microsoft.SharePo...  2

**Congratulations on using the list data REST API!**

Today, December 07, 2011, 6:17:32 PM

**Get Started with Microsoft SharePoint Foundation!**

Wednesday, July 27, 2011, 3:31:08 PM

*Figure 9-5: List of announcements as displayed by Internet Explorer*

░ **Note**  The URLs you use with REST services in SharePoint Online are case-sensitive. If our URL had used a lowercase *a* in the word *Announcements*, we would have gotten no results.

See the "SharePoint Foundation REST Interface" article on MSDN (http://bit.ly/aGR1R3) for more information on working with the REST interface for lists and libraries.

The second REST service that's available to you is one for working with Excel Services. It exposes parts of Excel workbooks (charts, pivot tables, and so on) as addressable resources for you to work with. For more information, see the "Excel Services REST API" article on MSDN (http://bit.ly/mkCC5t).

## Using the ASP.NET Web Services

The ASP.NET web services available to you in SharePoint Online are listed in Table 9-1. These cannot be accessed by server-side code in sandboxed solutions, but can be accessed by client-side code such as Silverlight and JavaScript applications.

*Table 9-1. List of ASP.NET Web Services Available in SharePoint Online*

| Web Service | Description |
| --- | --- |
| WebSvcAlerts | Provides methods for working with alerts for list items in a SharePoint site. |
| WebSvcCopy | Provides services for copying files within a SharePoint site and between SharePoint sites. |
| WebSvcDWS | Provides methods for managing Document Workspace sites and the data they contain. The following method is not available in SharePoint Online: `FindDwsDoc` |
| WebSvcImaging | Provides methods that enable you to create and manage picture libraries. |
| WebSvcLists | Provides methods for working with SharePoint lists, content types, list items, and files. The following method is not available in SharePoint Online: `AddDiscussionBoardItem` |
| WebSvcMeetings | Provides methods that enable you to create and manage Meeting Workspace sites. |
| WebSvcPeople | Provides methods for associating user identifiers (IDs) with security groups for site permissions. |
| WebSvcPermissions | Provides methods for working with the permissions for a site or list. |
| WebSvcSiteData | Provides methods that return metadata or list data from sites or lists. |
| WebSvcsites | Provides methods for returning information about the site templates for a site collection. |

| Web Service | Description |
| --- | --- |
| WebSvcspsearch | Provides methods for accessing search results from client applications and web applications that are outside of the context of a SharePoint site. |
| WebSvcUserGroup | Provides methods for working with users and groups. |
| WebSvcVersions | Provides methods for working with file versions in SharePoint document libraries. |
| WebSvcviews | Provides methods for creating, deleting, or updating list views in SharePoint Online. |
| WebSvcwebpartpages | Provides methods for working with Web Parts. |
| | The following methods are not available in SharePoint Online: |
| | `AssociateWorkflowMarkup` |
| | `ExecuteProxyUpdates` |
| | `GetAssemblyMetaData` |
| | `GetDataFromDataSourceControl` |
| | *GetFormCapabilityFromDataSourceControl* |
| | *RemoveWorkflowAssociation* |
| | *ValidateWorkflowMarkupAndCreateSupportObjects* |
| WebSvcWebs | Provides methods for working with sites and subsites. |
| | The following method is not available in SharePoint Online: |
| | `CustomizeCss` |

See the "Web Services in SharePoint Online" article on MSDN (`http://bit.ly/gHKT2x`) for a list of web services and web methods that are available to you in SharePoint Online.

# The Client Object Model

The *client object model,* also referred to as the *client-side object model (CSOM),* represents a tremendous step forward in client-side development for SharePoint. Introduced in SharePoint 2010, the client object model gives us a development experience similar to that on the server with a true abstraction layer and recognizable SharePoint objects (Sites, Webs, and so on) that we can manipulate.

## The Highlights

Let's start by covering a few key aspects of the client object model.

## Three APIs, One Object Model

The client object model consists of three APIs targeting three platforms: Managed .NET, Silverlight, and ECMAScript (JavaScript). The APIs are remarkably similar, so you'll find the development experience to be pretty consistent, regardless of whether you're creating a simple WPF application that talks to SharePoint or developing eye-catching jQuery interfaces for your lists. There are still a few inherent differences among the APIs (for example, some syntax differences with the ECMAScript API), but they all work essentially the same way and contain the same set of objects.

## Comparison with the Server-Side Object Model

With an eye on performance, Microsoft included only a subset of the server-side object model's functionality in the client object model. Specifically, the client object model contains a subset of the functionality found in Microsoft.SharePoint.dll. Keeping download times small for Silverlight and JavaScript clients was a key ingredient in this design decision.

---

░ **Note** Remember that Microsoft.SharePoint.dll contains functionality for SharePoint *Foundation*, not SharePoint *Server*. That means the client object model does not contain support for publishing and other features found in the *Server* edition.

---

The three APIs in the client object model are all autogenerated from the server-side object model using attributes that decorate some of the classes. Therefore, they share many similarities with one another and also bear a close resemblance to their server-side counterpart.

Table 9-2 lists the names of some well-known server-side objects and their client-side counterparts.

*Table 9-2. Comparison of Well-Known Object Names Across APIs*

| Server-Side Object | Managed .NET Client API | Silverlight Client API | ECMAScript Client API |
| --- | --- | --- | --- |
| SPSite | Site | Site | Site |
| SPWeb | Web | Web | Web |
| SPList | List | List | List |
| SPListItem | ListItem | ListItem | ListItem |
| SPField | Field | Field | Field |

As you can see in the table, the objects have almost the same names. The only difference is that the *SP* prefix is omitted in the client-side object names. Many of the objects in the client object model follow this same pattern.

Another observation you might make is that there are no client-side equivalents for the SPFarm and SPWebApplication server-side objects because the client object model is scoped to the site collection level and below. You can't manipulate anything at the farm or web application levels in SharePoint Online.

## Architecture

Figure 9-6 depicts the architecture of the SharePoint 2010 client object model.

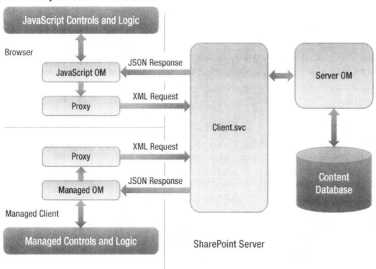

**Figure 9-6.** *Architecture of the client object model (Source:* http://bit.ly/N4WEC2)

---

■ **Note** The ECMAScript API is referred to as the JavaScript OM (Object Model) in Figure 9-6.

---

As shown in the figure, all communication is routed through a WCF service called client.svc. Commands are serialized into XML and sent to the server as a single HTTP request. For each command issued by the client, a corresponding server call is made, and a response is returned in JavaScript Object Notation (JSON) format. The proxies shown in the diagram are responsible for the details of communicating with the server and serializing/deserializing objects.

Because of how the client object model is architected, we have to do a few things differently than we would on the server. First, we have to be explicit in requesting exactly what data we want. If we don't ask for something to be loaded, it often won't be. The idea there is to cut down on network chatter and save bandwidth. Second, operations are batched into a single XML request, and we control when it's sent to the server. Sometimes we may need to send multiple requests in order to complete a task. Finally, we have to route all communication to and from the server through a central object.

## ClientContext: The Hub of the Model

When using the client object model, all communication with the server is routed through a central object called the *ClientContext object*, which encapsulates all the details of communicating with the server and acts as a liaison between the object model and the runtime (referred to as a "proxy" in Figure 9-5).

When using the ClientContext object, it operates in the context of a single web or site collection. In the Managed .NET API, you must pass the full URL of a site or site collection to the constructor, for example:

```
ClientContext content = new
ClientContext(http://contoso.sharepoint.com/sites/MySiteCollection);
```

You can use the same constructor in the Silverlight API, but if your Silverlight application is running in the context of a SharePoint page or web part, you can also use the static property ClientContext.Current to get a ClientContext object for the current site.

When using the ECMAScript API, you can't specify a URL. Your ClientContext object must operate within the context of the site in which your page lives. Therefore, you get a reference to a ClientContext object like this:

```
var context = SP.ClientContext.get_current();
```

Once you have a ClientContext object, you can use the client objects you retrieve through the context to define what you want to do on the server (similar to building a query with SQL or LINQ). Once you define what you want to do, you must invoke a method on the ClientContext object to send your request to the server where your instructions will be carried out.

The Managed .NET API provides the ExecuteQuery method to send your request in a synchronous fashion. The ECMAScript API provides the executeQueryAsync method to send it asynchronously (so the browser doesn't hang). The Silverlight API gives you a choice. If you're not operating on the UI thread, you can use the ExecuteQuery method to send the request synchronously. Otherwise, you should use the ExecuteQueryAsync method to send it asynchronously as in JavaScript. The latter tends to be the one most often used in Silverlight applications.

Finally, the ClientContext object provides two important methods related to loading data: Load and LoadQuery. Up until now, we've talked about using client objects to define what you want to do and then explicitly telling the server when to do it. However, there's still one more piece of the puzzle: telling the server what data you need returned to you. Until your client objects are filled with data returned from the server, you can think of them as being empty shells that are simply used to define operations. The Load and LoadQuery methods tell the server which property values and collections you'd like initialized so you can use their values when the request completes. We'll discuss these methods in more detail and explain how to use them a little later in this chapter.

# Developing with the Client Object Model

Next, we cover how to develop solutions for SharePoint Online using the client object model. For the most part, the process is similar to developing solutions for on-premise SharePoint environments. However, there are a few differences when developing for the cloud that that we'll cover here as well.

# Requirements

The first thing you'll need when developing client-side solutions for SharePoint Online is a development environment. If you haven't already done so, see Chapter 3 for instructions on how to set up your development environment.

While it's possible you could do your development on a machine that doesn't have SharePoint installed and then do your testing directly in the cloud, we recommend against that approach. Having your own SharePoint development environment ensures you can develop and test everything thoroughly before deploying and also allows you to use the F5 debugging experience that's built into Visual Studio 2010.

To use the Managed .NET API, you need to reference the following dynamic link libraries (DLLs) in your project:

- Microsoft.SharePoint.Client.dll

- Microsoft.SharePoint.Client.Runtime.dll

Assuming you're developing on a machine that has SharePoint installed, you can find those DLLs at the following location: `%Program Files%\Microsoft Shared\Web Server Extensions\14\ISAPI`. If not, you'll need to copy them to your development machine. The "Runtime" DLL is the proxy we saw referenced back in Figure 9-5.

To use the Silverlight API, you need to reference the following DLLs:

- Microsoft.SharePoint.Client.Silverlight.dll

- Microsoft.SharePoint.Client.Silverlight.Runtime.dll

Again, if you're using a machine with SharePoint installed, you can find these at the following location: `%Program Files%\Microsoft Shared\Web Server Extensions\14\TEMPLATE\LAYOUTS\ClientBin`.

Using the ECMAScript API requires a slightly different approach. You simply need to reference "_layouts/sp.js" in your page (via a ScriptLink tag or other means). Once that script is loaded, you have everything you need to use the ECMAScript API.

---

**Tip** If you're developing with the Managed .NET or Silverlight APIs, remember to distribute the client object model DLLs with your application since they'll be needed at runtime.

---

# Authentication

Because you're accessing SharePoint remotely when you use the client object model, you need to consider authentication in your solutions.

## Authentication with the Managed .NET API

Unfortunately, the Managed .NET API is the only one where authentication to SharePoint Online isn't all that straightforward. What makes it that way is the need for a user to interactively log in. That means your application will need to include an embedded web browser control that displays the standard

Office 365 login page and captures the authentication cookie that's set after the user logs in (similar to what other apps such as SharePoint Designer 2010 do when they connect to SharePoint Online).

At the time of this writing, the best information on this topic comes from the following article on MSDN: http://bit.ly/jBws8Q. As the article explains, part of this approach also involves making calls into unmanaged code because the cookie that's returned from Office 365 is marked as *HTTPOnly* and can't be directly accessed by the .NET Framework.

If you really want to pursue a "headless" authentication solution (one that would work even without a user interacting with your application), see this blog post on MSDN for a proposed approach: http://bit.ly/lL9yzQ. In effect, you're still doing what we outlined a moment ago (interactively logging in), but your application is playing the role of the user.

### Authentication with the Silverlight API

Authentication with the Silverlight API is much easier. As long as your XAP file is served from the same domain (for example, www.contoso.com) or site that you're connecting to, the client object model will reuse the authentication cookie from the user's browser session.

If you desktop-enable your Silverlight application, and a user installs it on the desktop, Windows will issue its standard authentication prompt when the app tries to connect to SharePoint Online. (The experience is similar to that of the Get-Credential PowerShell cmdlet, if you've ever used that.)

### Authentication with the ECMAScript API

In the case of the ECMAScript API, your code always executes within the context of a page in the browser, so no explicit authentication is required. The API simply uses the authentication cookie of the logged-in user.

# Performing Common Tasks with the Client Object Model

This section covers how to perform some common tasks with the SharePoint client object model. The examples provided here are designed to show how the object model works and get you started using it. For more examples and detailed information on using the Client Object Model, see http://bit.ly/NhfZnk.

## Creating New Items

The process of creating new items (sites, lists, and so on) with the client object model follows a pattern, regardless of the type of item you're creating. To create an item, you create an instance of its "creation information" object and add that object to a parent collection of that type of item.

For example, Listing 9-1 demonstrates how to create a new site using the Silverlight API.

*Listing 9-1. Creating a new site (Silverlight API)*

```
ClientContext context = ClientContext.Current;
WebCollection webs = context.Web.Webs;

WebCreationInformation webCreateInfo = new WebCreationInformation();
webCreateInfo.Title = "New Site";
webCreateInfo.Description = "Description of new site.";
```

```
webCreateInfo.Language = 1033;
webCreateInfo.Url = "NewSite";
webCreateInfo.UseSamePermissionsAsParentSite = true;
webCreateInfo.WebTemplate = "STS#0"; // Team Site Template

webs.Add(webCreateInfo);
context.ExecuteQueryAsync(OnSuccess, OnFailure);
```

Something else this listing points out is that the ExecuteQueryAsync method (present in the Silverlight and ECMAScript APIs) takes two parameters. The first parameter is a delegate of type ClientRequestSucceededEventHandler and is invoked if the request is successful. The second is a delegate of type ClientRequestFailedEventHandler and is invoked if the request fails for some reason. The arguments passed to the latter include details about the error (error code, message, stack trace, and so on) that can be used for troubleshooting.

Listing 9-2 shows how to create a new calendar item (event) using the ECMAScript API.

*Listing 9-2. Creating a new calendar item (ECMAScript API)*

```
private void CreateNewCalendarItem()
{
    var context = SP.ClientContext.get_current();
    var list = context.get_web().get_lists().getByTitle("Calendar");
    var createInfo = new SP.ListItemCreationInformation();
    var evt = list.addItem(createInfo);

    evt.set_item('Title', 'My Event on September 20, 2011');
    evt.set_item('EventDate', new Date(2011, 8, 20, 8));
    evt.set_item('EndDate', new Date(2011, 8, 20, 9));
    evt.update();

    context.executeQueryAsync(ListItemCreateSuccess, ListItemCreateFailure);
}

private void ListItemCreateSuccess(object sender, ClientRequestSucceededEventArgs e)
{
    // Code that executes when the operation was successful
}

private void ListItemCreateFailure(object sender, ClientRequestFailedEventArgs e)
{
    // Code that executes when something caused the operation to fail
}
```

## Retrieving List Items

Listing 9-3 demonstrates how to use the ECMAScript API to query the "Shared Documents" library for all items created by the current user.

*Listing 9-3. Querying a list (ECMAScript API)*

```
var context = SP.ClientContext.get_current();
var list = context.get_web().get_lists().getByTitle('Shared Documents');
var query = new SP.CamlQuery();
query.set_viewXml("<View><Query><Where><Eq><FieldRef Name='Author' /><Value
Type='Integer'><UserID /></Value></Eq></Where></Query></View>");

var items = list.getItems(query);
context.load(items);

context.executeQueryAsync(
    Function.createDelegate(this, function() {
        alert('Success: ' + items.get_count());
    }),
    Function.createDelegate(this, function(sender, args) {
        alert('Failure: ' + args.get_message());
    })
);
```

This time we passed in anonymous functions for our success and failure delegates so we can easily access the *items* variable and display the number of items we got back.

Notice that we called context.load before sending our request to the server. Had we not done that, we would have received a JavaScript error (about the collection not being initialized) when trying to access the *count* property in our success delegate.

Listing 9-4 is similar except this time we're loading properties on the list items that aren't loaded by default. JavaScript doesn't support lambda expressions such as .NET, so we have to use the Include operator instead.

*Listing 9-4. Loading additional properties when querying a list.*

```
var context = SP.ClientContext.get_current();
var list = context.get_web().get_lists().getByTitle('Shared Documents');
var query = new SP.CamlQuery();
query.set_viewXml("<View><Query><Where><Eq><FieldRef Name='Author' /><Value
Type='Integer'><UserID /></Value></Eq></Where></Query></View>");

var items = list.getItems(query);
context.load(items, 'Include(DisplayName, HasUniqueRoleAssignments)');

context.executeQueryAsync(
    Function.createDelegate(this, function() {
        var item = items.get_item(0);
        alert('Success: ' + item.get_displayName() +
            ', ' + item.get_hasUniqueRoleAssignments());
    }),
    Function.createDelegate(this, function(sender, args) {
        alert('Failure: ' + args.get_message());
    })
);
```

If we hadn't used the Include operator to load the DisplayName and HasUniqueRoleAssignments properties of our list items, trying to access those properties would've thrown a PropertyOrFieldNotInitialized exception. Also note that even though the property names don't start with uppercase letters in the JavaScript syntax, we spelled them that way within the Include operator anyway. The Include operator expects the same spelling (title case) that's used in the server-side object model.

## Updating and Deleting List Items

Listing 9-5 demonstrates how to update a list item.

*Listing 9-5. Updating a list item with the ECMAScript API.*

```
var context = SP.ClientContext.get_current();
var list = context.get_web().get_lists().getByTitle('Test List');
var item = list.getItemById(2);
item.set_item('Title', 'New Title');
item.update();

context.executeQueryAsync(
        Function.createDelegate(this, function() {
                /* Do something when update succeeds */
        }),
        Function.createDelegate(this, function(s, args) {
                /* Do something when update fails */
        })
);
```

Listing 9-6 demonstrates how to delete a list item.

*Listing 9-6. Deleting a list item with the ECMAScript API.*

```
var context = SP.ClientContext.get_current();
var list = context.get_web().get_lists().getByTitle('Test List');
var item = list.getItemById(2);
item.deleteObject();

context.executeQueryAsync(
        Function.createDelegate(this, function() {
                /* Do something when deletion succeeds */
        }),
        Function.createDelegate(this, function(s, args) {
                alert(args.get_message());
                /* Do something when deletion fails */
        })
);
```

## Summary

The goal of this chapter was to introduce you to the client-side development landscape for SharePoint Online. We began the chapter by discussing when it makes sense to go client-side and talking about the options we have for client-side development. After a discussion about accessing SharePoint data with services, we dove into a discussion about the client object model and its three APIs (Managed .NET, Silverlight, and ECMAScript). We wrapped things up with a few examples of using the client object model.

# CHAPTER 10

# Client-Side Development with Silverlight

One particularly nice feature of SharePoint Online is the capability to develop and deploy Silverlight client applications within it. Silverlight allows you to create rich Internet applications (RIAs) within SharePoint and can significantly enhance the user experience of your site. You can also access and work with SharePoint data within your Silverlight application by using the SharePoint client object model or Representational State Transfer (REST) services (see Chapter 9). Among other benefits, using Silverlight can improve the performance of your site because Silverlight code runs on the client rather than on the server.

The topic of Silverlight integration with SharePoint is pretty broad and is impossible to cover in just one chapter, so we had to be fairly selective in what we chose to include here. For example, because there are already a lot of great resources available for learning Silverlight, we chose not to cover that topic here. We assume if you're reading this, you at least have a passing familiarity with Silverlight development (XAML, data binding, out-of-browser applications, .xap files, and so on). However, if you need a primer on Silverlight development, a great place to start is http://www.silverlight.net.

In this chapter, we'll cover the following topics, all of which relate specifically to developing Silverlight applications for SharePoint Online:

- Preparing Your Development Environment for Silverlight

- Building a Silverlight Application with the Client Object Model

- Deploying Silverlight Applications to SharePoint Online

- Hosting Silverlight Applications in SharePoint Online

## Preparing Your Development Environment for Silverlight

First, it's important to understand that although server-side code for SharePoint Online cannot exceed version 3.5 of the .NET Framework, Silverlight has no such restriction. Silverlight 4 and 5 will both work just fine with SharePoint Online. Because the most recent release of Silverlight at the time of this writing is Silverlight 5, we'll be using that version throughout the rest of this chapter.

# Getting the Necessary Tools and Software

If you haven't already done so, the first thing you need to do is install Service Pack 1 for Visual Studio 2010 because it's required by the Silverlight 5 Tools for Visual Studio. You can download Service Pack 1 at http://bit.ly/khSjYE.

Next, you need to install the Silverlight 5 Tools for Visual Studio SP1, which can be downloaded at http://bit.ly/rTuFvc. This package installs the Silverlight 5 SDK and runtime so you can use them for development.

Optionally, you can also download and install the Silverlight 5 Toolkit, which is available on CodePlex at http://silverlight.codeplex.com. Strictly speaking, the toolkit isn't required for Silverlight development, but it provides additional controls and examples you will likely find useful. *DataForm* and *BusyIndicator*, for example, are two controls that both come from this toolkit and are used in a lot of Silverlight applications.

*Expression Blend* is another optional tool you may want to consider using for Silverlight development. It's an integrated development environment (IDE) like Visual Studio, but is oriented toward designers rather than developers. Although Visual Studio 2010 now has a fairly decent XAML designer baked in for Silverlight, Expression Blend is still a far superior tool for developing sophisticated user interfaces (UIs), especially when themes or animations are involved. Expression Blend 4 is the current version at the time of this writing and is designed to work with Silverlight 4 projects. However, there's a preview version of Expression Blend 5 available for working with Silverlight 5 projects. Visit http://www.microsoft.com/expression for more details.

---

**Note**  Unless you're doing *only* Silverlight development (and someone else is doing the SharePoint work), your development environment also needs to be set up for SharePoint Online, as described in Chapter 3.

---

# Creating and Linking Your Projects

If you can get away with it, the easiest way to structure your projects is to place your Silverlight and SharePoint projects within a single solution in Visual Studio. Among other benefits, this structure lets you link the projects together. Linking the projects ensures the Silverlight project is built when the SharePoint project is built and also ensures the output (.xap file) of the Silverlight project is automatically added to the SharePoint project for deployment (via a *module* element in a feature). That way, you don't have to worry about keeping everything synchronized.

Note that if you plan to deploy the Silverlight application manually and have no other need for a SharePoint project in Visual Studio, simply creating the Silverlight project alone should be sufficient (and there's also no need to link it with any other projects in that case).

## Creating a SharePoint Project

First, we'll walk through creating a SharePoint project in Visual Studio. You can skip this step if you already have one or have no need for a SharePoint project in your solution.

1.  Open the **File** menu in Visual Studio and choose **New ➤ Project**.

2. On the New Project dialog, expand the **SharePoint** node on the left and choose **2010**. Select the Empty SharePoint Project template, give it a name, and click **OK**. See Figure 10-1 for an illustration of this step.

*Figure 10-1. Creating a new SharePoint project in Visual Studio 2010*

■ **Tip** If you're creating a new solution that will house both your SharePoint and Silverlight projects, we recommend checking the *Create directory for solution* box, as shown in Figure 10-1. This will create a parent folder (which we've named "Chapter 10") for the solution, and your two projects will both be subfolders.

3. After clicking **OK** to create the project, Visual Studio will display the SharePoint Customization Wizard, as depicted in Figure 10-2. Enter the URL of the site where you'll be testing/debugging your code, and select the *Deploy as sandboxed solution* deployment option (recall from Chapter 7 that farm solutions—the other choice–are not allowed in SharePoint Online even though Visual Studio doesn't specifically call that out).

4. Click **Finish** on the SharePoint Customization Wizard to finish creating the project.

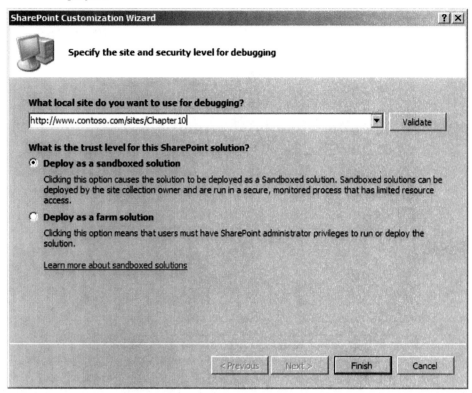

*Figure 10-2. SharePoint Customization Wizard in Visual Studio*

## Creating a Silverlight Project

The following steps will guide you through creating a Silverlight project in Visual Studio. Steps 2 and 3 are illustrated in Figure 10-3.

1. Open the **File** menu in Visual Studio, and choose **New ➤ Project**.

2. On the New Project dialog, select the **Silverlight** node on the left. Select a Silverlight project template (normally *Silverlight Application*) and give it a name.

3. If you're adding this project to an existing solution, select *Add to solution* from the **Solution** drop-down near the bottom of the dialog.

4. Click **OK** to create the project.

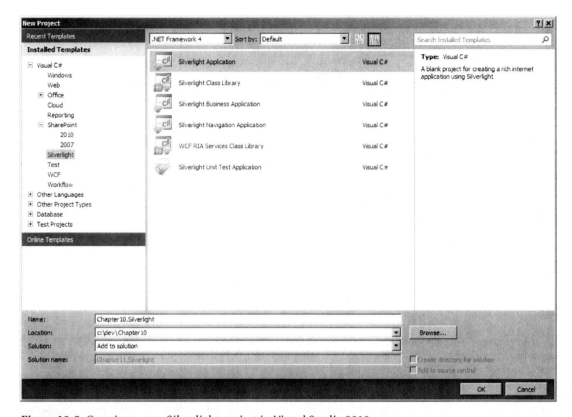

**Figure 10-3**. *Creating a new Silverlight project in Visual Studio 2010*

If you choose *Silverlight Application* or *Silverlight Navigation Application* for Step 2, a dialog similar to the one shown in Figure 10-4 will pop up during project creation. The dialog offers a couple of configuration options for your project, including whether you want a web project (website) created to host your Silverlight application. (The dialog will be slightly different if your solution already contains a web project. In that case, you'll be asked whether you want the Silverlight application hosted in the existing web project.)

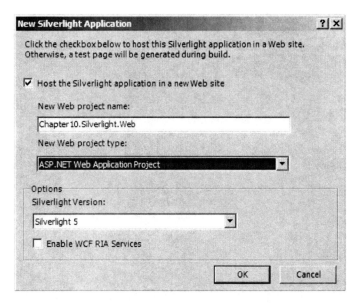

***Figure 10-4.*** *Dialog for creating a new Silverlight Application project*

It's up to you whether you want a separate web project created. Strictly speaking, you don't need one because you can do your testing and debugging in your local SharePoint environment. However, during the early stages of developing a Silverlight app, when you're building out the application framework and creating the UIs, having a separate website for testing can be helpful because you can spin it up and debug it pretty quickly. Just keep in mind that if your SharePoint site requires authentication and you connect to it through code in your Silverlight application, you'll be prompted to authenticate if you run the Silverlight app in another website outside of SharePoint.

Assuming you *do* want a web project created, the dialog also offers you the choice of enabling WCF RIA Services for your Silverlight and web projects. WCF RIA Services is an application framework that simplifies the development of n-tier applications by more tightly integrating ASP.NET with Silverlight (see http://bit.ly/1euj3T for more information). However, it's unlikely you'll need to enable WCF RIA Services because SharePoint Online doesn't provide any built-in support for it on the server side.

## Linking Your SharePoint and Silverlight Projects Together

If you plan to deploy your Silverlight application to SharePoint Online using a *module* element in a feature, linking your SharePoint and Silverlight projects together in Visual Studio will help ensure everything stays synchronized.

Follow these steps to link a Silverlight and SharePoint together in Visual Studio:

1.  Locate your SharePoint project in the Solution Explorer. As shown in Figure 10-5, select the module through which the Silverlight application will be deployed (be sure to select the actual SharePoint project item that represents the module, not any files or folders beneath it).

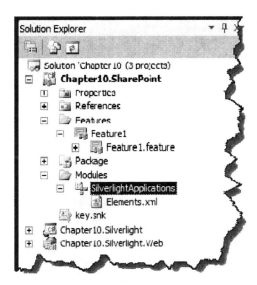

*Figure 10-5. Selecting Module project item in Visual Studio*

2. Once the module is selected, examine the Properties window and locate the **Project Output References** property, as shown in Figure 10-6. Edit the property to access the Project Output References dialog.

*Figure 10-6. Project Output References property in the Properties window*

3. Click the **Add** button on the Project Output References dialog. Select your Silverlight project in the drop-down next to the Project Name field and change the Deployment Type to **ElementFile** (see Figure 10-7).

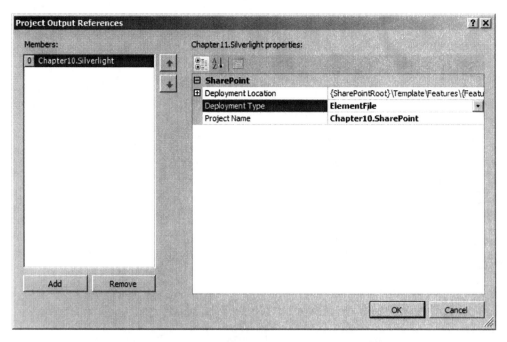

***Figure 10-7.*** *Project Output References dialog*

4.  Open your module's Elements.xml file and verify the .xap file from your Silverlight project was added. Tweak the Url attribute of the <File> tag for the .xap file as needed (for example, the path to the document library where you're deploying might need to be set).

Now your SharePoint and Silverlight projects are linked. When you're ready to test, you can simply build and deploy the SharePoint project to SharePoint Online. The Silverlight project will automatically be built as well and its output will be added to the module it was linked with.

# Building a Silverlight Application with the Client Object Model

If you aren't already familiar with the client object model in SharePoint Online, we recommend you first read Chapter 9 before continuing. Chapter 9 introduces and describes the client object model, including the Silverlight application programming interface (API).

In this section we'll walk you through building a simple Silverlight application that uses the client object model to retrieve data from a SharePoint document library and display it in a pie chart. Our goal here is to expand your horizons beyond simply reading and updating list data (of which you can find examples almost everywhere) and instead demonstrate how you might use Silverlight as a data analysis or business intelligence tool by helping you better visualize your data.

Although this section will show you snippets of the application, you can download a completed version of the entire application if you want. It's available as part of the download that accompanies this chapter.

# Referencing the Client Object Model

Before you can use the client object model in your Silverlight application, you must add the necessary assembly references to your Silverlight project.

The files you want are `Microsoft.SharePoint.Client.Silverlight.dll` and `Microsoft.SharePoint.Client.Silverlight.Runtime.dll`. When you open the Visual Studio Add Reference dialog, browse to the following location to find the assemblies: `C:\Program Files\Common Files\Microsoft Shared\Web Server Extensions\14\TEMPLATE\LAYOUTS\ClientBin` (assuming SharePoint was installed at `C:\Program Files`, as is common in development environments).

Once the references have been added, most of the classes you will need in your code can be found in the `Microsoft.SharePoint.Client` namespace.

# Getting the Chart Control

Silverlight 5 doesn't provide a built-in pie chart control, but you can use the one provided by the Silverlight toolkit. As we mentioned in the *Preparing Your Development Environment for Silverlight* section earlier in this chapter, you can download the toolkit for free at `http://silverlight.codeplex.com`. Make sure you download the toolkit for Silverlight 5, not the one for Windows Phone. At the time of this writing, the December 2011 version of the toolkit is the most current release.

Once you've downloaded and installed the toolkit, you'll need to add a reference in your project to the `System.Windows.Controls.DataVisualization.Toolkit.dll` assembly, which you can find in the `C:\Program Files (x86)\Microsoft SDKs\Silverlight\v5.0\Toolkit\dec11\Bin` folder.

The control you'll be using from this assembly is the `System.Windows.Controls.DataVisualization.Charting.Chart` control. The Chart control can be used to render several different types of charts, including pie charts.

# Adding the Chart to a View

The next step is to add the Chart control to a view (.xaml file) in your Silverlight application. Listing 10-1 shows the code we used to add a Chart control to the MainPage.xaml file in our application.

*Listing 10-1. Code to add a Chart control to MainPage.xaml*

```
<UserControl x:Class="Chapter10.Silverlight.MainPage"
    xmlns="http://schemas.microsoft.com/winfx/2006/xaml/presentation"
    xmlns:x="http://schemas.microsoft.com/winfx/2006/xaml"
    xmlns:d="http://schemas.microsoft.com/expression/blend/2008"
    xmlns:mc="http://schemas.openxmlformats.org/markup-compatibility/2006"
    xmlns:toolkit="http://schemas.microsoft.com/winfx/2006/xaml/presentation/toolkit"
    mc:Ignorable="d"
    d:DesignHeight="300" d:DesignWidth="400">

    <Grid x:Name="LayoutRoot" Margin="10" Background="White">
        <toolkit:Chart LegendTitle="{Binding LegendTitle}" Title="{Binding Title}">
            <toolkit:Chart.Series>
                <toolkit:PieSeries
                    ItemsSource="{Binding FileTypes}"
                    DependentValueBinding="{Binding Count}"
                    IndependentValueBinding="{Binding TypeName}" />
```

```
            </toolkit:Chart.Series>
        </toolkit:Chart>
    </Grid>
</UserControl>
```

As shown in Listing 10-1, the way to construct a pie chart using the Chart control is to add a PieSeries object to the Chart's Series collection. The PieSeries object has three important properties you'll need: ItemsSource, DependentValueBinding, and IndependentValueBinding.

The ItemsSource property will reference your collection of data objects. Each data object in this case will have two values: a file type name (e.g., .docx for a Microsoft Word 2010 document) and a count (e.g., 10 if there are 10 files of that type in the library). In pie chart lingo, the file type name is the *independent* variable in the chart and the count is the *dependent* variable (in that it determines the size of the "chunk" representing that file type in the pie).

# Presenting Data to the View

When it comes to modeling the data and presenting it to the view, we recommend following the Model-View-View-Model (MVVM) design pattern that's commonly used for Silverlight development. The MVVM pattern is designed to work well with XAML and data binding and helps ensure proper separation of concerns in your application.

Listing 10-2 shows a starting point for a PieChartViewModel class that could be used to present data to the view.

*Listing 10-2. PieChartViewModel class*

```
public class PieChartViewModel : BaseViewModel
{
    public List<PieChartFileType> FileTypes
    {
        get { /* Return a list of PieChartFileType objects */ }
        set { /* Set property value and notify view */ }
    }

    public string LegendTitle
    {
        get  { return "File Types"; }
    }

    public string Title
    {
        get { return "File Breakdown by Type"; }
    }

    public void Load()
    {
        // Get data from a service and load it into the ViewModel
    }
}
```

Although the code in Listing 10-2 isn't entirely complete, it illustrates the basic structure of a ViewModel class. It has properties to which the view can bind, and it has a mechanism for loading data into those properties. It also inherits from a "base" ViewModel class, which is pretty common practice. At a minimum, the base ViewModel class usually implements the INotifyPropertyChanged interface (required for data binding) and provides a method that child classes can call to invoke the PropertyChanged event (which tells a view bound to a property to refresh its value for that property).

## Modeling the Data

To create our pie chart, we need to construct a data series. For each data point in that series, we need two values: a file type and a count (the independent and dependent variables, respectively, which we're plotting on the pie chart).

Continuing with the sample code we showed in Listing 10-2, we present a PieChartFileType class in Listing 10-3 that could be used to model each data point in our series.

*Listing 10-3. PieChartFileType class that represents a data point for the pie chart*

```
public class PieChartFileType
{
    public PieChartFileType(string typeName, int count)
    {
        this.TypeName = typeName;
        this.Count = count;
    }

    public string TypeName { get; set; }
    public int Count { get; set; }
}
```

Now the FileTypes property we showed in Listing 10-2 should make more sense. If you set that property value to a list of PieChartFileType objects, you have a data series for plotting on your pie chart.

## Getting the Data from SharePoint

Once you have a way to model the data, the next step is to retrieve it from SharePoint. There are many ways to structure that logic. Listing 10-4 presents a PieChartDataService class as one possible way to do it.

*Listing 10-4. Sample PieChartDataService class for retrieving data*

```
public class PieChartDataService
{
    public void GetData(Action<List<PieChartFileType>> onSuccess, Action<string> onError)
    {
        try
        {
            ClientContext ctx = ClientContext.Current;
            List mpGallery = ctx.Web.Lists.GetByTitle("Shared Documents");
            CamlQuery query = new CamlQuery();
            query.ViewXml = "<View Scope='Recursive' />";

            ListItemCollection items = mpGallery.GetItems(query);

            ctx.Load(items);
```

```
                ctx.ExecuteQueryAsync(
                    (sender, successArgs) => {
                        // Process data and invoke onSuccess callback
                    },
                    (sender, failureArgs) => {
                        // Invoke onError callback
                    }
                );
            }
            catch (Exception ex)
            {
                // Invoke onError callback
            }
        }
    }
```

The class shown in Listing 10-4 is small and simply contains a GetData method for retrieving the necessary data from SharePoint. To simplify life for callers in light of the asynchronous nature of retrieving the data, the GetData method takes two parameters: onSuccess and onError. Both parameters use the generic System.Action<T> type to define callback functions that are called when the data is loaded successfully or when an error occurs, respectively. In the former case, a list of data points is passed to the caller; in the latter, a string variable containing an error message.

In both cases, whether the data is loaded successfully or not, we are returning from an asynchronous call and must marshal our subsequent calls back to the UI thread so we don't get exceptions when control values are updated on the view. Normally, that process involves getting a handle to a Dispatcher object, but Microsoft provides a SmartDispatcher class (available at http://bit.ly/dihIDd) that makes marshaling to the UI thread even easier by abstracting out the details of finding a Dispatcher object.

Listing 10-5 builds on Listing 10-4 by showing how the SmartDispatcher class can be used to process the data returned from SharePoint and pass it to the caller.

***Listing 10-5.*** *Using SmartDispatcher to process and return data from SharePoint*

```
SmartDispatcher.BeginInvoke(() =>
    {
        List<PieChartFileType> fileTypes = new List<PieChartFileType>();

        var groups =
        from item in items.ToArray()
        group item by (string)item["File_x0020_Type"];

        foreach (var group in groups)
        {
            fileTypes.Add(new PieChartFileType(group.Key, group.Count()));
        }

        if (onSuccess != null)
        {
            onSuccess(fileTypes);
        }
    }
);
```

---

■ **Note** To use the `SmartDispatcher` class, you must call its static `Initialize` method in the `Application_Startup` event of your Silverlight application.

---

Note the use of LINQ to Objects in Listing 10-5 to group the list items by file type. Grouping them this way makes it easy to count how many there are of each type.

Now that we have a data service for retrieving data, the Load method from Listing 10-2 could be written as shown in Listing 10-6.

*Listing 10-6. Body of Load method in the PieChartViewModel class*

```
PieChartDataService service = new PieChartDataService();

service.GetData(
    (fileTypes) =>
        {
            this.FileTypes = fileTypes;
        },
    (error) =>
        {
            // Display error to user
        }
);
```

Now you have all the core pieces you need to get started building a Silverlight application that displays SharePoint data in a pie chart. Figure 10-8 shows what the final application might look like.

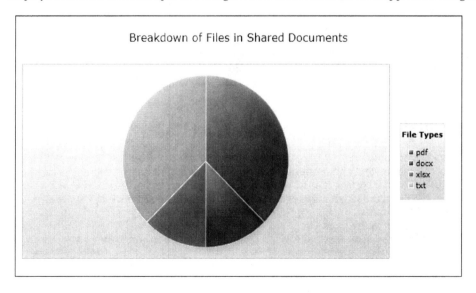

*Figure 10-8. Silverlight application with pie chart showing breakdown of file types*

The next two sections of this chapter discuss the options for deploying and hosting a Silverlight application in SharePoint Online.

# Deploying Silverlight Applications to SharePoint Online

There are two ways you can deploy a Silverlight application to SharePoint Online: manual deployment or feature-based deployment. Both approaches are presented here so you can choose the one that works best for your situation.

## Manual Deployment

Manually deploying a Silverlight application to SharePoint Online is as easy as uploading the .xap file to a document library. Once the file is uploaded, it is ready to be referenced and hosted in the browser. The steps for uploading a .xap file are no different from uploading any other type of file, so they aren't covered in detail here.

There's no specific library in which you have to store your .xap files, but we definitely recommend keeping permissions in mind when making your choice. If it's an important application you don't want accidentally deleted, for example, choosing a library with loose permissions (such as the *Shared Documents* library in a team site) is probably not the best approach. Creating a new dedicated library or using an existing one with more restrictive permissions (such as the Master Page Gallery) would be a better way to go.

In any case, anyone who has permissions to upload files to your site can upload a Silverlight application, making it a fairly easy and accessible approach.

## Feature-Based Deployment

Feature-based deployment is a more repeatable and controlled way of deploying a Silverlight application to SharePoint Online, but does require some SharePoint development knowledge.

Feature-based deployment consists of creating a feature (in a SharePoint solution package or .wsp file) that deploys the Silverlight application using a *module* element. As was mentioned in the "Creating and Linking Your Projects" section earlier in this chapter, the easiest way to do this is by having your SharePoint and Silverlight projects in a single solution and linking them together in Visual Studio.

Once you create your feature and solution package, you can upload it to the Solution Gallery of a SharePoint Online site and activate it normally.

# Hosting a Silverlight Application in SharePoint Online

Once you deploy a Silverlight application to SharePoint Online, the next decision you're faced with is how to host it (i.e., how to reference it and render the appropriate markup to the browser).

You have two options when it comes to hosting a Silverlight application. The first option is to use the Silverlight web part that's included with SharePoint Online. Using this web part is as simple as pointing it at a .xap file, and it renders the appropriate markup to the browser. The second option is to render your own HTML markup to the page just as you would in any website outside of SharePoint. This latter option can be implemented in a variety of ways, including emitting markup from a custom web part, adding markup to a page using SharePoint Designer, and adding markup with a Content Editor web part, just to name a few. Basically, any means you can use to inject HTML markup into a page in SharePoint Online will work with the latter approach.

This section focuses on two of the most common approaches: using the Silverlight web part and emitting markup from a custom web part. As usual, we recommend choosing the approach that best fits your specific requirements.

# Using the Silverlight Web Part

Using the Silverlight web part is a very common way to host Silverlight applications in SharePoint Online. It's simple to configure and can be easily added to a page by anyone with permissions to do so.

There are at least two ways we can use the Silverlight web part in SharePoint Online to host a Silverlight application. One way is to add the built-in Silverlight web part to a page and configure it using the web part's tool pane. Another way is to create a preconfigured version of the Silverlight web part that requires no (or minimal) configuration after being added to a page. We'll discuss both approaches in this section.

## Using the Built-In Silverlight Web Part

To use the built-in Silverlight web part, start by editing one of the pages on your site. On the **Insert** tab of the **Editing Tools** group in the ribbon, click the **More Web Parts** button, as shown in Figure 10-9.

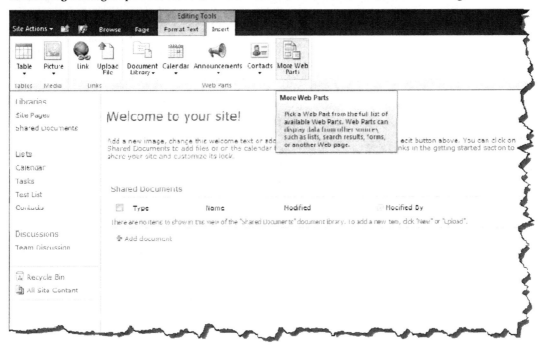

*Figure 10-9. The More Web Parts button on the page editing ribbon*

When the dialog window with more web parts appears, select the Silverlight web part from the **Media and Content** category (see Figure 10-10). Click the **Add** button to add the web part to the page.

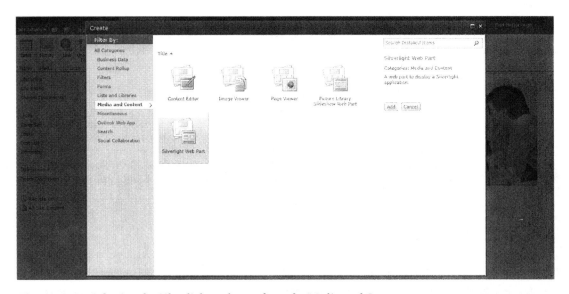

***Figure 10-10.*** *Selecting the Silverlight web part from the Media and Content category*

After being added to the page, the web part will display the message shown in Figure 10-11. Click the tool pane link in the message to open the web part's tool pane so you can configure it.

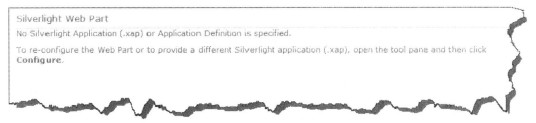

***Figure 10-11.*** *Configuration message displayed by the Silverlight web part*

---

■ **Note** When you click the tool pane link, you may get a message asking whether you want to save your changes (to the page) before continuing. Click **OK** to save and then continue with configuring the web part.

---

Once the tool pane is open, click the **Configure** button in the **Application** section at the top. Enter the URL (local or remote) of the .xap file you want to host and click **OK** to close the dialog. You must also enter a fixed height for the web part under the **Appearance** section (if you don't, you'll get an error when trying to save your changes). Click **OK** or **Apply** in the tool pane to save your changes.

## Using a Preconfigured Silverlight Web Part

Using the built-in Silverlight web part as-is is fine if you don't mind configuring it every time you use it. However, what if you have a Silverlight application that may get used repeatedly throughout your site? Or what if you just want to make life easier for your users by not requiring them to know how to configure .xap file URLs?

You can address both cases by deploying a preconfigured version of the Silverlight web part for your users. There's no server-side code involved here, and there's no need to deploy any DLLs.

You'll just deploy a custom .webpart file (XML file) to the Web Part Gallery in the top-level site of your site collection. The files in this gallery are designed to tell SharePoint how a web part should be configured when added to a page (i.e., which .NET web part class should be used and how its properties should be set). You can have multiple files in the gallery that reference the same web part as long as they're named uniquely.

The following steps help you create your own preconfigured version of the Silverlight web part and deploy it to the Web Part Gallery:

1. Edit a page on your site and add a Silverlight web part to the page, as discussed in the previous section.

2. Edit the web part. Under the Advanced section in its editing tool pane, look for the Export Mode property. Set the property value to Export All Data and save your changes.

3. Now, from the web part's menu (the right side of its header), choose the Export command. Save the resulting .webpart file where you can find it easily because you'll need it again in a moment.

4. Open the .webpart file in a text editor or in Visual Studio. Look for a <property> tag with a name of "Url" and a type of "string." Set the value of this tag to the URL of a .xap file. You should also find the property with a name of "title" and set its value to a descriptive title for the web part. Figure 10-12 shows a sample .webpart file and highlights these two properties. Note that the Url property can contain two special tokens (~siteCollection or ~site) to reference the base URL of the site collection or site (web) where the web part is used.

```
 1   <webParts>
 2     <webPart xmlns="http://schemas.microsoft.com/WebPart/v3">
 3       <metaData>
 4         <type name="Microsoft.SharePoint.WebPartPages.SilverlightWebPart, Microsoft.SharePoint, Version=14.0.0.0, Culture=neutral, PublicKey'
 5         <importErrorMessage>Cannot import this Web Part.</importErrorMessage>
 6       </metaData>
 7       <data>
 8         <properties>
 9           <property name="HelpUrl" type="string" />
10           <property name="AllowClose" type="bool">True</property>
11           <property name="ExportMode" type="exportmode">All</property>
12           <property name="Hidden" type="bool">False</property>
13           <property name="AllowEdit" type="bool">True</property>
14           <property name="Direction" type="direction">NotSet</property>
15           <property name="TitleIconImageUrl" type="string" />
16           <property name="AllowConnect" type="bool">True</property>
17           <property name="HelpMode" type="helpmode">Navigate</property>
18           <property name="CustomProperties" type="string" null="true" />
19           <property name="AllowHide" type="bool">True</property>
20           <property name="Description" type="string">A web part to display a Silverlight application.</property>
21           <property name="CatalogIconImageUrl" type="string" />
22           <property name="MinRuntimeVersion" type="string" null="true" />
23           <property name="ApplicationXml" type="string" />
24           <property name="AllowMinimize" type="bool">True</property>
25           <property name="AllowZoneChange" type="bool">True</property>
26           <property name="CustomInitParameters" type="string" null="true" />
27           <property name="Height" type="unit">400px</property>
28           <property name="ChromeType" type="chrometype">Default</property>
29           <property name="Width" type="unit" />
30           <property name="Title" type="string">Custom Silverlight Web Part</property>
31           <property name="ChromeState" type="chromestate">Normal</property>
32           <property name="TitleUrl" type="string" />
33           <property name="Url" type="string">
34             ~siteCollection/Silverlight Applications/Silverlight1.xap
35           </property>
36           <property name="WindowlessMode" type="bool">True</property>
37         </properties>
38       </data>
39     </webPart>
40   </webParts>
```

*Figure 10-12. XML for preconfigured Silverlight web part*

5.  Deploy your custom .webpart file to the Web Part Gallery in the top-level site of your site collection. One way to do this is to use a module element within a feature. However, it can also be done manually by following these steps:

    a.  Navigate to the Site Settings page of the top-level site in your site collection.

    b.  Click the **Web parts** link under the **Galleries** heading.

    c.  Upload your .webpart file into the gallery (go to the **Documents** tab in the ribbon and select **Upload Document**).

    d.  You'll be prompted to fill out a few properties for your file, including its name and group. Whatever name you give it is fine as long as it's unique within the gallery. The group value is the category that shows up on the left side of the web part dialog when adding the web part to a page (for example, the "Media and Content" group in Figure 10-10). If you don't supply a group name, SharePoint will create a group called "Miscellaneous" and add it to that.

## Using a Custom Web Part

Depending on your requirements, the Silverlight web part may not always be a good fit. Sometimes, you may need or want to create your own web part that hosts a Silverlight application.

To do so, you can emit your Silverlight application markup from the CreateChildControls method of your web part, as shown in Listing 10-7.

*Listing 10-7. Emitting Silverlight markup from a custom web part*

```
protected override void CreateChildControls()
{
    string markup = String.Format(
        @"<div id=""silverlightControlHost"">
                <object data=""data:application/x-silverlight-2,"" type=""application/x-
silverlight-2"" width=""100%"" height=""100%"">
                    <param name=""source""
value=""/_catalogs/masterpage/MySilverlightApp.xap""/>
                    <param name=""minRuntimeVersion"" value=""5.0.61118.0"" />
                    <param name=""initParams"" value=""MS.SP.url={1}"" />
                    <param name=""autoUpgrade"" value=""true"" />
                    <a href=""http://go.microsoft.com/fwlink/?LinkID=149156&v=5.0.61118.0""
style=""text-decoration:none"">
                        <img src=""http://go.microsoft.com/fwlink/?LinkId=161376"" alt=""Get
Microsoft Silverlight"" style=""border-style:none""/>
                    </a>
                </object><iframe id=""_sl_historyFrame""
style=""visibility:hidden;height:0px;width:0px;border:0px""></iframe>
            </div>",
            SPHttpUtility.HtmlEncode(SPContext.Current.Web.Url)
    );

    this.Controls.Add(new LiteralControl(markup));
}
```

The Silverlight markup in Listing 10-7 is essentially what Visual Studio generates when creating a web application with a test page to accompany a Silverlight 5 project. The two key differences are the source and initParams parameters that are passed to the <object> tag. The former was changed to reference the Silverlight app at its location within SharePoint, and the latter was changed to include a special variable called MS.SP.url. The reason for passing MS.SP.url (with the URL of the current site or site collection we're in) to Silverlight as an initialization parameter is so ClientContext.Current will work if the Silverlight app is using the client object model. Without that variable, ClientContext.Current would return null. SharePoint automatically adds the MS.SP.url variable when the Silverlight web part is used, but you must do it yourself if emitting your own markup.

# Summary

We began this chapter by helping you prepare your development environment for Silverlight. We then walked you through the process of creating SharePoint and Silverlight projects in a single solution in Visual Studio and linking them together to make deployment easier. We then discussed developing a Silverlight application using the client object model and concluded by discussing options for deploying and hosting Silverlight applications in SharePoint Online.

It's impossible to cover every possible scenario for using Silverlight in SharePoint Online in a single chapter because the topic is so broad. However, we hope we've given you some good information to help you get started on your own project.

# CHAPTER 11

■ ■ ■

# Developing with jQuery, HTML5, and CSS3

It's no secret that a big trend in web development today is making websites more responsive and more user experience-focused than in the past. Technologies such as jQuery, HTML5, and CSS3 are at the heart of that movement and will continue to be a core focus in creating modern websites for the near future. While SharePoint Online wasn't really designed specifically for use with these technologies, we can still leverage them in ways that hopefully help make our SharePoint sites more adaptive, more user-friendly, and more modern-looking.

This chapter discusses the following topics:

- Introduction to jQuery
- Using jQuery in SharePoint Online
- jQuery and the client object model
- Introduction to HTML5 and CSS3
- Using HTML5 and CSS3 in SharePoint Online

## Introduction to jQuery

## What Is jQuery?

Remember the days of struggling to write cross-browser client-side code in JavaScript? Yeah, neither do we. Why not? Because for years now, we've had JavaScript libraries at our fingertips that make the task much easier (and frankly, much more enjoyable). jQuery is one of those libraries and is also one of the most popular.

The definition on jQuery's own website (http://jquery.com) describes it well:

> *jQuery is a fast and concise JavaScript library that simplifies HTML document traversing, event handling, animating, and Ajax interactions for rapid web development. jQuery is designed to change the way you write JavaScript.*

The last sentence of that definition stands out because it captures exactly what jQuery has done: it changed the way developers write JavaScript.

## Where Can You Get It?

You can download the latest version of jQuery from the jQuery website at `http://jquery.com`. At the time of this writing, the current release is version 1.7.2. The website gives you a choice of downloading a production version of the library (slimmed-down or "minified" for best performance) or a development version for debugging (human-readable, uncompressed code).

Alternatively, you can also reference jQuery using a content delivery network (CDN). A list of publicly available CDNs you can link to is available on the jQuery website at `http://bit.ly/aqJ92n`.

The jQuery website also has some great documentation and tutorials that can teach you how to use the library if you haven't used it before.

## jQuery UI

In addition to the core jQuery library, you can also download and use the jQuery user interface (UI) that is built on top of the core jQuery library and provides controls and abstractions for building highly interactive UIs. You can download jQuery UI from `http://jqueryui.com`.

At the time of this writing, the jQuery UI home page provides a "Build custom download" button that lets you decide exactly how much of the library to download based on your needs. (For example, you might want the drag-and-drop behavior but not the resize, sort, and selection behaviors.) You can also choose the theme you want (or design your own), and the appropriate CSS will be included in your download.

## What Does jQuery Give Us?

At a high level, the core jQuery library provides the following capabilities and functionality (across browsers):

- Selectors (for finding and referencing elements in the DOM)

- Attribute manipulation (e.g., retrieving an element's value or changing its CSS class)

- Traversal of DOM elements (e.g., looping over a collection of elements or finding all the children of a parent element)

- Document Object Model (DOM) manipulation (e.g., adding and removing elements)

- Events (e.g., adding a `click` event handler to an element)

- Effects (e.g., making an element fade in or out of view)

- Ajax (e.g., loading data from a server without requiring a full page refresh)

- Utilities and other "core" functionality (e.g., manipulating arrays and strings, and associating arbitrary data with elements in the DOM)

As you can see, the core library gives us a lot. And if you download the jQuery UI, you also get the behaviors, themes, and controls that come with the jQuery UI library. All in all, it's a lot of functionality, and it's all free.

---

**Note** *DOM* refers to the *Document Object Model*, which is a model used by web browsers to represent the content and structure of an HTML document (web page). For more information, see `http://www.w3.org/DOM`.

---

# Using jQuery in SharePoint Online

## Referencing jQuery

There are two ways to reference, or "include," jQuery in a web page: by using a CDN or by referencing your own local copy of the library. Regardless of which approach you plan to use, you'll use a <script> tag to reference jQuery in your page. You can't run jQuery code on a page unless that page has a reference to the jQuery library.

Here's a quick example of a CDN reference (in this case hosted by Google):

```
<script src="//ajax.googleapis.com/ajax/libs/jquery/1.7.2/jquery.min.js"
type="text/javascript"></script>
```

And here's a quick example of a local reference (assuming in this case that jQuery resides in your site collection's style library):

```
<script src="/Style Library/js/jQuery-1.7.2.min.js" type="text/javascript"></script>
```

---

**Note** The server-side `<ScriptLink>` tag can also be used to reference jQuery. The *Name* attribute supports absolute URLs as well as URLs containing the `~site` and `~sitecollection` tokens.

---

If you're wondering how to actually add the jQuery reference to your page, there are several different approaches you can take. We've listed three common ones with pros and cons (to help you decide when each is appropriate) in Table 11-1.

*Table 11-1. Common Approaches for Referencing jQuery in SharePoint Online*

| Approach | Pros | Cons |
|---|---|---|
| Content Editor Web Part | Easy; anyone who can edit the page in a browser can do it; no special tools or editing skills required. | Must be done on each individual page in which jQuery will be used and doesn't work on pages in which web parts can't be added; can't use the server-side <ScriptLink> tag that supports URL replacement tokens such as ~site and ~siteCollection. |
| Content placeholder | Still pretty easy for someone with basic web design skills (requires editing a little ASP.NET markup); not tied to a specific web part and works even on pages where web parts can't be added; can use the server-side <ScriptLink> tag. | Must be done on each individual page (or page layout in the case of publishing sites) in which jQuery will be used; requires using a tool such as SharePoint Designer to edit markup. |
| Custom master page | Allows jQuery to be used on any page that references the master page (eliminates the need to add a jQuery reference to each page where it will be used); can use the server-side <ScriptLink> tag. | Requires some SharePoint branding knowledge (knowing how to create and deploy a custom master page); also requires a tool such as SharePoint Designer and more-advanced editing skills (mainly so you don't break something) |

Now that we've outlined three common approaches, let's take a closer look at each one so you know how to do it should the need arise.

## Content Editor Web Part (CEWP) Approach

To demonstrate this approach, let's start with a standard site page (like what you get with a team site). Begin by inserting a Content Editor Web Part (CEWP) from the *Media and Content* category of web parts into the page, as shown in Figure 11-1.

*Figure 11-1. Empty CEWP on site page*

Edit the web part (select *Edit Web Part* from the web part's menu). The web part body will now display a link that reads, "Click here to add new content." Click the link. Once a cursor appears within the web part, find the *Markup* group in the ribbon at the top of the page. Click the *HTML* button and select **Edit HTML Source**, as shown in Figure 11-2.

*Figure 11-2. Selecting* Edit HTML Source *command in the ribbon*

In the popup window that appears, enter your <script> as shown in Figure 11-3 (our script tag in the figure references a Microsoft-hosted CDN).

*Figure 11-3. jQuery <script> tag in HTML Source popup window*

Click **OK** to close the popup window. *Before* you stop editing the web part, take a look at the web part editing panel (which should still be visible on the page at this point, typically on the right side). Expand the *Appearance* category and change the Chrome Type to **None**, as shown in Figure 11-4. This effectively hides your web part on the page when the page isn't in edit mode. Because this web part does nothing except reference jQuery, there's no reason it needs to be visible.

---

**Note**  A web part's *chrome* is its border, header (title area), and menu. In essence, the chrome is everything that surrounds the web part's core content.

---

*Figure 11-4. Setting the web part's Chrome Type to* None

To test whether jQuery is working, you can add a second CEWP to the page (below the first one) and add the code from Listing 11-1 to it (again by using the HTML source window as before).

■ **Tip** As shown in Listing 11-1, we use $j rather than $ to reference the jQuery() function. If you've used jQuery before and are wondering why we did this, it's because re-aliasing the jQuery() function is considered a best practice when using jQuery in SharePoint. The reason is because SharePoint has a lot of JavaScript code behind it and occasionally makes use of the $ symbol in its own code, which jQuery also uses as its default alias for the jQuery() function. If you don't give jQuery a different alias besides $, you might encounter strange behavior in your code that's hard to debug. You might get lucky and have code that works fine with $, but it's better to not take any chances.

*Listing 11-1. Testing whether jQuery is working*

```
<script type="text/javascript">
    var $j = jQuery.noConflict();
    $j(document).ready(function() {
        alert('jQuery is working!');
    });
</script>
```

■ **Note** If you use a CDN to reference jQuery, and your browser warns about displaying mixed content, it's probably because the schemes of the URLs don't match (e.g., the CDN URL starts with http and your site's URL starts with https). You can usually prevent the warning by changing the CDN URL's scheme to match the one your site uses.

## Content Placeholder Approach

Content placeholders are a concept from ASP.NET (Microsoft's server-side web development framework, on top of which SharePoint Online is built). If you aren't familiar with master pages and content pages, we suggest you visit http://www.asp.net and view the relevant training materials on the subject.

The default master pages in SharePoint Online contain a placeholder called "PlaceHolderAdditionalPageHead" that you can use in your pages (or page layouts) to add additional markup to the <head> tag when your page is rendered in the browser. It's a convenient way to add references to things like JavaScript and CSS files when you need them only on a specific page.

Begin by opening SharePoint Designer and connecting to your site. Edit the page (or page layout in a publishing site) in which you want to insert the jQuery reference. (Make sure to choose the option to edit the page in *Advanced Mode.*) If your site is a team site, you'll likely be editing a page in the Site Pages library.

Search for "PlaceHolderAdditionalPageHead" to see whether the placeholder tag already exists in the page. If not, add it. Add your jQuery reference (<script> tag) within it. When all is said and done, the placeholder tag should look similar to the one following (in this example, we're referencing a local copy of jQuery stored in the Style Library of our site collection):

```
<asp:Content ContentPlaceHolderId="PlaceHolderAdditionalPageHead" runat="server">
  <script type="text/javascript" src="/Style Library/js/jQuery-1.7.2.min.js"></script>
</asp:Content>
```

The placeholder tag might already contain markup before you add your jQuery reference. If so, that's fine. Just add your <script> tag below the existing markup.

You can now add jQuery code elsewhere on the page (either directly in SharePoint Designer or by using web parts such as the CEWP if the page allows it).

## Custom Master Page Approach

If you want jQuery to be available on any page in your site, an easy way to accomplish that is by adding a jQuery reference to a custom master page. Simply edit your custom master page in SharePoint Designer and add a jQuery reference to the <head> tag. Now jQuery will be available on any pages attached to that master page.

# Using jQuery

This section quickly covers the basics of using jQuery to get you up and running quickly.

## The jQuery Function

Everything in jQuery revolves around the jQuery() function, which returns a new jQuery object when called. A jQuery object is a special object that wraps a collection of native DOM elements, provides additional functionality, and surfaces a cross-browser application programming interface (API) for manipulation of the elements it contains.

This function is aliased by default as $, allowing you to construct a new jQuery object simply by doing something such as $('div'), which creates a new jQuery object that wraps a native DIV element. Even though we also said that it's a best practice in SharePoint to re-alias jQuery with another identifier such as $j, we'll use $ here for the sake of readability because most people are accustomed to seeing $ associated with jQuery calls.

## Executing Code When Your Page Loads

The customary way to execute code with jQuery when your page finishes loading is to use the $(document).ready() function like this:

```
$(document).ready(function() {
    alert('DOM is loaded and can now be manipulated!');
});
```

This $(document).ready() function starts executing code as soon as the DOM is ready (fully loaded by the browser) and ensures that your code doesn't execute too soon in the page lifecycle. It is a common place to use jQuery to do things such as hook up event handlers to DOM elements on the page.

## Selecting Elements

A common operation in jQuery is selecting one or more DOM elements and returning the resulting collection as a jQuery object you can manipulate. For example, the following code selects the left panel area on a page in a SharePoint Online team site (the left panel area is the light gray area containing the Quick Launch menu, recycle bin link, and so on):

```
$('#s4-leftpanel')
```

The # selector in jQuery selects elements by ID, so in this case jQuery finds the element with ID s4-leftpanel, which is a DIV tag.

In this next example, we select the site logo in the header of a team site:

```
$('.s4-titlelogo > a > img')
```

The "." selector selects elements by class name, and the ">" selector selects child elements. Because the markup for the site logo in SharePoint Online consists of an <img> tag within an <a> tag within a <td class='s4-titlelogo'> tag, this code will find that <img> element for us.

For the full list of jQuery selectors, see http://api.jquery.com/category/selectors/.

## Simple DOM Manipulation

The following code adds a CSS class called highlighted to an <li> element with a class of first:

```
$('li.first').addClass('highlighted')
```

The following code removes the same class from the same element:

```
$('li.first').removeClass('highlighted')
```

The following code hides the left panel containing the Quick Launch menu:

```
$('#s4-leftpanel').hide();
```

This code snippet gets the value of the 'alt' attribute for the site logo in a team site:

```
$('.s4-titlelogo > a > img').attr('alt')
```

And this snippet sets that same 'alt' attribute to a new value:

```
$('.s4-titlelogo > a > img').attr('alt', 'New Alt Value')
```

There are also functions for inserting elements into the DOM, removing elements, getting the values of input controls such as radio buttons and check boxes, and so on. See the documentation on the jQuery website for a complete list of functions related to DOM manipulation.

# jQuery and the Client Object Model

As useful as jQuery is on its own, it really shines when integrated with SharePoint Online's client object model (see Chapter 9 if you're unfamiliar with the client object model). By combining jQuery with the client object model's ECMAScript API, you can easily write client-side code that interacts with data in SharePoint *and* has all the benefits of jQuery (such as cross-browser compatibility, slick UIs if using jQuery UI, and so on).

There are more possibilities for integration than what we could possibly describe here, but we'll toss out a few examples just to get your creative juices flowing:

- Creating a cool UI that lets users drag items from one list and drop them in another.

- Replacing a SharePoint list form with a slicker, more responsive one created with jQuery.

- Adding a new button to the ribbon that lets users perform a bulk rename operation on a group of selected files in a document library. For example, a jQuery dialog box could pop up, asking the user what the new filename pattern should be and then show a progress indicator as the rename takes place.

- Aggregating and reporting on list data (there are jQuery plug-ins you can download that let you create charts, graphs, interactive grids with sorting and filtering, and so on). If you've been looking for an alternative to Silverlight for this sort of interactivity, jQuery can be a good option.

# Introduction to HTML5 and CSS3

HTML5 is the latest version of the HTML standard. It's technically still under development at the time of this writing, but has matured enough that developers have begun using it, and browser manufacturers have begun supporting it.

CSS3 is the latest CSS standard, also still in development at the time of this writing and subject to change. Although it is often paired with HTML5 in articles and code samples you find on the web, it is *not* directly related to HTML5. The standards are independent of one another. HTML5 relates to the structure and semantic meaning of content. CSS3 relates to its layout and presentation on a page. (In even simpler terms: HTML5 defines the content, and CSS3 defines how it's displayed.)

In the end, both these new standards are geared toward making websites easier to code, more accessible, and better able to support mobile devices such as phones and tablets. With HTML5, for example, the new <video> tag allows you to embed videos in your pages without the need for plug-ins such as Flash or Silverlight. Improvements such as this will make websites much more "lightweight" by having native browser support for functionality we had to tack on before because it just wasn't there.

Finally, the group in charge of developing HTML5 and CSS3 is the World Wide Web Consortium (or W3C for short). You can visit its official website at http://www.w3c.org to learn more about the group or the standards.

## Browser Compatibility

Let's start with a list of the browsers that support the core elements (tags) in HTML5:

- Internet Explorer 9+

- Firefox 7+

- Chrome 14+

- Safari 5+

- Opera 11+

- Mobile Safari 3.2+

- Opera Mobile 5+

- Android 2.1+

While these browsers support the core HTML5 standard, be aware that they might *not* fully support the new CSS3 selectors or some of the HTML5 native browser features or canvas elements. To find out whether your browser fully supports a specific feature, check out one of the many cross-browser testing sites on the web, such as `http://www.browserstack.com` (paid service with a trial subscription) or `http://browserlab.adobe.com` (free but points you to a different service for testing mobile browsers). You can also visit `http://www.caniuse.com` for a detailed list of which HTML5 and CSS3 features are supported in various browsers (and you'll want to check that because even if your browser supports the core HTML5 standard, it might not support some of the JavaScript APIs or CSS3 features).

## HTML5 Highlights

This section covers some of the highlights in HTML5. It's not meant to be an exhaustive list (that's beyond the scope of this chapter and even this book), but it will help you get an idea of what's included in the new standard.

### Doctype

The doctype for HTML5 pages is *super simple* and is written as follows:

```
<!DOCTYPE html>
```

### New HTML Elements

Table 11-2 lists tags that are new in HTML5:

*Table 11-2. New Elements in HTML5*

| Category | Tag | Description |
| --- | --- | --- |
| Semantic/Structural | <article> | Independent piece of content (such as a blog entry or article) that can be syndicated (at least in principle) |
| | <aside> | Piece of content that is only somewhat related to the rest of the page |
| | <bdi> | Span of text that needs to be isolated from its surroundings for bidirectional formatting |
| | <command> | Command the user can invoke |
| | <details> | Represents content that can initially be hidden (for example, appearing under a collapsible node in a Tree view) |

| Category | Tag | Description |
| --- | --- | --- |
| | <summary> | Provides the summary/legend/caption for a <details> element |
| | <figure> | Self-contained flow content, optionally with a caption; used to annotate diagrams, code listings, and so on |
| | <figcaption> | Caption for a <figure> element |
| | <footer> | Represents a footer for a section |
| | <header> | Group of introductory or navigational aids |
| | <hgroup> | Section heading used to group h1–h6 tags that represent a hierarchy |
| | <mark> | Represents a run of text that's "marked" (highlighted) to bring attention to it because of a special relevance in the current context (such as marking keywords that appear in search results) |
| | <meter> | Measurement such as disk usage |
| | <nav> | Represents a major navigation block on the page (the word *major* is used because not all navigation menus or links have to be contained within a 'nav' tag) |
| | <progress> | Represents the amount of completion of a task |
| | <ruby>, <rt>, <rp> | Used for marking up Ruby annotations (for East Asian typography) |
| | <section> | Used to represent a generic section of a document or application |
| | <time> | Represents a date and/or time |
| | <wbr> | Indicates a line break opportunity |
| Media | <audio> | Represents a sound or audio stream |
| | <video> | Used for videos/movies and audio streams with captions |

| Category | Tag | Description |
|----------|-----|-------------|
| | <source> | Used to specify multiple alternative media resources for media content (such as different codecs for a video) |
| | <embed> | Used for plug-in content |
| | <track> | Used to specify text tracks for media elements |
| Form | <datalist> | Can be used with the new <list> element to create a drop-down list in a form |
| | <keygen> | Represents a key pair generator control |
| | <output> | Represents the result of a calculation |
| Other | <canvas> | Provides scripts with a resolution–dependent bitmap canvas |

## Obsolete Elements

The following is a list of elements that are now obsolete in HTML5:

- basefont
- big
- center
- font
- strike
- tt
- frame
- frameset
- noframes
- acronym
- applet
- isindex
- dir

## Other Differences in HTML5

Other differences in HTML5 include new and obsolete attributes for many elements and a host of new JavaScript APIs (see http://dev.w3.org/html5/html4-differences/#apis for information on the APIs). For a complete list of all the differences between HTML4 and HTML5, please see http://www.w3.org/TR/html5-diff.

## CSS3 Highlights

Similar to the way we introduced HTML5, we include some highlights of CSS3 in this section to help you get familiar with some of the key features included in the new standard. Again, this is not an exhaustive list, but we included a link at the end of this section to the complete list on the W3C website.

## New Selectors

Table 11-3 summarizes the new selectors in CSS3.

*Table 11-3. New Selectors in CSS3*

| Selector Pattern | Meaning |
| --- | --- |
| E[foo^="bar"] | Element whose "foo" attribute value begins with "bar" |
| E[foo$="bar"] | Element whose "foo" attribute value ends with "bar" |
| E[foo*="bar"] | Element whose "foo" attribute value contains "bar" |
| E:root | An E element, root of the document |
| E:nth-child(n) | An E element, the n-th child of its parent |
| E:nth-last-child(n) | An E element, the n-th child of its parent, counting from the last one |
| E:last-child | An E element, last child of its parent |
| E:nth-last-of-type(n) | An E element, the n-th sibling of its type, counting from the last one |
| E:last-child | An E element, last child of its parent |
| E:first-of-type | An E element, first sibling of its type |
| E:last-of-type | An E element, last sibling of its type |
| E:only-child | An E element, only child of its parent |
| E:only-of-type | An E element, only sibling of its type |

| Selector Pattern | Meaning |
|---|---|
| E:empty | An E element with no children (including text nodes) |
| E:target | An E element that is the target of the referring uniform resource indicator's (URI's) anchor identifier (for example, the element referred to by the "Recipes" identifier in the URI http://www.example.com/food.html#Recipes) |
| E:enabled | User interface element E that is enabled |
| E:disabled | User interface element E that is disabled |
| E:checked | User interface element E that is checked (e.g., check box or radio button) |
| E:not(s) | Element E that does not match simple selector 's' |
| E ~ F | An F element preceded by an E element |

## Other Goodness in CSS3

CSS3 also has new or improved functionality in a host of other areas, including the following:

- Rounded corners
- Background decorations
- Gradients and shadows
- Text effects
- Box model
- Web fonts

For more information on the latest developments in CSS3, visit http://www.w3.org/Style/CSS/ (the official website for the CSS3 standard) or do a web search on "CSS3 tutorials".

# Using HTML5 and CSS3 in SharePoint Online

As mentioned in the previous browser compatibility section, a modern browser (for example, Internet Explorer 9 [IE9] or 10 [IE10]) is required if you want proper support for HTML5 and CSS3, including in SharePoint Online. You'll either need to ensure that your user base meets the browser requirements or plan for a graceful downgrade experience for older browsers (which isn't a big problem if you're using only a few HTML5 tags here and there, such as the <nav> or <article> tags). In any case, *thoroughly* test any HTML5/CSS3 code you add to SharePoint Online! While modern browsers might support these newer standards, SharePoint Online wasn't designed to support them; it was designed to support XHTML 1.0 and CSS 2.1.

On a related note, if you plan to use Visual Studio 2010 for any SharePoint Online development work, you'll want to install the Visual Studio Web Standards update, available at `http://bit.ly/lWV98W`.

# "Turning On" HTML5 in SharePoint Online

To start using HTML5 in SharePoint Online, follow these steps:

1. Open SharePoint Designer 2010 and connect to your site.

2. Click the *Master Pages* node in the Navigation Pane.

3. Copy an existing master page you know is stable and works (such as v4.master). Figure 11-5 shows how we copied v4.master and named the copy "v4_html5.master."

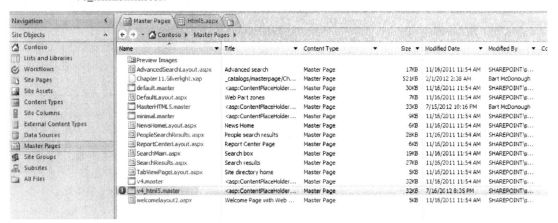

***Figure 11-5.*** *New master page that will be HTML5-compatible*

4. Edit the master page in advanced mode.

5. Locate the DOCTYPE tag near the top. Initially it will look like this:

```
<!DOCTYPE html PUBLIC "-//W3C//DTD XHTML 1.0 Strict//EN"
"http://www.w3.org/TR/xhtml1/DTD/xhtml1-strict.dtd">
```

6. Change it to `<!DOCTYPE html>`, the DOCTYPE for HTML5.

7. Next, locate the document compatibility tag. Initially it will look like this:

```
<meta http-equiv="X-UA-Compatible" content="IE=8"/>
```

8. Change "IE8" to "IE9". The result should look like this:

```
<meta http-equiv="X-UA-Compatible" content="IE=9"/>
```

9. That's it. You now have an HTML5/CSS3–enabled master page.

■ **Note** If you're using IE9 to view your SharePoint Online site, you might need to open the IE Developer Toolbar (by pressing F12) and change the document mode to "Internet Explorer 9 Standards." When we tested the previous changes in IE9, it still initially showed us the pages in IE8 mode, even though the compatibility tag had been updated.

## Trying It Out

We took our new v4_html5.master page from Figure 11-5 and applied it to a standard team site in SharePoint Online. At first glance, everything looked fine. However, it didn't take long to notice that a few things were amiss.

We noticed that a rich text field (called "Description") in one of our Calendar lists no longer worked in IE9. It was no longer editable, and none of the buttons in its toolbar were functional.

Figure 11-6 shows the field. (The field still worked in Firefox, but that's because Firefox doesn't support rich text fields in SharePoint. They're rendered as normal text boxes, but allow you to enter HTML markup to style your text.)

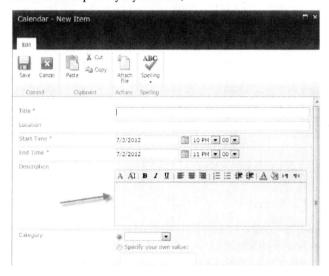

*Figure 11-6. Nonfunctional rich text field*

Another problem was that the "Send to" menu option for items in list views no longer worked in IE9, either (but did work in Firefox 9). Hovering over it wouldn't reveal the submenu that's normally present.

And that wasn't all. We encountered other issues in our testing (even though we hadn't added any HTML5 code yet other than turning it on!). For example, the popup dialog box that goes with the People Picker control didn't work correctly, either (it would display, but its content was sized wrong, and the Add button was missing for selecting a person or group).

# Argh! Now What?

The obvious question this leaves you with is this: "How do I fix the issues that enabling HTML5 introduced?" Unfortunately, the answer is that there is no well-defined answer at this point. If you do a web search on some of the issues we listed, along with any you find yourself, you'll likely find work-arounds for some of them (usually involving JavaScript code). However, you're just as likely to find an issue that *doesn't* yet have a documented work-around or solution. So what do you do?

The way we see it, you have at least four options:

1. Discover and correct each issue yourself (and then tell the rest of the world how you did it because we all want to know).

2. Search for a "ready-made" solution on a site such as CodePlex (http://www.codeplex.com). At the time of this writing, we saw some promising HTML5 master page solutions coming together, but none of them was completely solid. They all exhibited issues with certain built-in SharePoint functionality. However, they still might get you farther along in the test-and-fix cycle than starting from scratch.

3. Limit yourself to using HTML5 on publishing pages in publishing sites (because it's common in that scenario to hide a lot of the built-in SharePoint functionality, anyway, so the fact that it's broken won't matter as much).

4. Use multiple master pages for your site. Attach an HTML5-enabled master page to pages that need to use HTML5 functionality. Attach a non-HTML5 master page to other pages (especially the ones that include SharePoint functionality that breaks with HTML5, if you need that functionality).

If you go with option 4, the process of attaching a different master page to a content page is fairly straightforward. Suppose that you're dealing with a team site and a content page that resides in the Site Pages library. Start by opening the content page in advanced edit mode in SharePoint Designer. Change the value of the masterpagefile attribute in the server-side <Page> tag, as shown in Figure 11-7.

```
<%@ Page Language="C#" masterpagefile="../_catalogs/masterpage/MasterHTML5.master" title="Un
<%@ Register Tagprefix="SharePoint" Namespace="Microsoft.SharePoint.WebControls" Assembly="M
```

*Figure 11-7. Changing the masterpagefile attribute of a page*

You can also do this by using the SharePoint Designer UI rather than by editing markup directly. When the page is in edit mode, go to the Style tab in the ribbon. Expand the Attach menu under the Master Page group and select a master page to attach to your page. Sometimes this approach is easier because SharePoint Designer will figure out the correct path to the master page file for you.

This approach is also easier if you're editing a content page that has *no* master page attached to it yet. Using this approach, you can easily attach one for the first time. This might happen, for example, if you use SharePoint Designer to create a new ASPX page in the Site Pages library by using the Page button in the ribbon. By default, the new page won't be attached to a master page as it would be if you created it in the browser.

---

**Note** Be aware that changing the master page for a content page might cause problems if the placeholders in the new master page are different from those in the old master page. Be sure to check that before making the switch!

---

Regardless of how you ultimately get HTML5 enabled in your site (your own master page, one you download from CodePlex, or otherwise), you can start writing HTML5/CSS3 markup after it's enabled. Whether a page with HTML5/CSS3 code fully works will still be a function of your browser and whether the page has any built-in SharePoint functionality that breaks with these new standards. Hopefully, you've mitigated that latter issue by using one or more of the options we discussed a moment ago.

## Adding Some HTML5/CSS3 Markup

First, if you're planning to edit a wiki page (such as one in the Site Pages library of a team site) and add HTML5 markup to the wiki field on the page, don't bother. Even if you use the HTML source button in the ribbon to add your own markup, SharePoint Online edits the markup when the page is saved and removes what it thinks is "invalid" markup. As a result, your code will likely be lost or changed.

So how can you add your markup? There are at least two ways we've tested that both seem to work pretty well so far:

1. Add your markup directly to the page (for example, with SharePoint Designer or another editing tool). But even here you have to be careful because SharePoint Designer sometimes changes or removes "invalid" markup as well. Add small chunks of HTML5/CSS3 code at a time, save your changes, and see what happens. This will give you a sense of what markup SPD does and doesn't allow.

2. Use a web part such as a CEWP, which can be added to a web part zone or wiki field and allows you to add your own markup via an HTML source button (refer to Figure 11-2) in the ribbon. While it's still possible your markup could be lost or changed, our testing so far has shown the CEWP to be much more forgiving of the markup than the wiki fields we mentioned a moment ago.

As an example, try adding the HTML5 code in Listing 11-2 to an HTML5-enabled page in SharePoint Online. The resulting page should look like Figure 11-8.

*Listing 11-2. Sample HTML5/CSS3 code that makes a paragraph editable*

```
<style scoped>
  [contenteditable="true"] { padding: 10px; outline: 2px dashed #CCC; }
  [contenteditable="true"]:hover { outline: 2px dashed #0090D2; }
</style>
<div style="margin:10px;">
   <section>
      <p contenteditable="true">
      Everything within this paragraph is editable in browsers that support HTML5. All you
have to do is click on this paragraph and start making changes!
      </p>
```

```
    </section>
</div>
```

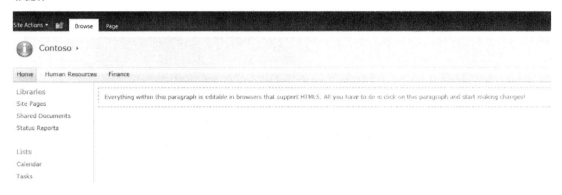

**Figure 11-8.** *Sample HTML5 page with editable content*

We tested this in IE9 and it worked perfectly! We clicked inside the paragraph (inside the dashed rectangle), and a cursor instantly appeared, allowing us to edit the text on the page just by typing! And we didn't have to put the page into edit mode to do it!

Now *saving* the changes across page refreshes is another story, and the code in Listing 11-2 doesn't address that. But consider the possibilities. Imagine integrating code such as this with the ECMAScript API of the client object model. We could offer users a way to edit content on their pages simply by clicking on it. We could then use the client object model to save their changes behind the scenes (perhaps when the editable region loses focus). Now that's pretty cool for SharePoint!

And this is just one little example. You can find lots of other great HTML5/CSS3 examples out on the web (demonstrating geolocation, drawing to a canvas, playing videos, and many other cool features of HTML5). One well-known site you can visit is `http://html5demos.com`. (Make sure to leave out the *www* because *http://www.html5demos.com* is a different site.)

## Dealing with Older Browsers

If your site needs to support older browsers that don't support HTML5 (think IE7 or IE8), you'll have to provide a way to gracefully downgrade your cool new functionality. Here are the key points you need to know:

- Doing this isn't easy or "built in" to SharePoint Online. Extra work and testing is required to support older browsers in HTML5/CSS3–enabled sites.

- Add-ins such as polyfills and shims are required. *Polyfills* are carefully crafted HTML, JavaScript, and CSS solutions that mimic the HTML5/CSS3 APIs and provide a graceful downgrade experience for older browsers (the idea being that you code against a single API and it "just works," even in non-HTML5 browsers). *Shims* are similar in nature but are more "stop-gap" in the sense that they might not exactly mirror the equivalent HTML5/CSS3 API for the functionality they're providing; they're more of an abstraction layer that might provide additional functionality.

If supporting older browsers for your HTML5/CSS3 solution is a requirement, start looking at solutions such as Modernizr (`http://modernizr.com`), which is an open-source library that provides feature-detection capabilities as well as shims, polyfills, and other cross-browser goodness you'll need to support both older and newer browsers.

# Summary

We began this chapter with a discussion about jQuery and its role in modern web development. We talked about how to get it into SharePoint Online, showed some simple examples of using it to get you started down that path, and talked about its real power when combined with SharePoint's client object model.

The rest of the chapter introduced the new HTML5 and CSS3 standards being developed by the W3C and talked about some of the pros and cons of using these new standards in SharePoint Online.

Considerations such as the browsers your users are using and the way HTML5 sometimes interferes with out-of-the-box SharePoint functionality all come into play. For those of you who do choose to go the HTML5/CSS3 route in SharePoint, we provided instructions for "turning on" HTML5 and CSS3 in your site and provided some sample code that illustrates just one of the ways HTML5 and CSS3 can significantly improve the user experience on your site.

# Hybrid On-Premise/Online Solutions

A *hybrid* SharePoint environment is one that combines an on-premise SharePoint 2010 environment with SharePoint Online. Although both types of SharePoint environments can certainly be used independently of each other, there are times when it makes sense to use them together.

This appendix covers the following topics relating to hybrid SharePoint environments:

- When does a hybrid environment make sense?

- Design patterns for hybrid environments

- Planning your hybrid environment

## When Does a Hybrid Environment Make Sense?

There are several scenarios in which a hybrid environment can make sense, including the following:

- Implementing a phased migration approach for migrating existing sites and content to Office 365 (from an existing on-premise environment)

- Using an on-premise environment to offer functionality to users that's not available in the cloud (such as PerformancePoint Services or Word Automation Services)

- Supplementing SharePoint Online with heavy customizations or third-party add-ons that must be deployed to an on-premise environment

- Compliance or security requirements that dictate where data resides

With these or any other hybrid scenarios, remember that you are dealing with two completely separate SharePoint environments, even though a key goal is usually to make them appear integrated to your users. With that in mind, we'll talk next about some design patterns for hybrid environments.

# Design Patterns for Hybrid Environments

One of the challenges of designing a hybrid environment is deciding where the boundaries are and how much crossover is allowed. Table A-1 lists six common design patterns for hybrid environments. More than one pattern can be used at a time; they are not mutually exclusive.

*Table A-1. Common Design Patterns for Hybrid Environments*

| Pattern Name | Description |
| --- | --- |
| Partitioning | This approach involves partitioning the environments (on-premise and online) so that *crossover* (a user needing to access both) happens as rarely as possible. This can lead to a better user experience by minimizing the differences users encounter in the two environments. There are multiple ways to partition, including these: <br><br>• By user type (e.g., internal users use an on-premise environment and external users use an online environment) <br><br>• By workload (e.g., collaboration and publishing workloads online and business intelligence workloads on-premise) <br><br>• By organization (e.g., Legal may use on-premise environment due to security concerns while other departments use the online environment) <br><br>• By date (e.g., new content created in online environment but existing content maintained in on-premise environment) |
| Smooth Transition | This pattern assumes that users will regularly access both environments (or that they will someday and you want to plan for it in advance). The goal is to make the transition as smooth and seamless as possible. Authentication, branding, navigation, information architecture, and governance all come into play when ensuring as seamless an experience as possible. |
| Encapsulation | This pattern uses client-side mashup technologies and techniques (such as iframes, RSS feeds, JavaScript, and so on) to combine information from both environments into a single view that resides in one environment or the other. For example, a page in your SharePoint Online environment might display information from your on-premise environment. |
| Federation | This pattern says that whenever functionality can be delegated to an authoritative system, it should be. An example of this is how single sign-on works with Office 365. It makes use of your existing Active Directory infrastructure (the authoritative system) and allows users to sign into Office 365 with their existing AD credentials. |

| Pattern Name | Description |
|---|---|
| Shared Source | This pattern helps ensure consistency by having both environments (on-premise and online) use common systems-of-record (authoritative systems) whenever possible. This has the effect of making the environments look synchronized, when in reality they're simply reading from and writing to the same source. Active Directory is a good example of a system-of-record for user profile information in both environments. |
| Replication | When environments can't directly access each other's content or access the same system-of-record, sometimes a replication solution makes sense. Replication involves either a one-time or ongoing synchronization process in which data from one environment is copied to the other. This will generally require either a third-party tool or custom code. |

■ **Note** See the Microsoft whitepaper, "Designing Hybrid SharePoint Environments," at `http://bit.ly/NjJuI4` for more detailed explanations of these patterns.

# Planning Your Hybrid Environment

This section covers key questions and considerations involved in planning your hybrid environment. The way your environment is architected and deployed will depend heavily on the decisions made during the planning stage.

## Authentication

If you want your users to have a single sign-on experience between your on-premise and online environments, you'll need to plan for and deploy Active Directory Federation Services (AD FS) and the directory synchronization tool. See `http://bit.ly/OKeZK8` for more information.

## SharePoint Workload Distribution

Part of planning your hybrid environment is deciding how SharePoint *workloads* (sets of related features) will be distributed between the two environments.

SharePoint 2010 includes six primary feature sets: Sites, Composites, Insights, Communities, Content, and Search. Part of the reason Microsoft grouped features into these workloads is due to how the features are deployed and managed, which comes into play when planning a hybrid environment.

Considerations include the following:

- Some workloads can run in both environments simultaneously (e.g., creating sites, pages, and libraries can be done in both environments at the same time).

- Some workloads can run in either environment, but shouldn't be run in both environments at the same time (e.g., User Profiles and My Sites should be deployed only in one environment or the other).

- Some workloads can (or should) be run only in an on-premise environment (e.g., PerformancePoint Services must be deployed on-premise because it isn't available in the cloud).

For a thorough list of which workloads are available in which environments and how they can be distributed, see the Microsoft whitepaper, "Designing Hybrid SharePoint Environments," at `http://bit.ly/NjJuI4`.

## Considerations and Limitations

Certain considerations and limitations come into play when planning your hybrid environment, including these:

- Some SharePoint service applications—such as the User Profile Service, Managed Metadata Service, and Search Service—cannot be shared across environments. The whitepaper mentioned in the previous section gives more detailed information about which service applications can and cannot be shared.

- Full-trust code solutions (a.k.a. *farm solutions*) cannot be deployed in Office 365. Only sandboxed solutions (discussed in Chapter 7) are allowed.

- Much of what's exposed through Central Administration in an on-premise SharePoint 2010 farm is not exposed in Office 365 for SharePoint Online. The SharePoint Online administration portal is much simpler than Central Administration and offers only a subset of the administration capabilities.

- Much of what PowerShell offers in an on-premise environment is not available to you in Office 365. For a list of what *is* available, see `http://bit.ly/r2TDoE`. Note that although PowerShell lets you manage many aspects of your Office 365 environment (user accounts, mailboxes, single sign-on, and so on), there are no cmdlets for SharePoint Online.

## Branding and Navigation

The strategy you use for branding and navigation will depend largely on the consistency requirements for your hybrid environment.

For example, consider a scenario in which an organization will be deploying collaboration and content management capabilities in the cloud, but will deploy business intelligence dashboards on-premise in order to use PerformancePoint Services. Because the two environments are intended to be perceived by end users as a single environment, a high degree of consistency is required. In that case, there needs to be global navigation deployed to both environments, as well as common master pages, styles, and other branding elements.

On the other hand, consider a scenario in which a company will continue to host its intranet on-premise, but will host its partner extranet in the cloud. There may be some overlap in the user base, but for the most part there will be two separate sets of users. In that case, there's probably not a great need for a highly consistent user experience across the two environments, so having separate navigation and branding is probably fine (and even desirable) so it's clear which one a user is accessing.

## Governance and Information Architecture

Governance and information architecture become especially important in hybrid environments. Users need to be able to find content quickly and need to know where new content should go. Your governance policy should provide guidance on where content should go in your hybrid environment, and your information architecture (and site design) should help enforce that policy with users.

An example can be something as simple as posting announcements on subsites and having them roll up to a home page. If that's a requirement for both environments, your information architecture needs to account for it and provide that capability to users. You may even end up deploying some of the exact same site columns, content types, and other structural elements to both environments.

Some guiding principles to help you in this area include the following:

- Similar content should often be grouped together and managed the same way (i.e., content with similar security and retention requirements should go together).

- Content in each environment is indexed separately for searching, so it's important that your search strategy account for this.

- Taxonomy terms (managed metadata) cannot be shared across environments (content migrated across environments must be retagged), so content in each environment should align to that environment's taxonomy.

- Content should be organized in a logical fashion (e.g., by department, by geography, by compliance requirements, and so on).

## Summary

This appendix provided an overview of hybrid on-premise/online SharePoint environments. We began by talking about what a hybrid environment is and when a hybrid environment might be appropriate. The rest of the discussion focused on planning a hybrid environment. We also listed some additional resources in the next section to help you dive deeper into this topic. While we provided a good overview of hybrid environments, some topics (such as architecting User Profiles and My Sites) require in-depth technical planning that can be done using the resources we list.

## Additional Resources

- "Designing Hybrid SharePoint Environments" (Microsoft whitepaper):

  - http://bit.ly/NjJuI4

- "SharePoint Online Administration Center" (TechNet):

  - http://bit.ly/Ujs8ua

- "Planning Guide for SharePoint Online for Enterprises":

  - http://bit.ly/S98XWH

- "Service Descriptions for Office 365 for Enterprises":

  - http://bit.ly/JvWrFD

# APPENDIX B

■ ■ ■

# Office 365 Preview (Office 2013)

This book focuses on the version of Office 365 that was released in mid-2011 and is based on the Office 2010 product suite. However, we also want to acknowledge that Office 365 Preview was released recently and is available for you to try. Office 365 Preview is based on the Office 2013 product suite. At the time of this writing, Microsoft has not publicly announced an official release date for Office 2013.

You can get started with Office 365 Preview by visiting `http://www.microsoft.com/office/preview/en/whats-new` and clicking the Try It link that's on the page.

Some key updates in Office 365 Preview include the following:

- Based on the Office 2013 product suite (currently in the Release Preview phase of its lifecycle)

- Now targets consumers as well as businesses with the addition of a Home Premium plan

- Plan offerings now include these:

  - Office 365 Home Premium

  - Office 365 Small Business Premium

  - Office 365 ProPlus

  - Office 365 Enterprise

- Skype integration is planned for the final release

If you sign up for a Preview plan, be aware that data in Preview plans will be deleted when the Preview period is over. Microsoft will send out notifications as the final release date approaches to give you time to prepare by moving any data you want to keep to another location. Also be aware that if you install any of the Preview desktop applications, they will need to be uninstalled before installing the final applications once they're released.

# Index

# ■ W

# ■ X, Y, Z

CPSIA information can be obtained at www.ICGtesting.com
Printed in the USA
LVOW110741041112

305742LV00003B/57/P